LEADERSHIP

FOR THE
TWENTY-FIRST
CENTURY

LEADERSHIP

FOR THE
TWENTY-FIRST
CENTURY

JOSEPH C. ROST

Foreword by James MacGregor Burns

PRAEGER   Westport, Connecticut
                                        London

Library of Congress Cataloging-in-Publication Data

Rost, Joseph C. (Joseph Clarence), 1931-
    Leadership for the twenty-first century / Joseph C. Rost.
       p.   cm.
    Includes bibliographical references and index.
    ISBN 0-275-93670-8
    ISBN 0-275-94610-X (pbk.)
    1. Leadership.   I. Title.
HM141.R685 1991
303.3'4—dc20   90-40961

British Library Cataloguing in Publication Data is available.

Library of Congress Catalog Card Number: 90-40961
ISBN: 0-275-93670-8
    0-275-94610-X (pbk.)

First published in 1991
Paperback edition 1993

Praeger Publishers, 88 Post Road West, Westport, CT 06881
An imprint of Greenwood Publishing Group, Inc.

Printed in the United States of America

The paper used in this book complies with the
Permanent Paper Standard issued by the National
Information Standards Organization (Z39.48-1984).

20 19 18 17 16

To
James MacGregor Burns,
who changed
my whole way of thinking about
leadership

Contents

Foreword   xi

Preface   xiii

1   *The Problem with Leadership Studies*   1

2   *An Overview of Leadership Studies*   13

3   *Definitions of Leadership: 1900–1979*   37

4   *Leadership Definitions: The 1980s*   69

5   *The Nature of Leadership*   97

6   *Leadership and Management*   129

7   *Leadership and Ethics in the 1990s*   153

8   *Leadership in the Future*   179

References 189

Index 215

Foreword

James MacGregor Burns

Imagine the following: that you, as a student of leadership, have been invited to spèak to doctoral candidates at a prestigious graduate program in leadership; that you are welcomed by the director of the program with more than the usual warmth and hospitality; that he presents you to his students with words of praise that you know are exaggerated several-fold but which, if only 20 percent true, offer you a gratifying little ego trip; but that, halfway through his introduction, his tone changes, he begins to critique your work, and it seems that—well, the guest speaker made a valiant and worthwhile effort, but he did not quite make it, did not quite get it right through, did not produce a breakthrough, but still, he is worth listening to, scholarly warts and all.

Imagine all that and you will have entered the iconoclastic world of Joseph C. Rost's doctoral program in leadership at the School of Education of the University of San Diego. But you need not share my rather daunting experience to gain a sense of the intellectual creativity and critical spirit of that school. You need only read this book. It is a biting critique of the great majority of writings on leadership, and certainly not sparing of my own. It will be, I expect, an intellectual blockbuster.

Rost contends that most of the works on leadership are describing not leadership but something else, such as management. He quotes approvingly Chester Barnard's comment that leadership "has been the subject of an extraordinary amount of dogmatically stated nonsense.'' Rost indicts scores of authors for not defining—or even trying to define—leadership, for succumbing to a series of fads that have dominated the history of the study of leadership, for failing to sense that we must enter a whole new ''paradigm'' of leadership as we approach the next decade and the next century, for seeing the trees and not the forest, and thus missing the main point. And what is that? For Rost the main point that has been missed is the role of followership in a dynamic interplay of leader-follower activism.

But *Leadership for the Twenty-first Century* is no mere polemic. Rost offers a fascinating section on the origins of the word *leadership*—it is old in usage but relatively recent in importance—and many pages on shifting definitions of leadership. He demonstrates how, over the decades, the study of leadership has been dominated in turn by great man theories, group leadership as facilitative, psychologists' trait theories (mainly), political scientists' behavioral theories (mainly), historians' contingency/situation theory (mainly), and excellence theory. All these fundamental concepts Rost criticizes with gusto. These pages alone make the work indispensable for teachers of leadership studies, and for their students.

Since the vast majority of leadership studies these days are not about leadership, in Rost's view, but management, writers on that subject will feel challenged—indeed, infuriated—by Rost's views on the matter. Those studies, he contends, narrow and oversimplify a complex set of influence relationships, leader-follower interactions, and mutual purposes. They lack an adequate concept of power. They underestimate the multiple and complex relationships in which leader and follower activists are involved. Rost makes clear his own distinction between management and leadership—one that many management theorists, I expect, will not accept.

This work, in my view, is the most important critique of leadership studies in our time, and as such will stand as one of a half-dozen indispensable works on leadership. Will it also stand as a major positive contribution to the understanding of leadership? For some time the jury—the many jurors—will be out before rendering this verdict. But I expect that Rost's call for a ''post-industrial'' concept of leadership—the most important concept in the book—will put him in the vanguard of a whole new force and direction in leadership theory.

In the spirit of Rost and his school, I cannot refrain from seizing this golden opportunity of being the first to criticize Rost's own argument in this volume (ah, sweet revenge!). I suggest that despite his intense and impressive concern about the role of values, ethics, and morality in transforming leadership, he underestimates the crucial importance of these variables. Even more I miss (and this reflects my own strong bias) a grasp of the role of great conflict in great leadership; Rost leans toward, or at least is tempted by, consensus procedures and goals that I believe erode such leadership. But Rost's main theme towers over such criticism. In this work he calls for a new school of leadership to face the leadership demands of the twenty-first century. This book could well become the Bible of such a school.

Preface

This book has taken a long time to write. Not the actual writing, but what has happened in my mind and in my life, which is the heart and soul of what is in this book.

I can remember very distinctly thinking about leadership as a high school student in the 1940s. More reflection occurred in college, especially when I wrote a thesis on the events in Japan that led to World War II. When I began teaching history and social studies in high school in the Midwest, I facilitated discussions about leadership among the students. I also have done leadership. I became very involved in a thirteen-state effort to infuse the study of non-Western cultures into the secondary social studies curriculum. I also spearheaded a youth movement to liberalize Roman Catholicism through the development of lay persons as church leaders.

As part of a master's degree, I wrote a thesis on Franklin D. Roosevelt's attempt to pack the Supreme Court in 1937, which was clearly a study of leadership although I did not frame it in that conceptual context.

When I became a Catholic school principal and later a public school district superintendent, leadership was constantly on my mind. And I was always involved in reform movements to make high schools more educationally relevant and effective. During a two-year leave of absence to complete my doctoral studies at the University of Wisconsin-Madison, I studied leadership explicitly and intensely. For my dissertation, I researched the successful attempt of Governor Patrick Lucey and the Wisconsin Legislature to merge the state's two university systems in 1972. I used Lindblom's (1968) reconstructive leadership model to make sense of that policy-making process.

When I came to the University of San Diego in 1976, I helped inaugurate a leadership doctoral program, a master's program in educational administration, and a leadership minor for undergraduates. Starting an educational administration program was an ordinary experience. Inaugurating the leadership doctoral program was a heady experience, the most extraordinary in my life. Since it was a leadership program (not a management or administration program), and since we wanted to study leadership from a multidisciplinary perspective with doctoral candidates from different professions but house the program in the School of Education, we were involved in double-duty (and at times multiple-duty) change processes simultaneously. There were no models in other universities that we could find, so we had to create the program and the curriculum from the ground up. With that kind of challenge, leadership had to be one's life, not one's job or profession.

Leadership for the Twenty-first Century is a critique of the efforts of leadership scholars and practitioners in the twentieth century to understand leadership based on the values and cultural norms of the industrial paradigm. It is also an effort to move our understanding of leadership forward, toward the postindustrial paradigm that will take hold in the twenty-first century.

Chapter 1 introduces three themes that are addressed throughout the book. Chapter 2 begins the critique of the leadership literature since 1930.

The first section in Chapter 3 details an investigation into the origins of the word *leadership* in English-speaking countries. Then definitions of leadership written in each decade from 1900 through 1979 are given, grouped in patterns of thought about leadership, and analyzed.

Chapter 4 is devoted to understanding how the concept of leadership was viewed in the 1980s, when an explosion of literature about leadership appeared in the bookstores. Again leadership definitions are grouped in patterns of thought and are followed by a more extended analysis of the views of leadership in the 1980s. The chapter ends with an explication of what I call the industrial leadership paradigm.

Chapter 5 begins with some ideas about the postindustrial era and its connection to our concept of leadership. Then I propose a new definition of leadership that is consistent with what some futurists see as the postindustrial paradigm of the twenty-first century. The definition has four essential elements, each of which is explained and amplified. The chapter ends with some thoughts on transformational leadership.

In Chapter 6, I deal with the issue of leadership and management. Past attempts to distinguish between the two have not been entirely successful, and I propose a conceptual framework that works because it uses the essential elements of the definitions—not traits, behaviors, and styles of leaders and managers—to make the distinction. Such a distinction, of course, is crucial to a postindustrial paradigm of leadership.

Chapter 7 develops some notions about the ethics of leadership. A distinction is made between the process and the content of leadership. Ethical perspectives concerning the process of leadership are fundamental to the nature of leadership as a relationship. The ethical content of leadership, which involves the changes that leaders and followers intend, poses severe problems because traditional ethical frameworks are only minimally helpful in confronting the ethical issues that leaders and followers must face in proposing changes in their organizations and societies. Finally, I propose two tentative ways out of this dilemma, but clearly there has to be much more thought given to this critical area of concern.

The final chapter, Chapter 8, summarizes the analysis and conclusions given throughout the book, and I make some suggestions to academic scholars, transition specialists (consultants and trainers), and practitioners for improving the study and practice of leadership in the twenty-first century. Actually, in the 1990s it is not too soon to start these efforts to transform our understanding of leadership. Thus, the final plea is for those of us concerned about the future to begin now.

While I have benefited enormously from the interactions with and the intellectual stimulation I have received from the leadership professors and students at the University of San Diego, and from the intense collaborations with educators as we have attempted to exert leadership in secondary and higher education, the analysis and proposals in this book are my responsibility alone. I am happy to take the credit and the blame for them, as the case may be.

I am indebted to several colleagues who reviewed the manuscript during various stages of its preparation and who made numerous helpful suggestions to improve the work. Their names shall remain anonymous. However, Alison Bricken of Praeger Publishers deserves special mention for her original evaluation of this book's merits, and she and Bert Yaeger were immensely helpful in editing and publishing the work. I also want to thank Edward DeRoche, dean of the School of Education at the University of San Diego, for supporting this work by awarding several faculty research grants and a sabbatical leave to facilitate the research for and the writing of this book.

Finally, there are family members and close friends who have been very supportive: with encouragement in times of what seemed to be a never-ending research project; with pressure in times of fatigue and letting go; with love and care in times of difficult analysis and writer's block, or fear. Thanks to one and all.

LEADERSHIP

FOR THE
TWENTY-FIRST
CENTURY

1

The Problem with Leadership Studies

Leadership studies is an emerging discipline devoted, as the name suggests, to the study of leadership as it is practiced in different organizations and societies. Most of the people who call themselves leadership scholars study leadership in one academic discipline or profession. Numerous examples abound: Bailey (1988) in anthropology, Bass (1985) in social psychology, Hersey and Blanchard (1988) in human relations/resources, Selznick (1957) in sociology, Sergiovanni (1990) in education, Tucker (1981) in political science, Whitehead and White-head (1986) in theology, and Zaleznik (1989) in business. By far, most leadership scholars are in schools of business and write for corporate executives and business students.

These one-discipline scholars are easily recognized because they almost always put an adjective in front of the word *leadership*, such as business leadership, educational leadership, or political leadership; and they strongly hold the assumption that leadership as practiced in the particular profession they are studying is different from leadership as practiced in other professions.

The same can be said for leadership practitioners—those who lead organizations—and those who are responsible for professional training and development in leadership. Most of these leadership experts are heavily involved in only one profession either as trainers or as leaders, and by far the largest percentage are in business organizations. Educational and political organizations have their share of such experts, but they are comparatively few in terms of numbers and influence.

In the 1980s a cadre of academics, trainers, and practitioners appeared on the scene who rejected the single profession and single academic discipline approach to the study and practice of leadership. These people increasingly use the term *leadership studies* to explain what they do because the title connotes a multidisciplinary, if not an interdisciplinary, approach to understanding and practicing leadership. These scholars have inaugurated university programs in leadership studies at both the undergraduate and graduate levels, and these programs enroll undergraduate students with different academic majors or graduate students in different professions. There are also several doctoral programs in leadership studies throughout the United States that are graduating academics who teach in other leadership programs, training and development professionals who head their own consulting firms or professional development programs in large organizations, and practitioners who put leadership to work in many public and private organizations. The University of San Diego has such a program.

In 1991, the University of Richmond (Virginia) will inaugurate the first undergraduate program in the United States leading to a bachelor's degree with leadership studies as a major. It will not be the last.

Examples of multidisciplinary scholars who have written books on leadership are still somewhat rare, but their numbers are increasing. Burns (1978) is probably the most widely read. Maccoby (1981), Gouldner (1950), Greenleaf (1977), McCall and Lombardo (1978), and Paige (1977) were other early advocates of the interdisciplinary approach. More recently, Adams (1986), Cleveland (1985), Ford (1990), Gardner (1990), Heller, Van Til, and Zurcher (1986), Henrickson (1988), Kellerman (1984b), and Rosenbach and Taylor (1984) have used such an approach. To some extent, Bennis (1989a), Nanus (1989), and Peters (1987) have developed a more generalized view of leadership that reaches across professions, although they are more noted for their studies of business leadership. Conger and Kanungo (1988) and Willner (1984) used a multidisciplinary approach to study charismatic leadership.

An increasing number of practitioners are able to engage in leadership in a variety of contexts. And an increasing number of training and development experts offer interdisciplinary professional development programs in leadership for practitioners. Many of these people have graduated from the leadership doctoral programs that tend to take a multidisciplinary approach to leadership studies.

This new trend in leadership studies brings with it a promising breakthrough in our understanding of leadership. The study of leadership has been mired in a single disciplinary view for most of the twentieth century; the leadership studies approach allows scholars and practitioners to think radically new thoughts about leadership that are not possible from an unidisciplinary approach.

There are many problems confronting leadership scholars and practitioners in the 1990s. Some of these stem from the study and practice of leadership since the 1930s. Those problems will be discussed in detail in subsequent chapters. For the present, I want to discuss three overarching problems that leadership scholars and practitioners must confront in the 1990s. Solving these problems is crucial to the development of leadership studies as a serious academic area of inquiry. Dealing with these problems is extremely important to the practice of leadership in the twenty-first century.

These three problems actually introduce the themes that appear over and over again in this book. They did not suddenly come on the scene at the beginning of the 1990s. Rather, they evolved out of the ferment generated in leadership studies during the 1980s, the inadequacies in our understanding of leadership as it has been defined over the years, and the transition from an industrial to a postindustrial paradigm in the United States and other Western countries.

THE IMPORTANCE OF PERIPHERY AND CONTENT IN LEADERSHIP STUDIES

The first problem of leadership studies has been the emphasis that writers on leadership have placed on (1) what is peripheral to the nature of leadership and (2) what I call the content of leadership—the ideas and information that leaders and followers in particular professions or organizations must know in order to influence one another in a leadership relationship. Traditional leadership scholars and the theories they have developed have been almost totally concerned with the peripheries of leadership: traits, personality characteristics, "born or made" issues, greatness, group facilitation, goal attainment, effectiveness, contingencies, situations, goodness, style, and, above all, the management of organizations—public and private. These peripheral elements are, for the most part, visible and countable, susceptible to statistical manipulation, accessible in terms of causality probabilities, and usable to train people in the habits of doing what those in the know may think is the right thing.

The emphasis on peripheral elements allows leadership practitioners to seize something tangible in their quest to define and practice leadership and to believe in the effectiveness of the prescribed behaviors. That emphasis allows followers to feel good about following because they can see leaders taking charge of organizations according to scripts written in their minds. Finally, the peripheral emphasis allows scholars to feel good about themselves because these theories were developed using the best scientific methods known to researchers and conformed to the best logical positivist framework for research. Whether the theories and research actually dealt with the essence of leadership did not seem to have been overly important to these researchers. Rather, what seems to have been important was that the research was based on empirical data and that it was done according to the traditional, quantitative methods.

On another level, traditional leadership scholars and practitioners are very interested in the content of leadership—what leaders need to know about a particular profession, organization, or society in order to be influential in it. The content of leading—the knowledge that leaders must have—is almost always thought of as more important as a determinant of leadership effectiveness than the process of leading. Such things as knowing the state-of-the-art theories and practices in a profession; understanding human behavior, situations, environmental stress, and future trends; having a grasp of the technical information needed in an organization; knowing the critical data needed to introduce change; and even an intuitive understanding of what all these new ideas mean for the profession or organization one is leading—these are the real essence of leadership, the stuff that separates the real people from the quiche makers. The process of leadership, the understanding of leadership as a relationship, the connection among leaders and followers—all these are far down on the list of priorities that scholars and practitioners must have in order to understand how to put leadership to work.

That this "periphery and content" syndrome is so pervasive can easily be illustrated by counting the number of workshops or seminars on the content of leadership as opposed to the process; by analyzing the number of class hours spent in educational, business, or public administration programs on the content of leadership as opposed to the process; by paying attention to media coverage of the content of leadership instead of the process; or by counting the number of books or journal articles with leadership in the title that deal primarily with the content of leadership and not the process.

The upshot of all this is that leadership scholars have spilled much ink on the peripheral elements surrounding leadership and its content instead of on the nature of leadership as a process, on leadership viewed as a dynamic relationship. Most of the research on leadership has emphasized the same two items—the peripheral aspects and the content of leadership—and almost none has been aimed at understanding the essential nature of what leadership is, the process whereby leaders and followers relate to one another to achieve a purpose.

Many scholars have wondered why we have not been able to get a conceptual handle on the word *leadership*. Stogdill (1974) and later, Bass (1981) collected and analyzed some 4,725 studies of leadership that Bass listed on 189 pages of references in his handbook. Stogdill concluded that "the endless accumulation of empirical data has not produced an integrated understanding of leadership" (p. vii). Bass, in his update of Stogdill's *Handbook*, came to the same conclusion, but ended on a note of optimism:

Some disparage the thousands of research studies of leadership completed with the supposed lack of progress. Yet, when we compare our understanding of leadership in 1980 with what it was thirty years earlier, we can agree with T. R. Mitchell (1979) that "there seems to be progress in the field. Theory and research are developing and much of what is being done is being used in practice. There is reason for controlled optimism. Yet, the challenges are still there for the years ahead." (p. 617)

Three years earlier, Burns saw little reason to be optimistic after analyzing past leadership study and practice. He wrote:

The crisis of leadership today is the mediocrity or irresponsibility of so many of the men and women in power. . . . The fundamental crisis underlying mediocrity is intellectual. If we know all too much about our leaders, we know far too little about *leadership*. We fail to grasp the essence of leadership that is relevant to the modern age. (1978, p. 1)

"Leadership," he concluded, "is one of the most observed and least understood phenomena on earth" (p. 2).

In 1984, Burns returned to the same theme: We know much about our leaders, he opined, but we know very little about what leadership really is. He criticized the media for spending "twice as much time commenting on trivial personality and tactical matters as on substance," newspeople who are "fascinated by little blunders" or "matters essentially lacking in substance or significance," and media coverage that is "perverse, superficial, unfair, [and] often biased" (Burns, 1984, pp. 155–156). In sum, we relate to our leaders by "mass spectatorship and personalism or personalismo" (p. 156). And why are these tendencies disturbing? Because their long-run effect undermines "effective, committed, collective, and durable leadership in politics" and has "dire implications for governance" (p. 156). Because these tendencies lead to a "politics of personality [rather] than of policy, program, authority, governance . . . , a politics that . . . seeks votes by appealing to short-run, superficial, and narrow needs and hopes," a "leadership [that] is classically short-run, unstable, ineffective, irresponsible" (p. 156).

Bennis and Nanus (1985) complained that "thousands of empirical investigations of leadership have been conducted in the last seventy-five years alone, but no clear and unequivocal understanding exists as to what distinguishes leaders from nonleaders" (p. 4). They opined that "books on leadership are often as majestically useless as they are pretentious," and insisted that they did not want "to further muddle the bewildering melange of leadership definitions" (p. 20) in their book.

Smith and Peterson (1988) cited 451 references in their study of leadership theory and research, and they review many of them in the first four chapters. They warned their readers: "Cumulatively, the chapters delineate the impasse which many researchers of leadership have diagnosed in recent years, and which has lead quite a few practitioners to conclude that research into leadership has little to offer them" (p. 1).

My own view is that it should be no surprise that scholars and practitioners have not been able to clarify what leadership is, because most of what is written about leadership has to do with its peripheral elements and content rather than with the essential nature of leadership as a relationship. If scholars and practitioners have not focused on the nature of leadership, it should not surprise any of us who are interested in the subject that we do not know what leadership is.

Thus, in the 1990s, it is absolutely crucial that scholars and practitioners interested in leadership studies de-emphasize the peripheral elements and the content of leadership, and concentrate on understanding its essential nature. There is no indication that anyone is anxious to change the emphasis of leadership studies if the books published in 1989 and the early months of 1990 are an indication. At least twenty such books were published in those fifteen months, and not one of the scholars and/or practitioners who wrote those works attempted to explicate the essential nature of leadership.

The reality is that, as of 1990, scholars and practitioners do not know, with certainty, what leadership is. This uncertainty about such an essential question must end in the 1990s. There is no possibility of framing a new paradigm of leadership for the twenty-first century if scholars and practitioners cannot articulate what it is they are studying and practicing.

DEFINING LEADERSHIP

The second problem with leadership studies as an academic discipline and with the people who do leadership is that neither the scholars nor the practitioners have been able to define leadership with precision, accuracy, and conciseness so that people are able to label it correctly when they see it happening or when they engage in it. Without an agreed-upon definition, all kinds of activities, processes, and persons are labeled as leadership by both scholars and practitioners. The word *leadership* (and, to some extent, related words such as *lead*, *leader*, and *leading*) are used in scholarly and popular publications, organizational newsletters and reports, and the media to mean very different things that have little to do with any considered notion of what leadership actually is.

The worst part of the present situation is that many scholars do not see this inability to agree upon a definition of leadership as a problem. While there have been some researchers who have taken scholars to task for not being able to come up with a definition of leadership, the large majority of leadership scholars accept definitional ambiguity and confusion as something that behavioral and social scientists have to put up with and work around. Indeed, as I shall argue later, leadership studies as an academic discipline has a culture of definitional permissiveness and relativity. One scholar's definition is as good as another's; the third scholar's definition is as good as the second scholar's definition; and so on for as many scholars as choose to give definitions of leadership. The culture allows anyone to give a definition of leadership, and ipso facto it is as accurate and acceptable as anyone else's definition.

There are almost no arguments about definitions in the literature on leadership. There are almost no critiques of other scholars' definitions, and what little there is, appears in the literature of the 1980s. There have been no criteria established to evaluate leadership definitions. There certainly has been no heuristic development of leadership definitions from one decade to the next so that for instance, the 1970s definitions are more accurate and real than those of the 1960s. "The existing [leadership] literatures do not 'add up' (Argyris, 1979)," Hosking and Morley stated, "partly for the reason that diverse phenomena have been studied in the name of leadership" (1988, p. 89).

There is surprisingly little discussion of leadership definitions in the literature. In fact, over 60 percent of the authors who have written on leadership since about 1910 did not define leadership in their works. There is an impression that one picks up from reading a leadership book, chapter, or journal article: Giving a definition of leadership will not do any good, since nobody will pay attention to it. Or, giving a definition will not matter, since most scholars ignore their definitions after they give them, so why should I give a definition and then ignore it in the rest of the book? Besides, doing research that is based on definition will only cramp my ideas and opinions, cause difficulties for my statistical procedures and sample population and/or phenomena, and create problems when I do the analysis and formulate the conclusions. Taking definitions seriously only gets in the way of doing the research I need and want to do.

Practitioners tend to be more intuitive about this issue because they believe they can accurately label phenomena as leadership even if they cannot define the concept in words: "I know leadership when I see it." The difficulty with this approach, however, is that the phenomena that one person judges experientially to be leadership often are not evaluated as leadership by other people who see the very same phenomena. As a result, the experiential approach to defining leadership is no better than the ambiguous approach of scholars because there is no agreement among practitioners on what phenomena should be labeled as leadership.

In 1990, *leadership* is a word that has come to mean all things to all people. Even worse, *leadership* has increasingly become a very "hot" word since about 1960, with an ability to produce a passionate reaction that draws people to it through an emotional attraction. Leadership has been "in" for so long, I cannot remember when it was "out." University programs, seminars, conferences, speeches, books, training activities, people, products, positions, and many relationships (group, marriage, counseling, teaching, friendship, etc.) are called *leadership* in order to present a positive image of these phenomena so that people accept them more readily and voluntarily, and to attract people to them for the purpose of selling them, dignifying them by putting them on some kind of pedestal, or pushing them into the limelight when they might not otherwise be able to gain that light.

Part of the reason that leadership has such a powerful attraction is that it has taken on mythological significance. According to Campbell, "Myths are stories of our search through the ages for truth, for meaning, for significance. We all need to tell our story and to understand our story. . . . We need for life to signify, to touch the eternal, to understand the mysterious, to find out who we are" (Campbell, 1988, p. 5). On an earlier television program, Campbell, in speaking of the American Indians, said that myths are "symbolic stories that reconcile for the Indians the harsh realities of life" (Moyers, *The Hero's Journey*, 1987). Campbell's understanding of mythology helps explain what has happened to the concept of leadership in the United States. Leadership helps Americans find significance in their search for the meaning of life, helps them reconcile the harsh realities of life. It helps people explain effectiveness and concomitantly allows them to celebrate the people who achieve that effectiveness; the lack of leadership helps them explain ineffectiveness and concomitantly allows them to blame certain people for that ineffectiveness.

In the 1980s, leadership helped the people of the United States understand what went wrong when the nation lost its domination of the world's economy. Leadership helped Americans reconcile themselves to the harsh reality that the United States is no longer number one in the world. It also helped Americans understand the significance of excellence. Thus leadership would be the savior, the way the United States would regain its lost power and prestige, the magic that would help restore confidence and bring it back to the number one spot again.

In the twenty-first century, the harsh reality may be that there might not be a number one country in the world. Is the mythological story of United States leadership going to reconcile Americans to that possibility? What is the significance of life if that scenario comes to pass?

In his books and in the interviews with Bill Boyers, Campbell insisted repeatedly that correctly interpreting the mythological stories was critical to the well-being of the group or society and to the lives of its people. That interpretation was the primary responsibility of the high priests and elders, who instituted rituals to make sure the correct interpretations were passed down from generation to generation. Such is the case with leadership studies as a mythological narrative. It is the responsibility of the leadership scholars and practicing leaders (the high priests and elders of leadership studies) to pass on an accurate understanding of leadership to succeeding generations. Read in that light, the leadership literature since the 1930s has been amazing successful. It has generated a mythological story of leadership that has been told over and over again and that almost everyone believes. Whether the stories are accurate and the interpretations correct are different issues. I will have more to say about those issues in other chapters.

Whether leadership studies is considered an academic discipline or a mythological story, the importance of understanding the true meaning of leadership—having a clear understanding of the essential nature of leadership by agreeing upon an accurate definition—is crucial to studying and doing leadership. A clear understanding of leadership is crucial to the concept adding up—making more sense—from one generation to another. A clear definition of leadership is crucial to leaders' and followers' making a difference in organizations and societies in the twenty-first century.

The facts are that in the 1990s, the concept of leadership does not add up because leadership scholars and practitioners have no definition of leadership to hold on to. The scholars do not know what it is they are studying, and the practitioners do not know what it is that they are doing. A high priority for the 1990s is to reach a consensus on a clear, concise, easily understandable, researchable, practical, and persuasive definition of leadership.

And, finally, the leadership literature does not add up because there is no easily recognizable school of leadership that makes sense of the concept of leadership, a comment that leads to the third theme in this chapter.

A NEW SCHOOL OF LEADERSHIP?

The third problem that besets those of us interested in leadership is the failure of scholars and practitioners to develop a readily recognizable school of leadership that integrates what we know about leadership from the research and writings of scholars and practitioners, a school of leadership that frames an understanding of leadership which makes sense to people who want to study leadership and put the concept to work in organizations, societies, and the world.

Burns called attention to this problem in the introduction to his monumental study of leadership.

There is, in short, no school of leadership, intellectual or practical. Does it matter that we lack standards for assessing past, present, and potential leaders? Without a powerful philosophical tradition, without theoretical and empirical cumulation, without guiding concepts and without considerable practical experience, we lack the very foundations for knowledge of a phenomenon—leadership in the arts, the academy, science, politics, the professions, war—that touches and shapes our lives.

Although we have no school of leadership, we do have in rich abundance and variety the makings of such a school. An immense reservoir of data and analysis and theories has been developed. No central concept of leadership has yet emerged. . . . I believe, however, the richness of the research and analysis and thoughtful experience, accumulated especially in the past decade or so, enables us now to achieve an intellectual breakthrough. Vitally important but largely unheralded work in humanistic psychology now makes it possible to generalize about the leadership process across cultures and across time. This is the central purpose of this book. (1978, p. 3)

Unfortunately, Burns did not achieve his purpose, and none of the authors of the hundreds of books, chapters in edited books, and journal articles on leadership published in the 1980s and in early 1990 have, individually or collectively, achieved it either. No one has presented an articulated school of leadership that integrates our understanding of leadership into a holistic framework.

In doing research for this book, I made notes on 312 books, chapters, and journal articles written during the 1980s (not all of which are in the References). I also have notes on five works that were published in the early months of 1990. Management and administration textbooks were generally excluded from that list (although there are a few exceptions I felt were important, and thus included them). If the chapters from such textbooks were included in the list, the total number would be over 500.

I am certain that there are, again conservatively, another fifty chapters and journal articles from the 1980s that were not uncovered. There may be a few leadership books that I did not find, but they would have to be very few in number. If one wanted to complete the list by adding the articles on leadership from hundreds of popular magazines, there would easily be another 300 or more sources from which to gather data. And there are another 200 or so unpublished papers on leadership available from computerized retrieval systems, dissertations, consulting firms, and training and development departments in organizations, conventions/meetings of professional associations, and personal contacts, all of which were written in the 1980s. The amount of written material on the subject of leadership generated in the 1980s is staggering by any standard.

The published materials on leadership from the 1950s, 1960s, and 1970s are not nearly so numerous as those from the 1980s, but nevertheless there were many published during those decades. I also made notes on those works, as well as those I could find from the period 1900 to 1949. I did not read or make notes on many of the journal articles on leadership that were published in the 1930s and 1940s. To some extent this was a decision based on my own time-management problem and the difficulty of finding many of these articles in libraries. Much of this literature is well summarized in the two leadership handbooks (Stogdill, 1974; Bass, 1981) and in Gibb's (1969) lengthy analysis, and I did not feel it was necessary to go through all that literature again. Having read Gibb, Stogdill, and Bass, I know the literature of the 1930s and 1940s quite well, even though I have not studied most of it directly.

After poring over those notes and doing several cuts in analyzing those materials, I came to a startling conclusion. There is a school of leadership in the literature since 1930 that has been hidden by the obvious confusion and chaos of the literature as it is presented in the books, chapters, and articles. Under the surface, I found a consistent view of leadership in the background assumptions (Gouldner, 1970) and in the meanings behind the words used in the definitions and the models. This school conceptualizes leadership as good management. I will call it the industrial paradigm of leadership and will discuss it in depth in upcoming chapters.

Previously, no one had been able to tie this literature together and make sense of it. If, indeed, there has been a school of leadership there all along, but it has never been articulated well as an integrated framework, it seems to me that we have an entirely new situation. Instead of criticizing leadership scholars and practitioners, individually and collectively, for not developing a school of leadership, we can now criticize them for not articulating the school well (for confusing both themselves and us by not being straightforward about the whole thing) and then criticize—in both the positive and the negative senses—the understanding of leadership embedded in the school's conceptual framework and its practice in organizations and societies.

Viewed in that light, a reinterpretation of Burns's important work (1978) may well be in order. With twelve years hindsight at this writing, and with the recognition of a previously existing but not well-articulated school of leadership operating since the 1930s, Burns's real purpose may not have been to construct a school of leadership after having evaluated the past literature as lacking one. His real purpose may have been to build a *new school of leadership*, having consciously or unconsciously rejected what he saw as confusion and mediocrity in the study and practice of leadership in a school of leadership that is all but unrecognizable. In sum, Burns's work is perhaps better interpreted as *reconstructing* the concept of leadership, not constructing it for the first time.

While Burns did not express his purpose in that way, nothing else makes sense if, in truth, a school of leadership already existed at the time he wrote his book. He certainly did not adopt the mainstream view of leadership and build that into his framework. His understanding of leadership and his model of it based on that understanding were very different from the traditional concept as found again and again in the literature. Yet in analyzing his leadership framework, I am struck by the significant bits of industrialism that are still embedded in it. In the end, I have to say that Burns was not successful in his attempt to build a new school of leadership. Nevertheless his work is extremely important as a transitional statement that has immense possibilities to lead us toward a new school of leadership.

Be that as it may, the sad fact is that leadership studies as an academic discipline did not produce a new school of leadership in the 1980s. Only a few of the authors who wrote the 312 books, chapters, and articles reviewed in this study made a significant contribution to our understanding of leadership, because the large majority of them did not concentrate on the nature of leadership. Only a few authors began to articulate a new school of leadership; the large majority of them still embraced the old school of leadership, the industrial paradigm.

The authors of these books, chapters, and journal articles come from most of the academic disciplines that have something to say about leadership: anthropology, history, literature, philosophy, political science, psychology, sociology, theology, and such applied disciplines as business, educational, health, military, public administration, and communication studies. They also come from practitioner communities that attempt to put leadership to work: professional associations, public and private organizations and institutions, training and development personnel, and consulting groups. While I have not analyzed the popular media for this book, my strong impression is that the concept of leadership articulated by the professionals in the media and arts would be the same. These professionals include television, radio, magazine, and newspaper commentators and reporters, novelists, nonfiction writers, playwrights, artists, and composers.

If this analysis is at all accurate, the conclusion is obvious: A new school of leadership is as elusive in 1990 as it was in 1978, when Burns wrote his book. This is a problem that must be solved in the 1990s as the people in our organizations and societies prepare for the twenty-first century.

2

An Overview of Leadership Studies

It is almost a ritual for the authors of books and articles on leadership to make two statements at the beginning of their works. The first statement goes like this: ''Many scholars have studied leaders and leadership over the years, but there still is no clear idea of what 'leadership' is or who leaders are.'' The second statement usually takes the form of several paragraphs summarizing the popular theories of leadership: great man, traits, group, behaviorist, and situational.

The first of these statements reveals indisputable evidence of the cultural permissiveness imbedded in the academic discipline called leadership studies. It is permissible for leadership scholars not to know what leadership is. The second statement shows the cumulative state of the art of the discipline—where scholars are as a group in the study of leadership—and the state of the art is not good. Both statements show signs of a malignancy that has been, and still is, very detrimental to achieving any worthwhile body of scholarly knowledge about the phenomena called leadership.

While I will document this malaise in Chapters 3 and 4, I believe there needs to be some discussion of the disease prior to that exposition, so that the definitions in the next two chapters can be put into a context.

CULTURAL PERMISSIVENESS ABOUT THE NATURE OF LEADERSHIP

The first statement repeats the idea that there have been many studies of leaders and leadership, but leadership scholars still have no clear understanding of what leadership is. I have made such statements myself. The problem with the statement is not that it is inaccurate but that, having made it, 95 percent of the scholars ignore the statement and write their book, chapter, or article as if they know what leadership is. Worse, many scholars write as if their readers know what leadership is and their readers' understanding is the same as their own. These scholars generally do not even attempt to give a definition of leadership, and the reader often has a difficult time trying to gain a clear understanding of the author's view of leadership.

As a result of the preponderance of this kind of leadership literature, leadership scholars and practitioners have been enculturated into a view of leadership as "anything anyone wants to say it is" and a notion of leaders as "anyone who is so designated." Leadership scholars and practitioners are no longer offended by an academic discipline whose scholars study a phenomenon they cannot adequately identify. We are no longer offended by a profession (using that term loosely) whose practitioners do not know what it is they are practicing. Would we put up with oenologists if they did not know what wine was? Would we trust medical scientists if they were not able to identify various diseases by name? Would we accept musicologists who did not know the nature of a symphony or an opera? Or would we believe archaeologists if they were unable to identify specific bones as those of human beings and not those of other mammals?

One could say, Those scientists are all dealing with things—objects that can be touched or seen. Leadership scholars are dealing with socially constructed reality, which cannot be seen or touched, but only inferred through the actions of human beings. A better comparison, then, might be with other behavioral scientists. Do political scientists actually know what politics is? Are anthropologists able to adequately identify culture? Do psychologists have a clear definition of the psyche or the psychic? Do sociologists know the nature of an organization, institution, or society? Probably not.

Thus, the point is well taken. Perhaps the basic problem of leadership studies— an inability to know and agree upon what leadership is—is pervasive in all the behavioral sciences. Many behavioral scientists seem to be unable to define the nature of the basic phenomena they are studying and to agree upon that definition. It may well be that the major reason leadership scholars have this problem is that social psychologists, organizational behaviorists, and political scientists have had this same problem. Leadership studies as an academic discipline was born when several social psychologists, organizational behaviorists, and political scientists decided to make leadership study a subspecialty. These disciplines had already been enculturated into an academic frame that allows these scholars to live with ambiguity in the basic understanding of fundamental phenomena, and they transmuted that frame of reference to the new discipline of leadership studies.

If this analysis is accurate, the basic problem is that behavioral scientists have established a scientific culture wherein they are not expected to clearly articulate an understanding of what it is they are studying. It is acceptable for them to research something without having a clearly articulated notion of what that something is. Or, often, a definition of that something is given, but the definition is ignored by the researcher because it is not possible to research that something using the articulated definition, since that something, as defined, is not quantifiable. Mainstream behavioral scientists adopted the logical positivist framework of research, which required quantification for validity and replicability. Another variation on the same theme is the practice of researchers' giving a definition of whatever they are researching that allows the subject to be quantified even though they have no guarantee that the quantifiable definition actually describes the reality the researchers say they are studying.

Both research strategies have been used in leadership studies hundreds of times. The first was used, for instance, in studies that defined leadership as influence behavior and then included in the research all kinds of behaviors that were not influence-oriented. The second has been used, for example, in studies that define leadership as management behavior. In this kind of strategy, the researcher amasses the managerial behaviors, observed or collected from survey instruments, and puts them in some kind of two-factor or three-factor model, calling the entire thing *leadership*.

Of course, the easiest way to deal with the definitional problem in researching leadership is to not give a definition. This no-definition approach has been the most common strategy of all, as will be obvious from the data in Chapters 3 and 4.

I have neither the expertise nor the motivation to try to solve this fundamental problem for all of the behavioral sciences. Since I am a leadership scholar, my primary responsibilities are to that area of study, and so this book is an attempt to address this fundamental issue in leadership studies. The difficulty of attacking this issue is that leadership is, by its very nature, a multidisciplinary subject because it has important ramifications for more than one of the behavioral sciences and liberal arts (history and literature, philosophy and theology, for instance). Yet, the great majority of leadership scholars study the subject from a unidisciplinary perspective. Indeed, I believe that this perspective is part of the overall, fundamental problem. The reality is that there are very few leadership studies scholars. Rather, there are anthropologists, educators, historians, management scientists, organizational behaviorists, political scientists, social psychologists, and sociologists who have developed an expertise in leadership. Thus, the leadership literature is primarily a mixed bag of subspecialized literatures from these disciplines. It was only during the 1980s that some scholars began to approach leadership from an interdisciplinary perspective—one scholar using several disciplines to study leadership—but they are still in the minority of those who are known as leadership scholars.

One of the basic views pervasive throughout this book is the categorical imperative that leadership studies is an interdisciplinary subject of inquiry. When this perspective is taken seriously, it means that scholars and practitioners can gain a clear understanding of the nature of leadership only by studying it from the framework of several different disciplines. Those who study leadership from an unidisciplinary perspective have blinders on, and the blinders prevent them from understanding what leadership is. Those who practice leadership as if it was different in the profit sector than in the nonprofit sector have blinders on, and those blinders prevent them from understanding what leadership is. (They have, to reiterate a point made in the last chapter, confused the content of leadership with its nature as a relationship.)

With those blinders on, scholars do research on phenomena they think constitute leadership and then write about what they have found concerning those phenomena, and the circular problem continues. Without any clear concept of leadership guiding the research that has been conducted since the 1930s, the reality may be, and very possibly is, that much of this research is not about leadership at all. For instance, in the 1930s many social psychologists became interested in groups and started researching them to find out how they operated. In the process, they equated group facilitation with group leadership, researched the equation in hundreds of studies, and developed a group theory of leadership. The group understanding of leadership is still accepted and popular. No one has ever asked, "Is facilitating groups leadership?" The nature of leadership as facilitation has been taken for granted because, in part, social psychologists and, later, other scholars have worn disciplinary blinders that automatically assumed that group facilitation was leadership. Since about 1930, we have agreed that facilitating groups is leadership because a large body of leadership literature has assumed this, and no one has bothered to question that basic assumption. This is dramatic testimony to the cultural laxity of leadership scholars in conceptualizing leadership. The ethos is: Anything that anyone proclaims to be leadership is leadership.

Practitioners have done the same thing. On the basis of cultural imperatives from Western societies and the particular organizations to which people belong, as well as influences based on race, gender, religion, family, and professional education, people develop an idea of what leadership is. They then do what they think is leadership, and later make assessments as to whether what they did, and what they thought leadership was, actually worked. For several decades practitioners have, for instance, thought that certain basic traits are endemic to leadership; that having a plan, aggressiveness in pushing the plan, persistence in getting it through whatever bureaucratic bottlenecks had to be gotten through, single-mindedness of purpose, and a certain cleverness of style are what leadership is all about. And many people have acted that way because they believed it was leadership. No one ever thought to question the assumption that such behaviors are indeed leadership. Such assumptions were not questioned because practitioners had their organizational blinders on, and these blinders equated the traits listed above with leadership. Again, this is dramatic testimony to our cultural permissiveness, which allows people to believe that anything they say is leadership, is leadership.

Clearly, this kind of tolerance has gotten us nowhere. While such an attitude may have been acceptable for some years while scholars were trying to determine the nature of leadership by experimentation and other scientific strategies, that kind of cultural laxity has outlasted its usefulness. Scholars and practitioners of leadership are no more sure of what leadership is in 1990 than they were in 1930, and that state of affairs is completely unacceptable. This kind of ignorance (literally ignoring the issue of what leadership is) has to stop. It is no longer acceptable for leadership scholars to begin their book, chapter, or article with statements such as "Leadership has been one of the most researched topics in management. Yet the research results have also been among the most disappointing" (Boal & Bryson, 1988, p. 10). Or "Leadership is one of the most talked about, written about, and researched topics in the area of management and organizational behavior. A vast number of articles and books about the leadership phenomenon have been written from a wide variety of perspectives over the years" (McElroy & Hunger, 1988, p. 169). It is no longer acceptable for authors to write such introductory sentences and then not do something about the problem. It is no longer acceptable for leadership scholars to ignore the issue of what leadership is.

Scholars need to attack the issue head-on. Only when they do that and resolve the issue will their research make any sense or have any impact on how the word *leadership* is used in both the scholarly and the popular literatures and in everyday language. It is time for some exacting criteria to be employed in making decisions about the nature of leadership. It is time for a reconceptualization of leadership based on clear, consistent, and easily identifiable criteria that can be used by scholars and practitioners alike in assessing whether some process or activity qualifies as leadership. In sum, it is time for us to find out what leadership is.

MOVEMENTS IN STUDYING LEADERSHIP

The second statement that many writers on leadership make has to do with the history of studying leadership. These writers often begin their book, chapter, or article with several paragraphs or pages on the different theories or movements of leadership. These summaries are frequently boiled down to the great man theory that was popular in the early part of this century, group theory in the 1930s and 1940s, trait theory in the 1940s and 1950s, behavior theory in the 1950s and 1960s, contingency/situational theory in the 1960s and 1970s, and excellence theory in the 1980s. (The last-mentioned movement is not as universally recognized as the others.)

These summaries of leadership theory movements are ritualistically repeated by author after author, especially textbook writers. As with other things that are repeated over and over, people begin to accept them as facts. These movements are part of the folklore of leadership studies and, like other folktales and myths, they are believed because leadership high priests have told us they are true. Writers of management textbooks for schools of business, education, nursing, and public administration (among others) are particularly fond of explaining leadership by devoting a page or two to these movements in a chapter on leadership.

The reality is quite different and much more complex. A critical analysis of the leadership literature suggests that these oft-repeated formulas for categorizing leadership research and theory are not accurate at all. Like other myths, these oft-repeated narratives of leadership theory movements may be the stories we want to hear, but they are not representative of what actually happened.

In reading the narrative, it is obvious that the story is told in such a way as to give the impression that we leadership scholars have been making progress in our understanding of leadership. In exaggerated form, the story reads like this: In the beginning, around the turn of the century and the first few decades of the twentieth century, the people who knew about leadership thought that only great men (and a few women) could be leaders. But in the depths of the Great Depression in the 1930s, some bright social psychologists found from their studies of groups that democratic leadership was not only possible but also more effective. So the great man theory gave way to a more egalitarian view of leadership. During and after World War II, people wanted to know what essential traits leaders needed to have in exercising leadership so that the ''good guys'' would win the war and then not lose the peace in the postwar world. When the researchers could not agree on the essential traits of leadership, behaviorist scholars in various disciplines decided in the 1960s to concentrate on leadership as a behavior act, and so they studied what specific behaviors in what combinations produced effective leadership.

After numerous studies, the scholars found that leader behaviors were not the only variables that produced effective leadership, so in the 1970s they added the situation upon which the leadership behaviors were contingent, and many people were pleased with these three-dimensional models. When the 1980s came around and Americans found that their country had taken second place to other, more prosperous nations, certain leadership scholars discovered that other theorists had not been able to put all the theories together in one holistic framework, so they packaged the excellence theory of leadership. Leadership produces excellent organizations because leaders are great executives who have certain traits (high energy, trustworthiness, charismatic persona, visionary purpose, honest communication, obsession with goals) that help them choose the correct behaviors (challenge the process, model the way, manage by walking around, position the organization, manipulate the culture, encourage the heart, empower collaborators, and stick to the knitting) so that they do the right thing in key situations (mergers, international economic competition, lower productivity, consumer dissatisfaction, volatile times) by facilitating the work group democratically but forcefully.

The telling of the leadership story (done in less fanciful form than above) is misleading because it gives the impression that our understanding of leadership is more sophisticated and advanced in the 1980s than it was in the 1950s and that we have certainly come a long way from our naiveté of the 1930s. Such progress is simply not the case. There are more scholars and practitioners who think of leadership as group facilitation in the 1980s than there were in the 1930s. Using traits as an explanation of leadership in the 1980s is as popular as it was in the 1950s. And the great man/woman theory of leadership is as strong in 1990 as it was in 1890. Lee Lacocca is our Henry Ford, Malcolm Forbes is our J. Pierpont Morgan, Sam Walton is our John D. Rockefeller, and George Bush is our Theodore Roosevelt.

There are a number of leadership scholars, myself included, who believe, with Hosking and Morley:

The potential value of the leadership concept can be realized only by taking it seriously. The existing literatures does not ''add up'' (Argyris, 1979), partly for the reason that diverse phenomena have been studied in the name of leadership. Here it will be argued that the concept can be made useful when used with greater care and rigor than has typically been the case. However, this, of itself, will not be enough. Decisions must be made about what kind of concept leadership should be. (1988, p. 89).

In 1959, Bennis wrote this stinging critique of the leadership literature:

Of all the hazy and confounding areas in social psychology, leadership theory undoubtedly contends for top nomination. And, ironically, probably more has been written and less known about leadership than about any other topic in the behavioral sciences. Always, it seems, the concept of leadership eludes us or turns up in another form to taunt us again with its slipperiness and complexity. So we have invented an endless proliferation of terms to deal with it . . . and still the concept is not sufficiently defined. As we survey the path leadership theory has taken we spot the wreckage of ''trait theory,'' the ''great man'' theory, and the ''situationists critique,'' leadership styles, functional leadership, and finally leaderless leadership; to say nothing of bureaucratic leadership, charismatic leadership, democratic-autocratic-laissez-faire leadership, group-centered leadership, reality-centered leadership, leadership by objective, and so on. The dialectic and reversals of emphases in this area very nearly rival the tortuous twists and turns of child rearing practices. (p. 259)

In 1970, Jacobs made the same argument in a book he wrote on an exchange theory of leadership:

Perhaps the greatest weakness in the leadership literature has been the striking lack of precision in the use of the term ''leadership'' and probably even in what constitutes the concept. It is not surprising that the processes studied under the label of leadership have been quite varied. Analysis of conditions surrounding the measurements that have been employed, and the situational contexts in which they have been employed, indicates that the total range extends from what seem [*sic*] to be garrulousness, through coercive power, to authority relationships established by the "demand" characteristics of instructions provided by experimenters. With inputs . . . as different as these, it is not surprising that there is a substantial variety of outcomes in the literature concerning what leadership precursors are, and the conditions that facilitate its practice. (pp. 338–339)

In 1977, J. P. Campbell wrote the following critique of leadership studies and presented it at a leadership symposium:

We are in very grave danger of transforming the study of leadership to a study of self-report questionnaire behavior, if indeed, the transformation has not already occurred. The method is too quick, too cheap, and too easy, and there are now many such questionnaire measures that possess no construct validity whatever. (p. 229)

It would be advantageous for the field if a much greater emphasis were given simply to defining, describing, and measuring leadership phenomena. We need much more discussion and argument about what we are trying to explain, not whether a particular theory has been supported or not supported. We need many more descriptive studies that attempt to develop reasonable taxonomies of what leaders and followers actually do when they interact, not more correlations among self-report questionnaires. (p. 234)

In 1978, Pondy presented a critique in a chapter titled "Leadership Is a Language Game":

I find the concept of leadership "style" particularly disturbing. It connotes to me superficiality of action, without either sincerity of intent or substantive meaning. (pp. 88–89)

Nearly all theories of leadership identify only a small number of strategies to choose from. You can use either a democratic, autocratic, or laissez-faire style. You can emphasize either consideration or initiating structure. Or if you really want to get fancy, Vroom and Yetton (1973) offer *six* different things you can do. Now there is something profoundly troubling about this. . . . I believe that we have sacrificed the creative aspects of leadership for its programmatic aspects. (p. 90)

For the most part, leadership research has limited itself to looking at social influence that is of the direct, face-to-face variety. Perhaps this is why there has been so much emphasis on personal style. But some of the most important forms of influence are remote from the behavior being induced. (p. 91)

Mintzberg made some extended comments on the state of leadership literature at a leadership symposium in 1982:

So let me say that I think the literature on leadership is in great shape. But not the "establishment" research literature, by which I mean the material that fills the refereed journals.

When I first looked at that literature, in the mid-1960s, I was frankly appalled: traits pursued fruitlessly for decades, consideration and initiating structure being rediscovered in the research year after year, risky shifts that were eventually discredited, and so on. And what has changed since the 1960s? Every theory that has since come into vogue— and I shall not name them for fear of losing all my friends—has for me fallen with a dull thud. None that I can think of has ever touched a central nerve of leadership— approached its essence. Even the old ones endure. I find in these chapters, intended to move beyond establishment views, that consideration and initiating structure are not dead—they come up repeatedly. Sometimes I think I must be awfully dense: I just do not get the point, and never have.

Even the titles of the theories—new no less than old—reveal the nature of their content— plodding and detached. Since the beginning, there seems to have been a steady convergence on the peripheral at best, and all too often on the trivial and the irrelevant. (p. 250)

In 1984, Dachler made these comments at a leadership symposium:

Nevertheless, Mintzberg's (1982) prescriptions, overstated as they may be, clearly signal the fact that the *nature* of leadership and management in the real world does not fit well our conceptions of it and the methods we use to research leadership and management. (p. 101)

. . . Thus, unless we rethink not only our conceptions of leadership but also our assumptions about the nature of social systems in general, our attempts to refocus leadership will by necessity remain obscure and incomplete. (p. 102)

In 1988, Calas and Smircich developed this critique:

Too often, our solution to problems is the one proposed for the unfortunate Humpty-Dumpty—"more horses, more men." We propose rather than going forward with more horses and more men (a technical solution akin to more of the same), that we not go forward at all, but that we stop—to give attention to what it is we are doing, how we are doing it, and why.

One way out of our stagnation is to reexamine what we have taken for granted as we have produced the academic leadership literature. (p. 202)

Consider the academics doing leadership literature. There are many of them, and they are smart. Almost all of them, however, have been overheard to say at one time or another: "All those studies and what do we really know about the phenomenon?" . . .

Why are these smart people beating their heads against a wall? They claim they are not getting very far with what they are doing, yet they are redoubling their efforts and trying even harder. There must be some other way to understand this behavior [that is called leadership]. (p. 214)

Finally, Watkins, after surveying the literature in 1989, wrote this negative conclusion:

This chapter commenced with a brief survey of some of the major theoretical perspectives on leadership and power. This survey indicated a number of serious shortcomings which are manifest in the traditional functionalist view of these concepts. In particular the functionalist account was charged with being simplistic, ahistorical, static, and lacking in a sense of human agency, while neglecting basic concepts such as the class structure of society. In short, as Perrow has bluntly stated, "the history of research in this area is one of progressive disenchantment." (1986, p. 86). (p. 30)

These are only a few of the critiques that could be quoted. However, they are some of the most forthright and strong, and that is why I selected them. They destroy the notion that the leadership literature adds up and makes sense. It does not.

Another way of telling the leadership studies story is to emphasize the experimental, scientific nature of the research that has been done since 1930, thus explaining the dead ends that leadership researchers have come up against. The point is, of course, that the experimental strategy is a time-honored scientific method, and the fact that leadership scholars have not yet discovered the "right stuff" does not mean they are on the wrong track or headed in the wrong direction. Researchers, like other human beings, follow one of life's most valuable maxims: If at first you don't succeed, try, try again. This narrative of leadership studies is a variation on the old Edison tale we all heard or read in grammar school: that he tried countless filaments before he found the right one for the electric light bulb. Leadership scholars are like Edison; they have been trying to find the correct mix of variables that adds up to leadership.

The story, as told from the experimental, trial-and-error view, goes like this. The great man theory of leadership proved unacceptable by the 1930s, so social psychologists began a new approach to studying leadership. They looked at how leadership emerges and develops in small groups. That line of research reached a dead end when it became clear that the results were not transferable to large groups or organizations. Even before that, however, other researchers looked for universal traits of leaders in order to understand what really makes leadership tick, but that effort was demolished in the 1950s by Stogdill, who compared the results of numerous traits studies and found that they were contradictory and inconclusive. So he and others at Ohio State University declared that leadership should be conceptualized as behavior, but after years of study of initiation of structure and consideration, as well as of other two-dimensional behavior theories, scholars could not isolate key behavioral patterns that made any difference. There seemed to be no one best way for leaders to behave when leading.

With that approach laid to rest, researchers tried to determine what leader behaviors were the best in certain situations. But that approach fell apart, again after many studies and dozens of contingency/situational models were formulated, when leaders realized that they would have to consult decision trees or wheel charts to find out how to behave. There were also thousands of situations that researchers had not studied, so leaders were left on their own, which they did not find very appealing, in view of the fact that situational leadership theory was supposed to have the answers to all their questions about leadership behavior. Finally, in the 1980s, leadership scholars repudiated situational leadership theory and determined that leadership is, after all these false starts, being number one; so, really, leadership is simply doing the right thing to achieve excellence. That meant the researchers had to find out what the right thing is, so they set about researching excellent companies and CEOs, and developed lists of traits, behavior patterns, group facilitation strategies, and culture-shaping practices for would-be leaders.

The point of this narrative, of course, is not that leadership scholars have failed so many times to uncover the secrets of leadership, but that they have been acting like scientists all this time and doing exactly what scientists are supposed to do. If one experiment does not work, the scientists go on to the next until they find the combination that works—just as Edison did with the electric light bulb.

The Narratives: A Critical Analysis

Either of these stories would be fine if it reflected the reality of leadership studies as it has evolved in the twentieth century. Both narratives tell essentially the same story, but they emphasize different points of view, different perspectives. The trouble with the narratives—both the basic story lines and the two perspectives—is that they do not tell the real story. The narratives miss the mark in five important ways:

1. The narratives are about leadership theory as given to students and practitioners, the consumers of the leadership literature, by social psychologists and management scientists. They leave out the stories of leadership theory from other academic disciplines and from the popular press.

2. The narratives indicate that the different theories of leadership were separate and distinct movements in the history of leadership studies. The reality is that the movements and the models they produced were not distinct from one another. The theories are a mish-mash of the structural-functionalist framework of groups and organizations. The models feed on one another and are so intertwined that they are indistinguishable except to intellectuals who study leadership as a profession.

3. The narratives suggest that each of the movements had a beginning and an end. Such is not the case. The theories have not died; they have been living in leadership books, chapters, and articles for years, and continue to live in them in 1990.

4. The narratives tell us about the theories of the dominant paradigm; they say nothing about alternative leadership theories that have been on the scene for years. The stories tell us that these alternative views don't count.

5. The narratives are intended to communicate the view that progress is being made in our understanding of leadership. In this sense, these stories, like other mythological tales, produce a feeling of well-being, that all is well with leadership studies as an academic discipline and with the practice of leadership in the world. The message is this: We really do know more about leadership in 1990 than we did in 1960, or 1970, or 1980. That message is very comforting to hear, especially if one believes, as many do, that leadership is a crucial element in the survival and progress of our organizations, societies, and world.

Some comments on each of these five points will help to underscore the rationale for this critique. They will also help readers to understand why a new school of leadership must be developed if scholars and practitioners really want to understand what leadership is and how it operates in groups, organizations, societies, and the world.

Leadership as Social Psychologists and Management Scientists View It

The narratives outline a view of leadership articulated by social psychologists and management theorists. All of the theories, except the original great man theory, were developed by social psychologists and management scientists. The great man theory was what academics were presented with when they first began to think about leadership as a social construct in the early twentieth century. It is interesting to note that after berating the great man theory of leadership for decades, management scholars took it up again in the 1980s.

The group theory of leadership was developed by social psychologists, as Browne and Cohn's (1958) compendium makes abundantly clear. The trait theory was developed by both management scientists and social psychologists, with the latter having the dominant role in the trait research. Stogdill's penetrating analysis (1974, pp. 35–111) makes that point quite dramatically. Interestingly, Stogdill was a professor of both management and psychology at Ohio State University.

The behavioral theory movement was primarily the work of management theorists and social psychologists in the late 1950s who believed that they had to accept behaviorism as the overarching scientific perspective in order to be respected in the academic community. They were not the only behavioral scientists to hold that belief. For the same reason anthropologists, educators, political scientists, and sociologists adopted the behavioral perspective. Thus the study of leadership was infused with a large dose of behaviorism that has been retained to this day.

The contingency/situational theory movement was the work of management scientists who took psychology to heart and of social psychologists who dabbled in management science—a popular thing to do in the late 1960s and 1970s, with Tavistock, Escalan, and the National Training Laboratories doing sensitivity training and group dynamics, and with the popularity of human relations, organizational development, and pop psychology in organizations and management thinking. The marriage of management and psychology was, and still is, very evident in the work of the contingency/situational leadership scholars.

The excellence theory of leadership is almost completely the work of management scholars in business and educational administration. The proliferation of leadership books in the 1980s was overwhelmingly the result of these scholars' becoming interested in leadership studies.

While these stories are accurate as far as they go, they do not go far enough, so the narrative in toto represents an inaccurate picture of where leadership studies has been since 1930. The reality is that leadership theory has been developed in anthropology, history, military science, political science, and sociology as well as in the popular press (trade books, newspapers, and magazines) and in television programs. To some extent—though this has not been researched a great deal—there are leadership theories embedded in the literature, drama, music, and visual arts of the period since 1930.

Leadership is by its very nature a multidisciplinary concept. The narratives treat leadership as a bidisciplinary subject, and when social psychology and management science came together, it became an unidisciplinary subject. Hosking and Morley (1988) focus on how inaccurate the psychological/managerial view of leadership is: "We take the view that leadership processes represent a special kind of organizing activity, the organizing activity that is political decision making, construed in the widest possible sense. . . . In sum, leadership is an inherently political process" (p. 91).

There is no indication in the narratives that leadership is conceived as a political process. Management and psychological scientists do not take kindly to conceptualizing leadership as a political process. Zaleznik (1989), a management theorist of leadership with a Freudian bent, argues that politics is part of the problem, not the solution, in trying to conceptualize and practice leadership.

In business organizations as in the family, politics flourishes in the absence of content and expression of talents. Cooperation for self-protection, although an understandable tendency, is not true cooperation. One of the critical jobs of leadership is to overcome these political inclinations and to encourage the expression of talent and the performance of useful work. True cooperation then follows because people are working for a dynamic organization that has direction. Leadership also amplifies the motivation to work because people experience the fusion of rationality with talent. (p. 35)

Zaleznik opined that the political model of leadership as explicated by Neustadt (1980) "may reflect the realities of election politics and bureaucratic continuity, but is bizarre if applied to business" (p. 32). Out with Burns, Kellerman, Lindblom, Neustadt, Paige, and Tucker, who do not fit into the rational, technological, and psychological understanding of leadership propagated by the management theorists.

Many anthropologists, historians, political scientists, and authors in the popular press conceptualize leadership as a political process. The consistency with which management and psychological scientists have developed a worldview of leadership devoid of politics shows how narrow their unidisciplinary perspective is and how inaccurate their narrative of leadership theory is.

Sociologists and anthropologists have been very interested in the nature–nurture issues concerning leaders and leadership. The notion that leaders are born and not made has been dismissed summarily by management scientists and to some extent by social psychologists.

The idea that leadership is a natural phenomenon—as essential to human existence and progress as water and air are to human life—is taken for granted by management and psychological scholars, but much more hotly debated by sociologists and anthropologists. Miner, a management scholar, proposed a "heresy" (his word) in 1975 at a leadership symposium: that the concept of leadership has outlived its usefulness. Hence, I suggest that we abandon leadership in favor of some other, more fruitful way of cutting up the theoretical pie" (p. 200). The notion that the concept of leadership should be abandoned was unthinkable to the mainstream leadership scholars at the symposium and to those who commented on the heresy for years afterward. Not only would such a suggestion destroy their profession, but the very idea was unthinkable because leadership was natural to human existence and had appeared in human thought as long ago as biblical antiquity and ancient Greece and Rome. They were not willing to debate the idea, quite prevalent in the sociological literature, that leadership is a nurtured concept of quite recent origin.

The idea that certain people are born to be leaders remains quite prevalent in some of the anthropological, historical, and sociological frameworks of leadership, as well as in many views of leadership that have appeared in the popular press and in the arts since 1930. The great man/woman theory is far from dead, but management and psychological scholars have actively discredited the notion since the 1930s. Unwittingly, however, many management scholars resurrected the basic notion of the great man/woman theory in the 1980s in articulating the excellence theory of leadership and more recently in a charismatic theory of leadership. Central to both theories is the requirement that great women and men be leaders.

The narrow perspective of management and psychological scientists regarding leadership will be documented in Chapters 3 and 4. At this point, my objective has been to indicate that there was no room for other, quite legitimate frameworks of leadership in the narratives of mainstream leadership theory. As a result, the stories do not accurately reflect the real history of leadership studies as an academic discipline.

Distinct Theories of Leadership

The second inaccuracy in the narratives of leadership theory as told by mainstream theorists is that the stories present the theories as distinct and separate from one another. First came the great man theory, against which group theory reacted. Then came the trait, behaviorist, contingency/situational, and excellence theories, all of which reacted against and improved on the theories preceding them. The earlier theories were inadequate to explain leadership, so the psychologists and management scientists had to distance themselves from them in order to develop a theory that was new, distinct, and more sophisticated, and that did, finally, explain leadership.

The separate and distinct view is misleading. The group theories included traits in their explanations and prescriptions concerning group facilitation. The trait theories looked like great men caricatures in egalitarian dress. The behavioral theories were very group- and trait-oriented, and the contingency/situational theories merely added a third dimension to the two-dimensional behavior theories, thus continuing to be a hodgepodge of group, trait, and behavior explanations of previous theories. The excellence theories more or less integrate all the previous theories in a more elitist context, and, if anything, leadership scholars are more inclined to espouse the great man/woman theory in the 1980s than they have been since the Great Depression.

All of these theories have common elements. As critical theorists are wont to explain, all leadership theories have a structural-functionalist frame of reference in the hierarchical, linear, pragmatic, Newtonian background assumptions of what makes the world go around (Smyth, 1989b). As many commentators have indicated, the leadership theories are all very management oriented. They simply take for granted that leadership and management are the same. As Marxist scholars on the left and elite power theorists on the right have said, the leadership theories have been dominated by an almost total concentration on the leader, the consequence of which is that there has been almost no interest in the followers. In these theories, *leadership* and *leader* have been used as synonymous terms.

Other critiques of these leadership theories have pointed to the major points of view that they have in common: The theories have been goal-achievement-oriented, often in the most pragmatic, self-interested, individualistic, cost-benefit terms possible; they overemphasize face-to-face, dyadic, and small group relationships to the detriment of transforming, larger, symbolic, and political relationships that may be organizational and societal in their breadth and largely carried on through a medium that is not face-to-face; they are representative of male, even macho, characteristics that contain heroic, folkloric, Old West, and Hollywood images of what males do as leaders; they are utilitarian, short-term, and materialistic in their ethical base; and, finally, they are excessively rationalistic, technocratic, quantitative, and scientific in their background assumptions, as well as in the language used to formulate the concepts and the methods used to research leadership and then discuss the research conclusions in the literature.

In sum, all of the leadership theories have reflected the industrial paradigm very well. The descriptors that scholars have given to the industrial era are exactly those I have given above. Analyzed individually or in toto, these leadership theories have been (1) structural-functionalist, (2) management-oriented, (3) personalistic in focusing only on the leader, (4) goal-achievement-dominated, (5) self-interested and individualistic in outlook, (6) male-oriented, (7) utilitarian and materialistic in ethical perspective, and (8) rationalistic, technocratic, linear, quantitative, and scientific in language and methodology. In only one characteristic do they contradict the descriptors of the industrial paradigm: their penchant for concentrating on face-to-face and small group relationships. While that characteristic is pervasive in the management frame, it is not a descriptor of the industrial paradigm, which is much more oriented to impersonal and bureaucratic relationships.

The point is that the various leadership theories of the period since 1930 are not discrete and distinct conceptual frameworks. There are very strong background assumptions based on the industrial paradigm that are part and parcel of all of the leadership theories and make these theories more or less the same.

Separate Time Frames for the Leadership Theories

The narratives tell us that each leadership theory dominated a certain period in the history of leadership studies, and then disappeared after being discredited by the scholars who developed the new theories.

The facts are that while several movements were quite popular during certain periods of time, their dominance was far from total. Contrary to popular belief, none of the theories have become completely extinct. They reappear decade after decade, sometimes disguised, sometimes in another form, but basically intact and flourishing.

For example, many commentators see the 1980s as dominated by the excellence theory of leadership. But that theory is highly influenced by the great man/woman theory, as all the leadership books on CEOs demonstrate. Burns's transformational theory of leadership, very popular during the decade, is very political and ethical in its orientation. Bennis and Nanus (1985), Kouzes and Posner (1987), Kotter (1988), and Maccoby (1981, 1988) were very concerned with leader traits and behavior. J. G. Hunt (1984a, b, & c) was pushing a second generation of contingency theories. Fiedler and Garcia (1987) published a book revising and updating Fiedler's contingency theory of the 1960s. Smith and Peterson (1988) documented scores of recent publications on group, behavioral, and situational theories, and then spent the second half of their book trying to shore up those theories. Foster (1986a & b) and Smyth (1989b) articulated a critical theory of leadership that has clear Marxist roots. Tucker (1981) and Kellerman (1984a) developed political models of leadership. Bass (1985) and Conger (1989a) unearthed a charismatic theory of leadership. S. M. Hunt (1984) and McElroy and Hunger (1988) spread the news about an attribution theory of leadership. Blanchard continued to publish a spate of one-minute manager/leader minivolumes that further refined the situational theory of leadership developed in the early 1970s.

Now, if the excellence theory of leadership was so dominant in the 1980s, why were those authors publishing works on other theories during that decade? The facts are that any one theory did not unduly dominate any decade to the exclusion of other theories. The theories did not run riot in any one separate time period, nor did they disappear from the picture when the next so-called dominant theory appeared on the scene. Once the theories gained a certain currency, they remained in the literature, and they continue to remain there in 1990. The theories also remained in the behavioral habits of practitioners who continued to put the theories into practice long after they were discredited by researchers.

A much more accurate interpretation of these theories as a saga of popular movements is that there were periods of heightened popularity for certain theories, but when that popularity waned, the theories remained in the minds and hearts of scholars and practitioners alike because they appealed to the structural-functional frame within which most researchers operated and to the managerial psyche of most practitioners. In sum, they came out of the industrial paradigm and spoke to theoretical and practical purveyors of the industrial complex.

Alternative Leadership Theories

The theories that make up the narratives of leadership theory are all representative of the dominant conceptual framework in management science and social psychology. As a result, the theories that speak in a different voice, and that represent an alternative paradigm, are not part of the story.

I have already indicated that anthropological, historical, political, and sociological theories had not been allowed into the inner sanctum, not so much because they reflected a paradigm different from the industrial paradigm that dominates leadership studies, but because they had a different context, a different environment, a different worldview than did the theories of management and psychological writers. Many of the scholars from these other disciplines were as behavior-oriented and as committed to the structural-functional frame as were the management scientists and the social psychologists. As a result, the anthropologists, historians, political scientists, and sociologists were as caught up in the scientific, quantitative, rationalistic view of theory and models as the other scholars. But there were still fundamental differences. The anthropologists thought in terms of culture, the historians thought in terms of long time frames, the political scientists thought in terms of politics, and the sociologists thought in terms of institutions and societies. These worldviews were foreign to the management and psychological researchers. They did not think in terms of culture, long time frames, politics, and societies. Their worldviews extended from the individual to dyadic relationships to small groups, to departments, and to organizations; and their time frames were typically short-range.

The exclusion of alternative theories from the leadership studies narratives has not been a recent problem. It extends back to the 1930s, but it became particularly severe from the 1950s to the mid-1980s, during which time the field became a fairly exclusive club that a few management and psychological scholars controlled. The situation has improved a bit since the mid-1980s, primarily because so many people were attracted to Burns's theory, and he certainly was not a member of the club. The scholars who had alternative views of leadership could no longer be ignored except by the most dedicated empiricists (see Immegart, 1988). And, much to the credit of the 1980s scholars who articulated the excellence theory of leadership, they began using concepts such as culture, politics, and society, and they started looking toward a longer time frame.

Selznick (1957), a good example of a scholar who was ignored by the mainstream management and psychological scientists, was a political sociologist who wrote a landmark study of the TVA. In 1957 he produced a small book in which he distinguished leadership from holding an office/position and likened it to institutionalization, by which he meant infusing values and purpose into an organization (all of which is a very typical sociological point of view). "The institutional leader," he wrote, "is primarily an expert in the promotion and protection of values" (p. 28). Although popular with practitioners, the book and its understanding of leadership never penetrated the group and behavioral views of leadership that dominated the leadership studies narratives.

In the 1960s and 1970s, there were a number of leadership scholars who defined leadership in terms of influence, but that view never entered the mainstream literature because the concept was too political and slippery. It is very difficult to do an empirical study of influence. Leadership as influence is not part of the narratives.

Sociologists have developed an attribution theory of leadership. As an attribute, leadership is the name that people use to make sense out of complex events and the outcomes of events they otherwise would not be able to explain. In other words, people attribute leadership to certain individuals who are called leaders because people want to believe that leaders cause things to happen rather than have to explain causality by understanding complex social forces or analyzing the dynamic interaction among people, events, and environment (Calder, 1977; S. Hunt, 1984; McElroy & Hunger, 1988; Pfeffer, 1977). Such a notion calls into question the idea of leadership as something that is really real; and as such, the narratives of leadership studies could not accommodate attribution theory.

Finally, the saga of leadership studies does not mention Burns (1978), whose theory of leadership is politically based and to a large extent ignores most of the mainstream theories. His transactional leadership model has its antecedents in Hollander (1964; 1978a), who was part of the mainstream group, and in Jacobs (1970), who was not; both of them espoused an exchange theory of leadership. Even though the exchange theory was promoted by some management and psychological scholars, it was never accepted by the major scholars who told the narratives because the theory was based on power relations and required bargaining, trading, and compromising among leaders and followers. Exchange/transactional theory makes followers central to leadership because they are significantly involved in the negotiations that account for the exchange/transaction. In addition, they evidently have minds of their own. Mainstream theorists were unwilling to think of leadership as anything beyond leaders/managers doing leadership. Leaders and managers are the only people who count in these theories. In sum, Burns's transactional model of leadership, like its predecessor, exchange theory, was too political, and therefore unacceptable to management and psychological purists who told the leadership studies narratives.

Burns became famous among alternative leadership scholars because his model of transformational leadership included an ethical/moral dimension that, prior to 1978, had not been infused into any leadership theory. Selznick (1957) had equated leadership with the infusion of values into organizations, but values are not necessarily ethical or moral. There was certainly no room in the saga of the structural-functionalists, who eschewed any kind of value orientation as a bias that made scholarship unscientific, for a leadership theory that inserted a required moral component. Even after some management and psychological scholars discovered Burns, they sanitized his concept of transformation to include any kind of significant change, not just changes that had a morally uplifting effect on people (see Avolio & Bass, 1988; Bass, 1985; Conger & Kanungo, 1988; Peters & Waterman, 1982; Bennis & Nanus, 1985). Moral transformation then became performance beyond expectations, excellence, and charisma. Please understand what happened here—these authors didn't say, "We disagree with Burns because we don't believe that leadership must have a moral dimension." They changed the meaning of the concept of transformation, yet claimed they were being faithful to Burns's theory of leadership. Now that it had been so sanitized, management and psychological scholars could incorporate "transformational leadership" into the excellence theories of leadership and include the sanitized version in the narratives of leadership studies.

The narratives tell the story of leadership studies from a very narrow perspective and thus give a very inaccurate description of what scholars have thought about leadership since the 1930s. Since the 1960s particularly, there have been significant views of leadership that the mainstream scholars have ignored, much to the detriment of leadership studies as an academic discipline and to the practitioners who put leadership theory to work. To some extent, what is considered mainstream was expanded considerably in the 1980s; but old, worn, and narrow concepts of leadership die hard, as J. G. Hunt's (1984c) label of Burns's theory as radical (pp. 131–133) and Immegart's (1988) evaluation of Burns's theory as nonempirical (p. 260) attest.

Theoretical Quiescence

Myths and rituals, Edelman (1964, 1971) suggested in proposing a symbolic view of politics, serve either to induce quiescence or to cause arousal. The same myths and rituals are used by people on different sides of an issue or by people on the same side of an issue at different times in a policy-making process to make other persons (1) feel good about events, movements, and/or proposals, and thus feel satisfied about them, or (2) feel unhappy and dissatisfied about them, and thus become aroused to take action or somehow express their dissatisfaction. Satisfied people are generally quiet, accepting, calm, and inactive— in a word, quiescent. Dissatisfied people who are aroused generally express that dissatisfaction by grumbling, quarreling, agitating, speaking up, and making counterproposals—in sum, by taking action.

What is interesting about Edelman's model of symbolic politics is that the same myths and rituals can be used as tactics in the play for power by opposing groups. One group of leaders and followers can use them to quiet people by inducing satisfaction; another group of leaders and followers can use them to arouse people by inducing dissatisfaction. Or the framework can be put into two or more different time periods. In other words, the same group of leaders and followers can use the myths and rituals at one point in time to quiet people and at a later time to arouse them, and then, at a third point in time, to quiet them again. Either way, Edelman underscored the point that the myths and rituals are used to provide symbolic reassurance that the system (group, department, organization, society, world) is working or, alternatively, is not working. Interpreting what is happening in the present in light of the myths and rituals of the culture is the key to determining whether the system is or is not working, and whether quiescence or arousal is needed.

Another integral proposition in Edelman's symbolic theory of politics is that symbolic rewards are at least as important to people in the political process as are tangible rewards, and sometimes are more important. Since it is impossible to please all of the people all of the time with tangible rewards, leaders and followers use symbolic rewards to help keep people satisfied, thus providing symbolic reassurance that the system is working. Edelman indicated that there is considerable evidence to show that symbolic rewards actually work. They are appreciated and sought after; they help people feel good about themselves, their class, and the system; they allow people to accept decisions or events that are not personally appreciated; they develop confidence in the leader's ability to solve problems. In summary, they provide reassurance and maintain quiescence. They encourage people to say "We are making progress," even when there is considerable factual evidence to the contrary.

Edelman's model of symbolic politics fits perfectly with the myths and rituals that leadership scholars have promoted in the narratives about leadership studies.

The mythological narratives—the saga as told in either version—are designed to provide symbolic reassurance to the readers of the leadership literature that (1) the system of research has been working; (2) the leadership scholars have been doing what they are supposed to do—increase our understanding of leadership; (3) there has been progress toward that objective, and as a result both scholars and practitioners can rest assured that they have an increasingly sophisticated understanding of leadership; and (4) this better understanding of leadership will help make organizations more productive and, in the end, the United States and the world a better place to live and work. (Almost all of the researchers who were part of the narrative are from the United States.)

The myths are told over and over again in management textbooks used in business, education, health, and public administration programs throughout the United States. They are told over and over again in two major handbooks of leadership (Stogdill, 1974; Bass, 1981), in eight volumes from the leadership symposia (1973–1988), in three editions of the *Handbook of Social Psychology* (Gibb, 1954; Gibb, 1969; Hollander, 1985); in Cartwright's (1965) chapter in the *Handbook of Organizations*, in House and Baetz's (1979) chapter in *Research in Organizational Behavior*; in Immegart's (1968) chapter in the *Handbook of*

Research on Educational Administration; in Vroom's (1976) chapter in the *Handbook of Industrial and Organizational Psychology*, and in leadership books such as Boles and Davenport (1975), Smith and Peterson (1988), and Yukl (1989). And, of course, the myths are told over and over again in the books written by the major leadership scholars of the period since about 1960: Bass (1960), Blake and Mouton (1964), Fiedler (1967), Hersey and Blanchard (1988 and previous editions), Hollander (1964), Likert (1961), McGregor (1960), Stogdill and Coons (1957), and Vroom and Yetton (1973).

The major mythological message in these and other works is that the researchers and scholars are making progress in understanding leadership. To be sure, there usually are one-sentence or one-paragraph caveats that sometimes question the pace or the strength of the progress, but these authors leave no doubt that leadership researchers in general (and they in particular) have made significant contributions to the overall understanding of leadership, which is the work of leadership studies as a discipline.

For example, even after hundreds of commentators have faulted Fiedler and his associates for confusing leaders with managers and for producing a conceptual framework that has little or no validity and makes little sense in understanding leadership, Fiedler and Garcia (1987) remain firm that leaders and managers are the same and that their contingency model is an accurate construct of leadership:

There have been various proposals (e.g., Gibb, 1969) to reserve the term *leader* for those who lead by virtue of their personal charisma and the esteem in which their subordinates hold them. The term *head* supposedly designates the administrator or manager who holds the position by virtue of administrative appointment. Our research thus far does not demonstrate the need for this distinction. (p. 3)

The effect of all this reassurance is, of course, to induce satisfaction and thus quiescence among other leadership scholars and the practitioners of leadership. The message has been, and still is: "All is going well and we are making progress." And the mythological narratives have had their intended effect, at least until the late 1980s, when the number of scholars calling for a better understanding of leadership had, perhaps, reached a more critical mass.

The rituals surrounding leadership studies have had the same effect. The myths and rituals reinforce one another to provide the powerful symbolic reassurance that the system is productive and progressive.

The first ritual that became very popular, starting with the LBDQ in the 1950s, was giving tests. Several dozen of these self-report questionnaires were developed, including Fiedler's LPC questionnaire, tests to determine if the leader is Theory X or Theory Y or (later) Theory Z, Blake and Mouton's tests to place the leader on the managerial grid, Hersey and Blanchard's battery of tests for situational leaders, Kouzes and Posner's equally impressive package, and those used by the Center for Creative Leadership, the NASSP (and other) assessment centers, and consultants for organizations. Testing as a ritual plays to our penchant for quantification and for numerical symbols of how we are doing as leaders. It also accepts the concept of science as gathering empirical evidence and making conclusions only on the basis of such evidence. If the test shows *it*, whatever *it* is must be true. Since the tests are better and better as the years go by, the scholars are saying, we must be making progress.

An earlier ritual, which evidently is no longer acceptable, was to frame one's understanding of leadership in the context of people and results identified as letters of the alphabet. "If A did such-and-such to B, and C resulted from this interaction, D (leadership) occurred." Again, such objectification of people and processes was an attempt on the part of the behaviorists, particularly, to look scientific.

Developing diagrams of two-dimensional models of leadership has been a major ritual in leadership studies. Drawing two-by-two squares and giving each of the four squares a clever name was almost a necessity if a researcher wanted to sell his or her work. When the two-dimensional models became three-dimensional, the visual overlays of the third dimension were taken seriously, as the artwork shows. Models are a way of collapsing complex material into understandable pictures that present the research as a whole. What was ritualistic was not so much the practice of drawing models as the sameness of the models as they were diagrammed. Rituals are actions that are repeated over and over to ensure belief. The two-by-two models certainly did that. Everyone believed that a two-factor model was the basic way to understand leadership. When the two-dimensional models became three-dimensional, the third dimension showed progress.

Another ritual was drawing systems-oriented figures with squares, rectangles, triangles, and circles connected by arrows. These diagrams were intended to show how leadership as a process goes from one point to the next and finally ends up with, usually, goal achievement. Since the systems model was widely respected in the academic community, adopting the ritual in leadership studies helped to show that researchers were current in their scientific frame of reference.

Less popular, but still highly valued, were decision trees ritualizing how leaders should behave in certain circumstances. Variations on that kind of ritual were wheels that could be manipulated to show leaders what to do in any given situation. Other rituals were two- or three- or four-column charts with descriptors in each column, continuum lines showing various degrees of leadership behaviors, and short simulation exercises that allowed people to practice "leadership."

Another ritual is producing movies, audio- and videocassettes, workbooks, overhead/slides, and computerized software to train people in one of the leadership models. These audio and visual aids are intended to develop confidence in the leadership models as accurate and reliable. They also win disciples who support a particular model, and these disciples then convert other people to the approach.

Doing collaborative research is another ritual: Bennis and Nanus, Blake and Mouton, Browne and Cohn, Cartwright and Zander, Fiedler and Chemers, Fiedler and Garcia, Hersey and Blanchard, House and Mitchell, J. G. Hunt and Larson, J. G. Hunt and Osborn, Katz and Kahn, Kouzes and Posner, McCall and Lombardo, Peters and Waterman, P. B. Smith and Peterson, Tannenbaum and Schmidt, Tichy and Devanna, and Vroom and Yetton are but a few of the twosomes involved in leadership studies. The 1980s saw a number of threesomes and foursomes writing chapters and articles. Collaborative research by two or more scholars may be viewed as a way of building confidence in the output of the research.

Finally, a very important ritual was to focus on styles as a way to make leadership meaningful, especially to practitioners, who were assumed not to be interested in anything more substantial. This ritual was so important that leadership studies has been virtually identified with leadership styles. Styles are fairly easy to work with, both from a researcher's point of view, since they can be quantified and objectified, and from a practitioner's point of view, since they can be used to work on one's leadership ability. Again, these rituals give the impression that both the researchers and the practitioners are making progress in understanding and engaging in leadership.

On the other side of the coin, researchers like myself and others, especially since the mid-1980s, have used the myths and rituals contained in the narratives to arouse other researchers and practitioners so that they become dissatisfied with mainstream leadership research. If enough scholars express their dissatisfaction and if practitioners join in, a climate for change may develop and we may experience a transformation in our understanding of leadership. A shift in paradigm could result, which could give us a whole new understanding of leadership.

In this context, the myths and rituals are used to show that the mainstream leadership theories did not live up to the hopes and dreams, the basic objectives, that the mythological narratives have promised for leadership studies. Burns (1978) began the process, attacking the myths and rituals indirectly, and even more substantively by developing a completely new understanding of leadership that did not embrace any of the mainstream theories which make up the narrative. Greenleaf (1977) did the same thing in developing his servant leadership model. Pondy's (1978) "Leadership Is a Language Game" challenges the leadership narrative more directly. Dubin (1979) confronted the mainstream literature head-on in "Metaphors of Leadership: An Overview." So did Mintzberg (1982) in his "If You're Not Serving Bill and Barbara, Then You're Not Serving Leadership." Peters and Waterman's attack in "The Rational Model" (1982, pp. 29–54) was more generalized but no less effective. Feminists have been more effective in critiquing management theories than leadership theories, but lately several have distinguished leadership from management and as a consequence have hit the mainstream theorists in more vulnerable areas (see Buckley & Steffy, 1986; Calas & Smircich, 1988; Kellerman, 1984a; Sayre, 1986; Stewart, 1984). Hosking and Morley (1988) have a stinging critique of mainstream theories in "The Skills of Leadership." The chapters in Smyth's (1989b) book are filled with critical theorists slaying the myths and rituals of structural-functionalism as it relates to leadership studies. Manz and Sims (1989) also reject the dominant paradigm, as does Sergiovanni (1990), I think.

This book serves the same objective; its message is loud and clear. The leadership narratives may have served their purposes since the 1930s in reflecting the industrial paradigm, but they are no longer acceptable as our understanding of leadership is transformed in the twenty-first century to reflect a postindustrial paradigm. Leadership scholars need to develop a new leadership narrative with revised myths and rituals that fit the postindustrial paradigm. And practitioners of leadership need to adopt postindustrial leadership models that help them make sense of what they do as leaders and followers in the postmodern world of the twenty-first century. Only with these transformed leadership models in their minds will they be able to develop the skills—the practical ways of doing leadership—that are necessary to help make the future work.

3

Definitions of Leadership: 1900–1979

Definitions are boring to many people. But, as much as people are uninterested in a discussion of definitions, the issue of defining leadership is central to the problems both scholars and practitioners have had with conceptualizing and practicing leadership. Dealing with—better yet, confronting—this issue is central to the message of this book and the importance it may have in making a break-through concerning the study and practice of leadership.

Actually, the issue of leadership definitions is rather exciting, assuming that the notion of controversy is in one's understanding of exciting.

ORIGINS OF THE WORD *LEADERSHIP*

Stogdill (1974) included a short statement about the origins of the words *leader* and *leadership* in his *Handbook of Leadership*, and Bass (1981) repeated the information in his edition of the *Handbook*.

A preoccupation with leadership as opposed to headship based on inheritance, usurpation, or appointment occurs predominantly in countries with an Anglo-Saxon heritage. The *Oxford English Dictionary* (1933) notes the appearance of the word "leader" in the English language as early as the year 1300. However, the word "leadership" did not appear until the first half of the nineteenth century in writings about political influence and control of the British Parliament. (Bass, 1981, p. 7)

This information has been repeated in several books on leadership, but the recent origin of the word *leadership* is not generally recognized by scholars or practitioners. I think that the relatively recent appearance of the word in the English language has important implications for the study of leadership, so I decided to test Stogdill's conclusion by looking up the word in as many etymological reference books and dictionaries as I could find. Included in my research were several dictionaries in rare book collections. My research generally substantiates Stogdill's and Bass's statements, but some elaboration would be very helpful, I believe, since the brevity of their statements does not do justice to what is involved in the issue. What follows, then, is an extended discussion of the meanings of the words *lead*, *leader*, and *leadership* in the English language as those words have come down to us through the last few centuries.

Etymological dictionaries all say much the same thing. The verb "to lead" comes from the Old English word *leden* or *loedan*, which meant "to make go," "to guide," or "to show the way," and the Latin word *ducere*, which meant "to draw, drag, pull; to lead, guide, conduct." From all accounts, the words *lead*, *leader*, and *leading* have been used in several European languages with Anglo-Saxon and Latin roots from 1300 to the present. France seems to be the exception; there, even in the late twentieth century, the word *leader* does not translate well (see Blondel, 1987, pp. 12–13). Actually, several references given in the *Oxford English Dictionary* (1933) are dated earlier than 1300. The Latin word *ducere* was used in the Bible and other Christian books as early as 800, and perhaps even before then.

DICTIONARY DEFINITIONS

The earliest dictionaries I could find were Candrey (1604) and Cockeran (1623) and neither had the word *lead* in them. (Note: The references for the dictionaries used in this section appear at the end of this chapter, not at the end of the book.) However, both dictionaries were comparatively short, and so both lexicographers must have been selective in the words that were included. As a result, the two dictionaries do not allow one to draw any conclusions.

I found two dictionaries from the eighteenth century. The first was Samuel Johnson's (1755). The verb *lead* had several definitions: "to guide by the hand; to conduct to any place; to conduct as head or commander; to introduce by going first; to guide, show the method of attaining; to draw, entice, allure; to induce, to prevail on by pleasing motives; to pass, to spend in any certain manner." Literary examples of the use of the word from the Bible, Milton, Shakespeare, Swift, Bacon, and others followed the definitions.

Leader was defined as "one that leads; captain, commander; one who goes first; and one at the head of a party or faction." Johnson defined the noun *lead* as "guidance, first place" and noted in a famous statement which has been quoted quite often that the noun was "a low despicable word." The word *leadership* was not defined, giving us the first solid evidence that it was a word English-speaking people did *not* use in the middle of the eighteenth century.

Johnson's extensive treatment of the words *lead* and *leader* suggests that they were in common usage in the eighteenth century, at least among educated people. I would think that Johnson's literary examples also suggest that the words were in seventeenth-century dictionaries, but I just wasn't able to find them.

Perry's *Royal Standard English Dictionary* (1788), the second eighteenth-century dictionary I found, was not nearly so extensive in its treatment of the words. The noun *lead* was defined exactly as in Johnson's dictionary, but the verb *lead* was defined very simply: "to conduct, guide, go first." *Leader* was defined simply as "captain, conductor." *Leadership* was not defined.

The nineteenth-century dictionaries treat the three words extensively and with multiple meanings. The definitions are quite similar to those given by Johnson in 1755. Perry's *English Dictionary* (1805) gave eleven definitions for the verb *lead*: "to guide by the hand; conduct to any place; head; conduct as head or commander; introduce by going first; guide; show the method of attaining; induce; prevail by pleasing motives; pass; to go first and show the way." A *leader* was defined as "one who leads or conducts; a captain, commander, chief, chieftain; a conductor; one who goes first; one at the head of any party or faction." The word *leadership* was not defined.

Crabb, in his *English Synonymes* (1839), indicated that the word *lead* had an unsavory connotation. He compared the words *lead*, *conduct*, and *guide*:

These terms are all employed to denote the influence which one person has over the movements or actions of another; but the first implies nothing more than personal presence and direction or going before, the last two convey also the idea of superior intelligence; . . . In the literal sense it is the hand that *leads*, the head that *conducts*, and the eye that *guides*; one *leads* an infant; *conducts* a person to a given spot; and *guides* a traveller. (p. 191)

In his *New Dictionary of the English Language* (1844), Richardson lumped *lead*, *leader*, and *leading* together as meaning "to go before as guide or conductor; to show the way or induce to follow; to conduce or conduct; to induce, attract, or persuade; to regulate the course; to draw on; to cause to follow or pursue." Richardson's definitions are important because they are the first to include the words *follow* and *persuade*.

Webster's *An American Dictionary of the English Language* (1828) listed thirteen definitions of the verb *lead*, including all of those given by Perry (1805) plus the following: "to draw, entice, allure; to induce, prevail on, influence; to pass, spend, that is draw out; to exercise dominion." The words *influence* and *exercise dominion* were used for the first time to define the concept of leading. The word *leader* had the same definitions as in Perry, along with "a performer

who leads a band or choir.'' And, more important, the word *leadership* appeared
in an English dictionary for the first time (at least as far as I have been able to
determine). Webster defined *leadership* as ''the state or condition of a leader,''
a definition that initiated the notion of leadership as that which a leader does.
He did not include the word *leadership* in subsequent editions of his dictionary,
an interesting but unexplicable fact of lexicography.

In 1879 John Walker revised Samuel Johnson's dictionary of 1755. The definitions of *lead* and *leader* remained basically the same as in Johnson's original
dictionary, but the ''despicable word'' quip was removed. Again, *leadership*
was not defined.

The *Century Dictionary* (1889–1911) and the *Universal Dictionary of the
English Language* (Hunter & Morris, 1898) were both published at the turn of
the century and represented monumental efforts to codify the English language
as used in the United States at the beginning of the twentieth century.

The *Century Dictionary* has numerous definitions of the verb and noun forms
of *lead* that are similar to the definitions given in previous dictionaries. *Leader*
has six definitions:

(1) One who leads, guides, conducts, directs, or controls; a director or conductor, a chief
or commander. (2) One who is first or most prominent in any relation; one who takes
precedence by virtue of superior qualifications or influence; a recognized principal or
superior. (3) One who has charge of a ''class.'' (4) A conductor or director of music.
(5) That which leads or conducts; something that guides the course of a thing, or conducts
it to it. (6) That which precedes; something that has a leading or foremost place, whether
in actual position or in importance.

Leadership is defined briefly: ''The office of a leader; guidance; control.''

The *Universal Dictionary* follows the same pattern. There is a page of definitions for *lead* (verb and noun), *leader*, and *leading*. The definition of *leadership*
is short and to the point: ''The office or position of a leader; guidance, pre-
miership.''

Chamber's Twentieth Century Dictionary (1904) repeats the definitions found
in the *Century* and *Universal* dictionaries, but the treatment is less detailed.

Murray's *New English Dictionary Based on Historical Principles*, the fore-
runner of the *Oxford English Dictionary*, was first published in 1908. A monumental achievement modeled on Johnson's dictionary of 1755, it has numerous
definitions of *lead*, *leader*, and *leading*, and the lexicographers backed up their
definitions with examples from historical documents and books written by prominent authors throughout the centuries. The material on *lead* covers over five
pages. The definitions fall into the same pattern as in the *Century* and *Universal*
dictionaries, but the treatment is more complete and extensive. *Leader* has three
definitions:

(1) One who conducts, precedes as a guide, leads a person by the hand; (2) One who
leads a body of armed men, a commander, a captain; (3) One who guides others in action

or opinion; one who takes the lead in any business, enterprise, or movement; one who is followed by disciples or adherents; the chief of a sect or a party.

Leadership is given a short treatment: "The dignity, office, or position of a leader, especially of a political party; also, ability to lead." There are only three examples of the use of the word from written works.

The third definition of leader in the *New English Dictionary* stands out dramatically because it reflects the twentieth-century notion of leaders in organizations and movements. None of the other dictionaries gives such a definition. The dictionary was also ahead of its time in giving a psychological definition to leadership: "the ability to lead." All twentieth-century lexicographers have included that notion in their definitions.

Clearly, the four dictionaries published at the turn of the century agree on the meanings and importance of the words. The verb *lead* is the most important of the four, primarily because it is the root word, and it was given a thorough treatment by the lexicographers. Next in importance is the word *leader*, then *leading* (about which I have not given much information), and finally *leadership*, a new word that was defined simply in all four dictionaries. Leadership, all four dictionaries agree, is an office or a position that intimates guidance or control.

The twentieth-century dictionaries showed a steady pattern toward a standardization of the definitions listed for the word *leadership*. *Webster's New International Dictionary* (1915) has extensive definitions of *lead* and *leader*, but no definition of *leadership*. This exclusion is very strange since Webster was the first lexicographer to include a definition of leadership in his 1828 dictionary.

The *Thesaurus Dictionary* of March and March (1925) contains no listing for *leadership*, but synonyms listed for *take the lead* include "leading-following, management," and one synonym for *leader* is "manager." This thesaurus shows that the concepts *lead* and *leader* had entered the vocabulary of organizations.

The *New Century Dictionary*, revised and published in 1927, repeats the same definitions of leadership as the four turn-of-the-century dictionaries: "The office or position of a leader; guidance;" but adds "the ability to lead." The Funk and Wagnalls *New Standard Dictionary of the English Language* (1928) gives the first two definitions but not the third. Wyld's *Universal Dictionary of the English Language* (1939) has no definition of *leadership*, which seems inexplicable, since the word was certainly in common usage by that date.

The *Oxford English Dictionary* (1933) has six pages of definitions of *lead*, *leader*, and *leading*, as well as examples of the uses of the words from prominent authors throughout the centuries. *Leadership*, however, is defined in two lines: "The dignity, office, or position of a leader, esp. of a political party; also, ability to lead." There are five examples of the word as used from 1874 to 1885.

The second edition of Webster's *New International Dictionary of the English Language* (1955) still did not have a definition of *leadership*, but the third edition (1965) finally included several: "(1) The office or position of a leader; (2a) The quality of a leader, capacity to lead; (2b) The act or an instance of leading; (2c)

A group of persons who lead." The 2b definition reflects the behaviorist notion of leadership, and the 2c definition reflects the social psychological view of leadership.

Definitions of leadership in the dictionaries published since 1965 have been variations on the same theme. Almost all of them contain the two definitions found in earlier dictionaries: (1) the office or position of a leader and (2) the ability to lead. Several dictionaries, however, go beyond those elementary definitions. The *Supplement to the Oxford English Dictionary* (Burchfield, 1976) added: "The position of a group of people leading or influencing others within a given context; the group itself; the action or influence necessary for the direction or organization of effort in a group undertaking." Those definitions primarily reflect the understanding social psychologists have of leadership.

The second edition of the *Oxford English Dictionary* (1989) continued the treatment of the words found in the first edition. There are no changes in the definitions of *leadership* from the 1976 supplement. More examples (nineteen) are given of the word's usage between 1821 and 1973.

The second edition of the *Random House Dictionary of the English Language* (1987) gives four definitions of leadership: "(1) The position or function of a leader; (2) The ability to lead; (3) An act or instance of leading, guidance, direction; and (4) The leaders of a group." The third definition reflects the behaviorist notion of leadership, and the fourth gives the social psychologist's view.

The *American Heritage Illustrated Encyclopedic Dictionary* (1987) provides three definitions of leadership, the same ones that are in the popular and shorter editions of that dictionary beginning in 1969 and continuing through 1989: "(1) The position, office, or term of a leader; (2) A group of leaders; (3) The capacity to be a leader; ability to lead."

Webster's New Collegiate Dictionary has given the same definitions of leadership since the 1960s: "(1) The office of a leader; (2) The quality of a leader, capacity to lead."

Funk and Wagnalls' *New Comprehensive International Dictionary of the English Language* (1971, 1982) furnishes only two definitions of leadership: "The office or position of a leader; guidance."

The conclusions one can draw from this survey of dictionaries of the English language are clear, and they are very instructive. The first conclusion seems definite: that *leadership* did not come into popular usage until the turn of the century, and even then lacked the connotations people attach to the word today. Those connotations seem to have begun to take shape in the 1930s, but they did not have a great impact on scholars and practitioners until after World War II. This conclusion becomes obvious when we look at the definitions of leadership found in books and journal articles on leadership from 1900 to 1979.

The second conclusion is equally clear. The many writers on leadership who assume that the modern concept of leadership has been in use since Greek and Roman antiquity, are in error. Leadership, as we know it, is a twentieth-century concept, and to trace our understanding of it to previous eras of Western civilization (much less other civilizations) is as wrong as to suggest that the people of earlier civilizations knew what, for instance, computerization meant. Even the word *leader* had a different meaning to people of the seventeenth century than it does to the people of the twentieth, and that difference relates, in large part, to the democratization of Western civilization.

The third conclusion is that the dictionary definitions of leadership have been, and continue to be, very simple and, as a result, are not very helpful in understanding the concept. They have not reflected since 1940, nor do they today, the complexity of the concept as it is discussed in the books and journal articles on leadership. This may be the result of the ambiguity of the word as it is used in everyday language and its lack of precise definitions in the scholarly literature. After all, if leadership scholars have not been able to agree on a definition of the term, why should lexicographers be able to define it? It may also be a function of lexicography, which is essentially oriented to short, simplistic definitions.

The fourth conclusion is that the dictionaries have contributed to the view that leadership and management are synonymous terms. Every dictionary since the turn of the century has defined leadership as "the position or office of a leader," indicating that leadership involves little more than occupying a position of management or administration.

The fifth conclusion is similar. The dictionaries have contributed to the notion that leadership is a bundle of traits by defining leadership as "the ability to lead."

Finally, the dictionaries commit a third error in the "position or office of leader" and "ability to lead." The error is that leadership resides in the leader(s), rather than being a relationship among leaders and followers. Fowler (1965) was aware of this semantic problem in his *Dictionary of Modern English Usage*:

Membership, leadership. . . . Much less desirable is the extension from number of members to members, a practice now rife and corrupting other words, especially by the use of *leadership* for leaders. . . . Leadership is used this way so constantly that we seem to be in danger of forgetting that there is such a word as *leaders*. Examples like the following could be multiplied indefinitely. "They have refrained from making declarations that the union's policy is not in the best interest of the membership or that the leadership has failed to implement the policy. / It was decided to proceed against the leadership of the E.T.U. under Rule 13. / The new Soviet leadership now launched its propaganda campaign for peace. / The leadership of the Parliamentary Party behaves as though it were a Shadow Administration."

Needless substitution of the abstract for the concrete is one of the surest roads to flabby style. In the following quotation, where the correct use of the second *leadership* in its abstract sense might have been expected to put the writer on his guard, he seems to have been so bemused by the lure of the abstract that he could not bring himself, by writing *leaders* for the first, to clothe in flesh and blood those whom he was urging to act wholeheartedly and in good conscience. "If the present leadership will wholeheartedly and in good conscience give the country that leadership, they will not lack loyal and enthusiastic support.'' (pp. 357–358)

I shall have more to say about these conclusions after an extended discussion of the definitions of leadership in the scholarly literature since 1900, to which I now turn.

SCHOLARLY DEFINITIONS OF LEADERSHIP

I analyzed 221 definitions of leadership that I found in 587 books, book chapters, and journal articles which by title indicated that they were primarily concerned with leadership. These materials were written from 1900 to 1990. Definitions of leadership written in the 1900–1919 period were obtained from secondary sources, mainly Gibb (1954), Stogdill (1974), and Bass (1981). I could find only one definition of leadership from the nineteenth century. I do not doubt that definitions of leadership were given by authors of books and articles on leadership in the 19th century, although I now believe them to be in very short supply, but I could not find them. Large libraries, even research libraries, thin out their collections, and old books have a way of disappearing except for those placed in rare book collections. I found no books on leadership is any of the rare book collections in which I did research. The earliest books on leadership that I could find were from the 1930s.

The authors of the works that I reviewed were/are from the United States, Canada, Australia, and Europe. One author (Misumi, 1985) lives in Japan, but he studied at the University of Michigan under Likert, so his views of leadership are Western-oriented. The large majority of these works were written by authors from the United States, but the number of books, chapters, and articles from scholars in Great Britain, Canada, and Australia, in particular, and from continental European countries increased dramatically in the 1970s and 1980s. Regrettably, I do not read European languages, so I was not able to analyze several non-English books that were available. There are also a few books on leadership in English and other languages by authors who live in African nations. Most of these books are from the 1980s. While I skimmed some of these books, I did not read any of them. The number of works I had to review was already overwhelming, and I did not want to add to my problems. Also, I felt that it was best to limit this investigation to Western literature. There will be opportunities for others more familiar with other cultures than I to extend this study to non-Western literatures, and I welcome such an extension with great enthusiasm.

The authors of these books, chapters, and articles are overwhelmingly male. It is only in the 1980s that female authors appear in enough numbers to make an impact on the leadership literature. There are, of course, exceptions to this general statement throughout the century. I made it a practice to point out the female authors in this discussion as much as possible, in order to give the reader some impression of the contributions women have made to our understanding of leadership.

The works themselves represent every academic discipline that has had some interest in the subject of leadership: anthropology, business administration, educational administration, history, military science, nursing administration, organizational behavior, philosophy, political science, public administration, psychology, sociology, and theology. Some of the works written for popular consumption are hard to classify within a single, traditional academic discipline. Other scholars might dispute my including such works in this historical analysis of leadership definitions, especially since this section is labeled "Scholarly Definitions of Leadership." I would argue, however, that any book is to some extent scholarly, since one cannot write a book without doing conceptual thinking about its subject. Some scholars (e.g., Immegart, 1988) would restrict the word *scholarly* to those who have done empirical research on leadership. But that notion of scholarship is completely unacceptable, and I reject it out of hand. The main reason I included what might be called practitioner-oriented literature in this analysis is that many of these popular works have had more influence on people's understanding of leadership, particularly in the United States, than most of the books that academics label scholarly. If scholars are really interested in understanding the evolution of the meaning of leadership, they cannot ignore these books that have had considerable impact on our understanding of leadership.

Sorting these works by date of publication shows a steady increase over the years in the books, chapters, and articles dedicated to the subject of leadership and, by implication, a steady increase in the popularity of the topic among both scholars and practitioners. As Table 3.1 indicates, there was a veritable explosion of interest in the 1980s.

The table is misleading in several ways, however. First, there was no attempt to include every piece of literature written about leadership in the twentieth century. Stogdill (1974) and Bass (1981) have already done that. Bass has some 4,725 works in his reference list. Since only 587 works are listed in Table 3.1, it is obvious that I have not reviewed many published works on leadership for this study.

Second, I made a decision not to look into the many articles about leadership published in journals in the 1930s and 1940s. There are many such articles, and if they were included in Table 3.1, the numbers for those two decades would show a significant increase. Browne and Cohn (1958) did include some articles from these two decades that I reviewed but are not reflected in Table 3.1.

Third, I decided not to list dozens of works by one author. I tried to keep the number of works by any one author to three or four. That decision reduced the number of works listed in all of the decades.

Fourth, textbooks were eliminated from the list, although there are a few exceptions to this rule because several texts on leadership have had a large impact on the discipline of leadership studies.

Fifth, Table 3.1 emphasizes books and chapters over articles. In fact, *Table*

Table 3.1
Numbers of Works on Leadership, by Decade

Decade	Number of works with a definition	Number of works without a definition	Total number
1900 - 1909	1	2	3
1910 - 1919	1	0	1
1920 - 1929	8	4	12
1930 - 1939	9	4	13
1940 - 1949	13	6	19
1950 - 1959	19	21	40
1960 - 1969	23	28	51
1970 - 1979	37	99	136
1980 - 1989	110	202	312
Total	221	366	587

3.1 is best interpreted as the number of books and chapters available to someone in 1990 who wants to study the literature on leadership. There are a number of journal articles among the items tabulated, but they do not indicate what is available in libraries.

There are several reasons for this emphasis on books and chapters from books. First, they are better evidence of leadership thought than journal articles, especially since the 1950s. Second, readers have higher expectations of books. They expect more substance, more research, more penetrating analysis, and more extensive explanations of conceptual frameworks. Third, as far as definitions go—the major point of Table 3.1—readers expect a definition of leadership in a book on leadership, whereas they may not expect it in an article. Finally, much of the thought expressed in journal articles finds its way into books. I would argue that much of what has been written about the nature of leadership in the hundreds of journal articles can be found in books.

The major point made obvious by the numbers in Table 3.1 is that many authors in every decade did not define leadership in their works. The fact that so many authors have written works on a phenomenon that they have not defined is a scandal that should have been exposed prior to 1990. I will have more to say about this problem after the review of the definitions of leadership. In the meantime, one should keep in mind that 366 books, chapters, and articles on leadership are not included in this review of definitions because these authors did not give a definition of leadership. Some of those authors are the most influential leadership scholars of the twentieth century. Given that fact, they have had a considerable impact on the meaning of the word *leadership*. However, it is not possible to assess that impact in this study, since I am relying on definitions of leadership as the primary data for this research.

Definitions from 1900 to 1929

The definitions of leadership in the first three decades of the twentieth century emphasize control and centralization of power. A conference on leadership was held in 1927, and Moore reported that at the conference Steward defined leadership as "the ability to impress the will of the leader on those led and induce obedience, respect, loyalty, and cooperation" (Moore, 1927, p. 124). However, Schenk dissented from the dominant view by writing that "Leadership is the management of men by persuasion and inspiration rather than the direct or implied threat of coercion" (1928, p. 111). Notice the use of the word *management* in that definition.

Definitions in the 1930s

Bogardus (1934), Pigors (1935), and Tead (1935) wrote major works on leadership in this decade. All three books can still be found in libraries.

Bogardus, a social psychologist, developed a trait-and-group theory of leadership. "Leadership," he wrote, "is personality in action under group conditions. . . . It is interaction between specific traits of one person and other traits of the many, in such a way that the course of action of the many is changed by the one" (p. 3). Two pages later, he wrote:

Not only is leadership both a personality and a group phenomenon; it is also a *social process*, involving a number of persons in mental contact in which one person assumes a dominance over the others. It is a process in which the activities of the many are organized to move in a specific direction by the one. It is a process in which the attitudes and values of the many may be changed by the one. It is a process in which at every stage the followers exert an influence, often a changing counter-influence, upon the leader. (p. 5)

Pigors, in a book comparing leadership with domination, defined leadership as "a process of mutual stimulation which, by the successful interplay of relevant individual differences, controls human energy in the pursuit of a common cause" (1935, p. 16). That definition clearly indicates that Pigors did not equate leadership with domination. The book is an interesting statement, especially in view of the rise of totalitarian regimes in Europe at the time.

Tead, another major author of the decade, agreed with Borgarus and Pigors: "Leadership is the activity of influencing people to cooperation toward some goal which they come to find desirable" (1935, p. 20). Tead's book was directed at executives, and he set them straight in the first chapter:

Popular notions of leadership tend to be expressed in terms of power to command or ability to dominate. The whole contention of this book is, however, that commanding of itself is wholly inadequate as a basis for getting results from people working in association. . . . Leadership is interested in how people can be brought to work together for a common end effectively and happily. (pp. 11–12)

Cleeton and Mason, in another book for executives, stated: "Leadership is often associated with the ability to influence men and secure results through emotional appeals rather than through judicious exercise of authority" (1934, p. 10). "Leadership," they added, "does not always imply the making of wise decisions or the proper use of power in influencing men" (p. 10).

Writing in 1930, Bundel demurred, defining leadership as "the art of inducing others to do what one wants them to do" (p. 339). But the view of leadership as control and authority had clearly lost its dominance among those who wrote about leadership in the decade before World War II. That trend would continue in succeeding decades.

Schmidt, writing in the *Encyclopaedia of the Social Sciences*, stated: "Leadership may be broadly defined as the relation between an individual and a group built around some common interest and behaving in a manner directed or determined by him" (1933, p. 282). In distinguishing leadership from authority and demagoguery, he wrote: "Strictly speaking, the relation of leadership arises only where a group follows an individual from free choice and not under command or coercion, and secondly, not in response to blind drives but on positive and more or less rational grounds" (p. 282).

Definitions in the 1940s

The group approach to understanding leadership began to dominate the leadership literature in the 1940s. Whyte, in his enormously popular and acclaimed study of street gangs published in 1943, probably had a good deal to do with that dominance. He studied a group of street toughs and, among other things, their leadership. He made it clear that "leadership within the group consisted of influence attempts that avoided the invocation of power and relative status" (Jacobs, 1970, p. 233).

Reuter (1941), as well as Copeland (1942) and Redl (1942), made essentially the same point. Since they wrote their works before Whyte, they may well have influenced his notions of leadership. Reuter wrote: "Leadership is the result of an ability to persuade or direct men, apart from the prestige or power that comes from office or other external circumstances" (1941, p. 133). Copeland stated much the same idea, but more forcefully: "Leadership is the art of dealing with human nature. . . . It is the art of influencing a body of people by persuasion or example to follow a line of action. It must never be confused with *drivership*— to coin a word—which is the art of compelling a body of people by intimidation or force to follow a line of action" (1942, p. 77). Redl, incorporating a Freudian approach, restricted the term *leadership* to "that relationship which is characterized by love of the members for the central person, leading to incorporation of the personality of the central person in the ego ideal of the followers, i.e., they wish to become the kind of person he is" (1942, p. 576).

H. H. Jennings (1944) accepted the followers as the people who identified the leader in the group. In what she called a "dynamic redefinition" of the word *leadership*, she concluded: "Leadership thus appears as a manner of interaction involving behavior by and toward the individual 'lifted' to a leader role by other individuals" (p. 432).

Pennington, Hough, and Case (1943) expressed the military view of leadership at the time, and it was worlds apart from the group approach: "It is little wonder, then, that leadership has been defined as 'the art of imposing one's will upon others in such a manner as to command their obedience, their confidence, their respect, and their loyal cooperation' (United States Military Academy, 1925)" (p. 102).

The OSS (1948) expressed a view of leadership that was more group-oriented: "There is nothing novel in our conception of leadership. We thought of it as a man's ability to take the initiative in social situations, to plan and organize action, and in so doing to evoke cooperation" (p. 301). Knickerbocker (1948/ 1958), in an influential article, took a more functional approach to the group theory of leadership:

Functional leadership places emphasis . . . upon the circumstances under which the group of people integrate and organize their activities toward objectives and upon the way in which that integration and organization is [*sic*] achieved. Thus, the leadership function is analyzed and understood in terms of a dynamic relationship. A leader may acquire followers, or a group of people may create a leader, but the significant aspects of the process can only be understood in dynamic relationship terms. . . .

The leader . . . is the leader only in terms of his functional relationship to the group. Therefore, the part he plays in the total dynamic pattern of the behavior of the group defines him as a leader. . . . The leader is followed because he promises to get, or actually gets, his followers more nearly what they want than anyone else. (1958, pp. 4–5, 7)

R. C. Davis (1942) took an organizational (rather than a group) approach but gave somewhat the same definition as Knickerbocker: "Leadership is the principal dynamic force that stimulates, motivates, and coordinates the organization in the accomplishment of its objectives" (p. 27).

After the war, the Ohio State Leadership Studies Program was organized, and in 1949 Hemphill expressed the direction of this program by giving what has been the most basic definition of leadership from the group perspective: "Leadership may be said to be the behavior of an individual while he is involved in directing group activities'' (1949b, p. 4). Hemphill's definition was used in numerous research studies at Ohio State and elsewhere, and it is still quoted frequently. It therefore has a solid reputation among leadership scholars.

Were these definitions, except for the military one, a collective reaction to the horrors of World War II and thus a concerted attempt to exclude totalitarianism and other forms of coercive behavior in groups from consideration as leadership? One is hard pressed not to make this connection, but the validity of such a conclusion is open to question. Be that as it may, the 1940s represent a significant move away from viewing leadership as domination and control, continuing the trend of the 1930s. At the same time, the 1940s belong to those who promoted the group approach to leadership. Although the group approach lost some adherents in the 1950s to the behaviorists led by Halpin and his Ohio State colleagues, it continued to flourish in leadership studies for many years.

Definitions of the 1950s

There is no greater sign of the continued prominence of group theory in the 1950s than Gibb's chapter "Leadership" in *Handbook of Social Psychology* (1954). It is a strong endorsement of the group approach to studying leadership. Since the chapter was written for psychologists by a psychologist, the group emphasis is not surprising. As if to underscore the point, Gibb started this chapter with an extended discussion of the definition of the word *group*, underlining the importance of understanding the meaning of a group in order to understand leadership. He did not give a definition of leadership but did provide an extended discussion of the definitions of *leader* and *leader behavior*. However, it is clear from the discussion that Gibb approved of defining leadership in terms of an influence relationship (see p. 882). But Gibb's real definition of leadership is simply this: Leadership is what leaders do in groups. "Whether we couch our definition in terms of the leader or the leadership act it is, of course, leader behaviors with which the psychologist is concerned'' (p. 884).

Nevertheless, Gibb is quite eloquent about distinguishing leadership from headship and along the way insists that leadership is a noncoercive relationship between a leader and the followers.

Most basically, these two forms of influence differ with respect to the *source* of the authority which is exercised. The leader's authority is spontaneously accorded him by his fellow group members, the followers. The authority of the head derives from some extra-group power which he has over the members of the group, who cannot meaningfully be called his followers. . . . The business executive is an excellent example of a head exercising authority derived from his position in an organization through membership in which the workers, his subordinates, satisfy many strong needs. They obey his commands and accept his domination because this is part of their duty as organization members and to reject him would be to discontinue membership, with all the punishments that would involve. (p. 882)

The problem with Gibb's eloquence is that he did not adhere to his definition for the rest of his chapter. The researchers he reviewed did not make any such distinction. Neither does he make the same distinction in his conclusions and in his proposed interaction theory of leadership (pp. 913–917).

Cartwright and Zander's *Group Dynamics* (1953) contained several chapters on leadership. In their introduction to that section of the book, they defined leadership thus:

Leadership is viewed as the performance of those acts which help the group achieve its objectives. Such acts may be termed *group* functions. More specifically, leadership consists of such actions by group members as those which aid in setting group goals, moving the group toward its goals, improving the quality of interactions among the members, building the cohesiveness of the group, or making resources available to the group. In principle, leadership may be performed by one or many members of the group. (1953, p. 538)

That definition has more to do with group facilitation than with leadership, properly so called, but such distinctions were not made in the 1950s. In fact, for group theorists, facilitating groups well was group leadership par excellence. The inclusion of Lewin, Lippitt, and White's research on autocratic, democratic, and laissez-faire leaders of groups (1939) in the Cartwright and Zander book helped make it very influential among leadership scholars and practitioners in the 1950s. But as a matter of fact, the article did not contain a definition of leadership and actually did not use the word *leadership* in labeling the three styles.

Many leadership scholars of the 1950s defined leadership as a relationship that developed shared goals. Halpin and Winter (1952) defined leadership as "the behavior of an individual when he is directing the activities of a group toward shared goals" (p. 6). Shartle (1956) saw the "leadership act as one which results in others acting or responding to a shared direction" (p. 3). Hemphill and Coons (1957) defined leadership as "the behavior of an individual when he is directing the activities of a group toward a shared goal" (p. 5). The following year, Hemphill (1958) was even stronger: "To lead is to engage in an act that initiates a structure-in-interaction as part of the process of solving a mutual problem. Leadership acts do not include various acts of influence that occur outside mutual problem solving" (p. 98). Bellows (1959) defined leadership as "the process of arranging a situation so that various members of a group, including the leader, can achieve common goals with maximum economy and a minimum of time and work" (p. 14).

Gibb (1954) agreed that the influence in a leadership relationship has to be voluntarily accepted and thus be oriented to shared goals: "It is necessary to qualify 'influence' by insisting that the term applies only when this is voluntarily accepted or when it is in a shared direction. . . . There is almost general agreement in the literature of the last few years that leadership is to be distinguished, by definition, from domination or headship" (p. 882).

Not quite! In the only definition of leadership I could find throughout Bennis's writings, he stated in 1959 that "Leadership can be defined as the process by which an agent induces a subordinate to behave in a desired manner" (p. 259). Haiman (1951) wrote that "Leadership refers to that process whereby an individual directs, guides, influences, or controls the thoughts, feelings or behaviors of other human beings" (p. 4).

In 1958 Browne and Cohn edited a collection of articles about leadership. They concluded that the "leadership literature is a mass of content without any coagulating substance to bring it together or to produce coordination and point out interrelationships" (p. iii). That may be because scholars such as Carter (1953/1958), whose work was included in the Browne and Cohn book, stated that "Leadership behaviors are any behaviors the experimenter wishes to designate or, more generally, any behaviors which experts in this area wish to consider as leader behaviors" (1958, p. 24). The only agreement that Browne and Cohn could find in the papers included in the first section of their book was that "leadership is a term that applies not to an individual alone, but to a relationship between an individual in a group and the other members of the group. . . . In other words, leadership is not looked upon as a universal set of variables, but rather as a group of variables describing interactions among group members" (pp. ii–iii).

Titus (1950), writing eight years earlier, opined that political scientists had no such squabbles about the definition of leadership:

In spite of these frustrations in other areas of thought, for those working in the field of politics the term *leadership* possesses a reasonably definite meaning. . . . The politician and analysts ignore the subjective dualism and think of leadership, statesmanship and politics as synonymous terms. Leadership becomes, like politics, the art of getting what one (either a politician or a leader) wants and making people like it. . . . Leadership is the cement unifying men for cooperative action in order to achieve given objectives. The very purpose of leadership is to realize distinct objectives with the aid of followers who can be conditioned to act or refrain from acting according to a prearranged plan. (pp. 51, 52)

A third theme of leadership definitions in the 1950s emphasized effectiveness. Stogdill opened the decade with such a definition: "Leadership may be considered as the process (act) of influencing the activities of an organized group in its efforts towards goal setting and goal achievement" (1950/1958, p. 33). Cattell (1951) defined a leader as a person who has a demonstrable influence on group syntality and stated that leadership is "the magnitude of the syntality change produced by that person" (p. 175). Syntality is a measure of the group's effectiveness as a group, so Cattell ended up defining leadership by the magnitude of the change in group effectiveness. Campbell (1956) wrote: "Leadership may be defined as the contribution of a given individual to group effectiveness, mediated through the direct efforts of others rather than himself" (p. 1). On the other hand, Gordon, the great effectiveness expert of the 1950s and 1960s, did not include an effectiveness dimension is his definition of leadership: "Leadership can be conceptualized as an interaction between a person and the members of a group. . . . One person, the leader, influences, while the other person responds" (1955, p. 10).

Gibb (1954) strongly disagreed with those who included effectiveness in the definition of leadership, and so this battle began heating up in the 1950s. Effectiveness as a necessary ingredient of leadership was not a very pervasive concept in the 1950s, and those who included it in their definition seemed more interested in the effectiveness of the group's process than of the group's product. That would change, of course, as leadership scholars and practitioners increasingly equated leadership with excellence and equated excellence with quality products.

In summary, the 1950s saw the continued influence of group theorists on leadership studies, but the behaviorists, accepting much of what the group approach to leadership had already achieved, made considerable inroads into the group dominance of the field. Perhaps the most important development of the decade was the influence of democratic ideology on defining leadership. The bulk of the definitions reviewed here indicated that the scholars viewed leadership as an influence process oriented toward achieving shared purposes. This conclusion suggests considerably more agreement among scholars as to the nature of leadership than Browne and Cohn (1958) were willing to admit. The problem was—and this is not evident in any listing of the definitions—that the researchers did not stick to their definitions in doing leadership research. They tended to research any and all group facilitators, any and all managers, any and all politicians. That problem, as we shall see, was equally pervasive in the 1960s, 1970s, and 1980s.

Definitions of the 1960s

Leadership definitions of the 1960s show increasing support for viewing leadership as behavior that influences people toward shared goals. A surprisingly large number of definitions reflect this theme.

Seeman (1960) defined leadership as "acts by persons which influence other persons in a shared direction" (p. 127). Montgomery (1961) summed up his thoughts about the nature of leadership, which came from his experiences as a British field marshal in World War II: "My experience teaches me that the following definition is about right: The capacity and the will to rally men and women to a common purpose, and the character which inspires confidence" (p. 9). Note the traits embedded in the definition. Even so, it is still about influencing other people in a shared direction. Beal, Bohlen, and Randabaugh (1962) gave a simple definition: "Leadership is the process of influencing people by ideas" (p. 36). Lowry (1962) wrote: "Leadership is the ability (and potential) to influence the decisions and actions of others (followers) and therefore to exercise power over the decision-making process of community life" (p. 8).

N. E. Long's (1963) definition is worded differently but expresses, I believe, the same theme: "Leadership is concerned with the transformation of doubts into psychological grounds of cooperative common action" (p. 126). That definition does not make sense without some translation.

In 1964 Hollander defined leadership by defining a leader, a common mistake that many authors have made: "Leader denotes an individual with a status that permits him to exercise influence over certain other individuals" (p. 16). Tarcher (1966) felt strongly that "the definition of leadership [must] shift from "the power to influence the behavior of others' to 'the art of influencing others through persuasion and guidance' " (p. 20). This is the only definition from the literature that I found in which the word *guidance* was used, even though *guidance* was frequently used in dictionary definitions. Still, Tarcher's definition is a powerful statement.

Edinger (1967) edited an important book on leadership from a political perspective, and five or six of the chapters in that book are very forward-looking in the authors' views on leadership. In his introduction, Edinger complained about the limited view that most political scientists have of leadership:

In their view, leadership is more or less a function of the environment. . . . A leader is "a bus driver whose passengers will leave him unless he takes them in the direction in which they want to go. They leave him only minor discretion as to the road to be followed" (Simon, 1947, p. 134). Who leads, how, and why are thus believed to be more or less situationally determined. (p. 14)

On the following page, Edinger gave his own definition:

Leadership is a position within society which is defined by the ability of the incumbent to guide and structure the collective behavior patterns of some or all of its members. . . . It is at all times relational, interpersonal, and is based upon inequality of influence between the leader as the influencing agent and the followers as the objects of his efforts to cue their behavior so that it will conform with his personal objectives. (p. 15)

While Edinger's definition puts leadership in a position and suggests only unidirectional influence, he does reflect the theme that leadership is behavior that influences people toward shared goals.

Schlesinger (1967), a political economist who wrote a chapter in Edinger's book, stated: "In my view, the leadership–followership relationship is a rational exchange of values in which followers barter their supports for political decisions to their liking" (p. 266). But how can two abstractions be in a relationship? Be that as it may, the definition again includes the three key points of the theme.

Lasswell did not define leadership in his famous 1948 book, *Power and Personality*, even though the subject was discussed several times. He did, however, give an explanation of leadership in the chapter he wrote for the Edinger book, and the explanation contains a definition, I think.

If a term is to be useful in studying politics, it must be defined as a pattern of interaction; politics is, after all, part of a social process and "social process" is a term for all the ways that human beings affect one another. Leadership is a leader–follower pattern. . . . A leadership pattern can be identified in any interaction in which *orientation is given and received*. . . . In identifying leadership in politics we take more than a single incident into account, since we are concerned with *relatively* stable patterns of effective initiative for decision. . . . After clarifying our working conception of political leadership as a stable pattern of effective initiation for decision, . . . (1967: pp. 316–318)

Lasswell's concept of leadership is focused on a pattern of interactions as opposed to the behaviorists' concentration on a single leadership act. McFarland (1969) combined both notions in his definition. "The term 'leadership act' is used to designate a pattern of interpersonal behavior in which one person attempts to influence another and the other person accepts this influence" (p. 154).

Gibb (1969) stated that leadership involves "influencing the actions of others in a shared approach to common or compatible goals" (p. 270). And, finally, Merton (1969) defined leadership as "an interpersonal relationship in which others comply because they want to, not because they have to" (p. 2614).

The definitions just given all revolve around the view of leadership as behavior (some would say a pattern of behavior) that influences people toward shared goals. That so many scholars and practitioners were able to agree upon the definition of leadership has not been noted in previous literature reviews. In fact, as we have seen, the exact opposite was the case; the reviewers complained that there were no common elements in the definitions. It is time to reconstruct our notions of what people in the past have said about the nature of leadership. There was a great deal more agreement than has previously been acknowledged.

However, not all scholars understood leadership in that light. In fact, several of the more famous leadership scholars gave definitions in the 1960s that did not fit into this theme at all. Bass (1960) is a good example. In a widely read book on leadership, he wrote: "When the goal of one member, A, is that of changing another, B, or when B's change in behavior will reward A or reinforce A's behavior, A's effort to obtain the goal is leadership" (p. 14).

Quite a few authors from the late 1950s to the early 1970s were prone to define and explain leadership in terms of A & B or X & Y. These authors may have been influenced by political scientists, who were prone to define power and authority in the same way. These scholars were attempting to appear scientific in the positivistic sense, and they hoped that such definitions might help generate quantitative data for researching leadership. All of the effort, however, was for naught; there is no possibility of gaining any accurate and deep understanding of a complex subject such as leadership by viewing it in terms of A & B or X & Y. One reason such efforts were doomed to failure is that such formulations reduced leadership to dyadic relationships, which leadership clearly is not.

Tannenbaum and Schmidt wrote a very influential article on leadership styles in the *Harvard Business Review* in 1958 that was still used in the 1980s. They did not give a definition of leadership in that article, so their styles continuum is just as easily applied to other social processes as it is to leadership. Tannenbaum, Weschler, and Massarck (1961) did attempt a definition, but it is of questionable utility. They saw leadership as "interpersonal influence exercised in a situation and directed through the communication process, toward the attainment of a specific goal or goals" (p. 21). That definition reflects the view of leadership embedded in the 1958 article, and it is typical of many human relations scholars who write about leadership. One would be hard pressed to distinguish leadership based on that definition from countless other types of human interactions.

Perhaps the most famous of all leadership theorists is Fiedler, who in 1967 wrote: "By leadership behavior we generally mean the particular acts in which a leader engages in the course of directing and coordinating the work of group members" (p. 36). This definition, which has basically remained unchanged, through the 1980s, fails to distinguish leadership from other human interactions that coordinate group members' efforts. Fiedler is another researcher who defined leadership by defining a leader, thus confusing the two words.

Lippitt's (1969) definition is not much better and may be worse. It reflects the group approach to leadership. "Leadership is viewed as the performance by the leader of those acts which are required by the group" (pp. 84–85). That sounds like group facilitation to me. Organizational definitions of leadership started to become more popular in the 1960s. Bavelas's definition is typical of them: He viewed organizational leadership as the function of "maintaining the operational effectiveness of decision-making systems which comprise the management of the organization" (p. 492). Such definitions, of course, completely confuse management with leadership and buy into the effectiveness notion of leadership. Janda's (1960) definition emphasizes a power relationship and perception: "Leadership is a particular type of power relationship characterized by a group member's perception that another group member has the right to prescribe behavior patterns for the former regarding his activity as a member of a particular group" (p. 345).

E. E. Jennings (1960) criticized the group and organizational views of leadership and used a trait approach to define leadership in terms of personal initiative and risk of the leader.

We now arrive at the heart of the matter. The essential difference between a leader and an executive is the degree of personal initiative and personal risk that such initiative involves. Leadership theorists find it difficult to apply the term leadership to people who reduce risk considerably by attempting to move the group in a direction it has already taken. . . . We may put this differently by saying that risk and initiation have been taken out of leadership by our present demand for chairmen, coordinators, facilitators, diagnosticians, and therapists. We no longer appreciate leadership because of our emphasis on those qualities that largely identify executive behavior. (p. 16)

As much as Jennings may strike a responsive chord in our intuition, his definition is unacceptable because of his reliance on personal traits to define leadership, which is not a person but a relationship.

Gibb (1968), in a second review of leadership literature from a psychological perspective for the *International Encyclopedia of the Social Sciences*, wrote: "The concept of leadership has largely lost its value for the social sciences, although it remains indispensable to general discourse" (p. 91). My own view, as should be obvious by now, is that there is more to the leadership literature than has been uncovered by numerous reviewers and analysts. In fact, except for several high-powered leadership scholars who were on a different track, the scholars of the 1960s showed remarkable unanimity in understanding leadership. The bulk of those who were willing to put their ideas of leadership on paper to construct a definition of leadership rallied around the idea of leadership as behavior that influences people toward shared goals.

Definitions of the 1970s

There was a fairly healthy increase in the number of books and articles about leadership in the 1970s (see Table 3.1). The numbers do not compare with those of the 1980s, but the popularity of leadership studies was clearly growing in the 1970s.

Hunt and Larson contributed to this increased output of leadership literature through three leadership symposia they organized in the 1970s. Three books containing the symposia papers were published in 1975, 1977, and 1979. Their symposia were a sign that leadership had become a serious topic of study for management science and organizational behaviorists in the 1970s. The decade's literature shows an important shift from the group approach of the social psychologists to the organizational behavior approach of the management scholars, a dominance that would extend into the 1980s.

But important work was also done by political scientists, sociologists, and anthropologists who did not fit the mainstream mode. Paige (1977) and Burns (1978) wrote the first two book-length works on leadership by political scientists. Calder (1977), Pfeffer (1977), and House and Baetz (1979) developed an attributional theory of leadership, Jacobs (1970) and Hollander (1978a) proposed an exchange theory of leadership that linked political and behavioral concepts. Kracke (1978) published the first book-length anthropological study of leadership.

Finally, the 1970s are noted for the frequency with which the authors repeatedly commented on the lack of coherence in the leadership literature concerning the definition of leadership and then ignored the topic. Ninety-nine authors did not give a definition of leadership in their books, chapters, or articles. Two impressions come through loud and clear as one reads these ninety-nine works. The first impression is that the scholars found it increasingly difficult to define leadership, so they deliberately chose not to give a definition. In the process, they implied that everyone knew what leadership was, so it wasn't necessary to define it. The second impression is that as the decade wore on, leadership scholars were increasingly sloppy in their use of the words *leadership* and *leader*. Part of the problem, of course, was a more explicit melding of the concepts of leadership and management. The synonymous use of these words became increasingly pervasive during the decade, especially by the scholars who chose not to define leadership. But beyond the "leadership equals management" trend, there were many authors who used the word *leadership* to mean just about anything that had to do with human interaction.

Having said that, let us review some of the definitions that came out of the 1970s. First of all, it is important to note that the psychological and group definitions continued, although the notion of shared goals seems to have slipped out of the picture. But Saville (1971), for one, did not lose the emphasis in his definition of leadership "as a process of structuring, organizing, and guiding a situation so that all members of a group can achieve common goals with maximum economy and minimum time and effort" (p. 53). However, it seems that leadership processes are not allowed to be inefficient.

Cassel (1975) wrote:

For wherever and whenever two or more persons are involved in personal interactions, there is some form of leadership present. The concept present in leadership maintains that one or more of the participating members in an interacting relationship contributes more to the meeting and directing of emerging activities . . . and it is this contribution that describes leadership. (p. 87)

Cassel's definition allows for almost all human interactions to be called leadership, a characteristic quite common to many leadership definitions in the 1970s. When every interaction becomes leadership, the definition loses its validity.

Stogdill (1974) provided a behavioral definition of leadership, using Ohio State's two dimensions as its backbone. Leadership is "the initiation and maintenance of structure in expectation and interaction" (p. 411). Again, this definition does not help to distinguish leadership from other forms of social interaction.

Boles and Davenport (1975), writing for educators, incorporated the psychological and group dimensions of leadership in their definition: "Leadership is a process in which an individual takes initiative to assist a group to move towards the production goals that are acceptable to maintain the group, and to dispose of those needs of individuals within the group that impelled them to join it" (p. 117). Another educator, DeBruyn (1976), was less successful: "I choose to define leadership simply as 'causing others to want what you are doing to accomplish the work of the school' " (p. 14). Gordon's (1977) definition remained simplistic: "Leadership is an interaction between leaders and followers" (p. 17).

Moloney's (1979) definition stressed goal attainment: "Leadership is defined as an interpersonal process of influencing the activities of an individual or group towards goal attainment in a given situation.'' (p. 11). She added some other variables in an explanation of her definition: ''It is important to understand that leadership is not a synonym for either administration or management. Leadership is a process whereby the leader can influence others to perform beyond those activities commanded by individuals in formal authority positions'' (p. 11). While I applaud the ideas in the second statement, her explanation is different from her definition, and that is quite confusing. Wayson (1979) also stressed meeting goals in his group-oriented definition: ''Leadership is the process by which a member helps a group to meet its goals'' (p. 182). Plachy (1978) defined leadership as ''getting things done through people'' (p. 16), which provides a very good example of the sloppy thinking of the 1970s about the nature of leadership.

The behavioral definitions are variations on the same theme, but more organizationally focused (and more management oriented). Doll (1972), in the field of educational administration, wrote: ''Leadership is a function requiring human behaviors which help a school achieve its constantly changing purposes, some of which are oriented toward productivity or task performance and others of which are oriented towards interpersonal relationships, within the school's own social climate and conditions'' (p. 17).

Osborn and Hunt (1975) provided the only definition of leadership in Hunt and Larson's first symposium: ''Leadership is defined in terms of discretionary influence. Discretionary influence refers to those leader behaviors under the control of the leader which he may vary from individual to individual'' (p. 28). Again, discretionary influence operates in many human relationships other than leadership.

Engstrom (1976), whose book takes a religious approach to leadership, gave a classical behavioral definition: ''Leadership is an act by word or deed to influence behavior toward a desired end'' (p. 20). Corwin (1978), a political scientist, translated the dictionary ''ability to lead'' definition to organizations: ''Leadership consists largely of the ability to influence organizational policy and practice to manipulate organizational resources'' (p. 78). Filley (1978) provided a management-oriented definition. Leadership is ''the ability of an individual to establish and maintain acceptable levels of satisfaction and job-related performance so that organization needs are met as well'' (p. 52). With such definitions circulating in the literature, it is easy to understand how leadership and management were viewed as the same process.

These definitions are all fairly standard stuff, and if one looks at the textbooks of this period, they are endlessly (and mindlessly) repeated over and over. Leadership is initiating and maintaining groups or organizations to accomplish group or organizational goals. That was the standard, mainstream understanding of leadership in thousands of college and university classrooms throughout the country.

The more exciting material and the more substantive definitions of leadership came from scholars who were developing understandings of leadership that did not fit into the mold of the mainstream approaches. The first of these chronologically was Jacobs (1970), who developed an exchange theory of leadership and who insisted that leadership as a concept must be distinguished from the concepts of authority and power. The book is exceptionally well written, and Jacobs shows a deep understanding of leadership as well as an ability to do some crystal-clear thinking and analysis, qualities that are in stark contrast with much of the mainstream leadership scholars of the 1970s. Unfortunately, his book was not published by a major company, so it did not receive the widespread reading it deserved. As a result, Jacobs has had little impact on the field of leadership studies. Some extended excerpts from the book follow.

Leadership is taken as an interaction between persons in which one presents information of a sort and in such a manner that the other becomes convinced that his outcomes (benefits/costs ratio) will be improved if he behaves in the manner suggested or desired.

Communication skills are more important in leadership as here defined, than in influence attempts based on either power or authority, because its essence is the development of a new state of knowledge, belief, or attitude in the target of the influence attempt. . . . In the present system, the key distinction in the exercise of influence through leadership is the recognition that the influence recipient has the option of deciding for or against compliance with the leader's wishes, without incurring coercive penalties. (p. 232)

In the present system, perhaps the most important distinctions lie between leadership and each of the other two concepts [power and authority, which were defined on pages 230–231]. As defined, it is probable that leadership depends on the competence of the leader at the task at hand, on his ability to understand the motives of his followers in order to provide convincing evidence of the desirability of an act that he desires, and on his tolerance for counter-influence attempts. He will probably be more influential as a leader if his personal characteristics, whatever they may be . . . increase his capacity to be admired by his followers. (p. 233)

Perhaps the greatest weakness in the leadership literature has been the striking lack of precision in the use of the term "leadership," and probably even in what constitutes the concept. It is not surprising that the processes studied under the label of leadership have been quite varied. Analysis . . . indicates that the total range extends from what seems to be garrulousness, through coercive power, to authority relationships. . . .

The essence of social exchange is the development of relationships with other persons, such that the benefits of mutual value can be "traded" between participants of both equal and unequal status.

Leadership is a more "sophisticated" exchange than the more primitive process that leads to the differentiation of power, in that it involves persuasive communication of some sort—not necessarily verbal—which convinces the influence recipient that he will benefit in some way if he behaves as the influence initiator wishes, but probably with the special requirement that this not be "backed up" with the threat of coercive reprisal if he fails to behave as desired.

It is probable that the ability to lead must be based on the competence to make some kind of unique contribution to the success of the group being led. It appears, then, that leadership is a transaction between the leader and the group. (p. 339)

Perhaps the most important conclusion reached in this work is the importance of distinguishing between the concepts of leadership, power, and authority, and of identifying superordinated role behaviors that constitute each. . . .

Analysis of role theory findings relevant to leadership practices suggests that most superordinates fail to lead because they are not "open" to counter-influence attempts by their subordinates, or, in present terms have inadequate skills in social exchange. Lacking such skills, they resort to position power more often than they should, when the formal organization makes such a resource available, and thereby lose the capacity for positive influence by imposing barriers to communication between themselves and their subordinates. (pp. 340–342)

Hollander (1978a) also developed a social exchange theory of leadership.

The theme of this book is that leadership is a process of influence between a leader and those who are followers. While the leader may have power, influence depends more on persuasion than on coercion. A leadership process usually involves a two-way influence relationship aimed primarily at attaining mutual goals, such as those of a group, organization, or society. . . . Leadership is not just the job of the leader but also requires the cooperative efforts of others. (p. 1)

The behaviors recognized as leadership must include the reactions of followers. Therefore, leadership is not confined to a single person in a group but depends upon other members as well. Yet the terms *leadership* and *leader* are still used as if they were the same. For instance, the statement "We need new leadership" usually means that another leader, with different characteristics, is needed. (pp. 2–3)

Leadership is a process, not a person. Certainly, the leader is the central and often vital part of the leadership process. However, the followers are also important in the picture. Without responsive followers there is no leadership, because the concept of leadership is *relational*. It involves someone who exerts influence, and those who are influenced. However, influence can flow both ways. (p. 4).

Influence involves persuasion. It is not the same as power which leaves little choice. . . . The real "power" of a leader lies in his or her ability to influence followers without resorting to threats. This is one basis for distinguishing true leadership from the most basic level of supervision. (pp. 5–6)

The process of leadership involves a social exchange between the leader and followers. This social exchange, or *transactional approach*, involves a trading of benefits. (p. 7)

Leadership is a process of influence which involves an ongoing transaction between a leader and followers. (p. 12)

Hollander's definition (the last paragraph above) is not the same as his explanation of leadership, which places considerable emphasis on the followers' part in the leadership process.

Burns (1978) also used exchange theory to develop his transactional leadership model. "Such leadership occurs when one person takes the initiative in making contact with others for the purpose of an exchange of valued things. The exchange could be economic or political or psychological in nature" (p. 19). This statement, however, is not Burns's definition of leadership (which is given below). Lord, writing in the 1979 leadership symposium book of Hunt and Larson, also took a transactional view of leadership even though his definition does not entirely reflect that approach. "Leadership has been conceptualized [in this chapter] as a mutual influence process grounded in shared perceptions of followers" (p. 156).

Katz and Kahn (1966/1978) are social psychologists, but they wrote about leadership from a different perspective than their colleagues when they decided to tackle the subject in their classic work *The Social Psychology of Organizations*. Their chapter is also interesting insofar as they included some sharp criticisms of the leadership literature.

Among social scientists who emphasize the concept of leadership, there is no close agreement on conceptual definitions or even on the theoretical significance of leadership processes. . . .

Leadership appears in social science literature with three major meanings: as an attribute of a position, as the characteristic of a person, and as a category of behavior. . . . Leadership is a relational concept implying two terms: the influencing agent and the persons influenced. Without followers there can be no leader. Hence, leadership conceived of as an ability is a slippery concept since it depends too much on properties of the situation and of the people to be "led."

We consider the essence of organizational leadership to be the influential increment over and above mechanical compliance with routine directives of the organization. (pp. 300–301)

In fact, organizational leadership . . . is always a combined function of social structural factors and of the particular characteristics of the individual situation making up the structure. And yet, the social-psychological literature has been strangely silent in describing the operation of leadership processes in the real social world, i.e., within social systems. The literature of leadership has a disembodied, nonorganizational quality.

Three basic types of leadership behavior occur in organizational settings: (1) the introduction of structural change, or policy formulation, (2) the interpolation of structure, i.e., piecing out the incompleteness of existing formal structure, or improvisation, and (3) the use of structure formally provided to keep the organization in motion and in effective operation, or administration. (p. 308)

Every instance of leadership involves the use, interpolation, or origination of organizational structure to influence others. When people are influenced to engage in organizationally relevant behavior, leadership has occurred. When no such attempt at influence is made, there has been no leadership. (p. 309)

Another approach to leadership that gained a number of adherents in the 1970s, especially among sociologists, was an attribution theory of leadership. Pfeffer (1977) is probably the most notable among those embracing this approach, but he did not give a definition of leadership in his article. From the text, however, one can put a definition together: Leadership is a socially constructed label people attribute to others to make sense of happenings in their world that otherwise would not make sense. In other words, people attribute the causation of certain results to the behavior of leaders.

Calder's (1977) approach to leadership attribution theory is more complicated than Pfeffer's and others, but essentially develops the same basic notion. However, Calder is more straightforward as to how attribution theory fits into leadership studies. "While it might be possible simply to graft attribution theory onto one or more present approaches to leadership, the objective here is to propose a reorientation of the entire leadership area in which attribution would become the central construct. Indeed, in this reorientation, leadership itself would cease to be a scientific construct" (p. 181).

His definition is less clear. Calder provided only a few clues as to what leadership is from an attributional perspective. "Leadership is a label which can be applied to behavior" (p. 187). Leadership, he wrote, "refers to a set of personal qualities which are described in ordinary language" (p. 195). "Leadership is a disposition and cannot itself be observed" (p. 197). "By definition, leadership cannot describe everyone in the group; its very meaning calls for distinctive behavior" (p. 197).

In stating unequivocally that "Leadership exists only as a perception" and that "Leadership is not a viable scientific construct" (p. 202), Calder and other attribution theorists deny the essential notion of leadership as a relationship. They conceive of leadership as existing in the perception of distinctive behaviors of people who are called leaders who cause certain effects in people's lives and worlds. As with many other leadership scholars, the attribution theorists confuse leadership with the behavior of leaders, even though they filter that behavior through the perceptual lens of followers or observers.

House and Baetz (1979) wrote a chapter on leadership for the first volume of *Research in Organizational Behavior* in which they constructed an attributional approach to leadership in their definition. First, they rejected the view "that despite the fact that leadership has been the subject of speculation, discussion, and debate since the time of Plato and the subject of more than 3,000 empirical investigations (Stogdill, 1974), there is little known about it." They continued:

We disagree with this conclusion. It is our position that there are several empirical generalizations that can be induced from the wealth of research findings concerning leadership. Further, it is our position that when viewed collectively these empirical generalizations provide a basis for the development of a theory of leadership—a theory that potentially describes, explains, and predicts the causes of, processes involved in, and consequences of the leadership phenomena. While such a theory is not presently available, it is argued here that it is possible of attainment. (p. 342)

Thus, the construct of leadership is defined as the degree to which the behavior of a group member is perceived as an acceptable attempt to influence the perceiver regarding his or her activity as a member of a particular group or the activity of other group members. To qualify as a leadership behavior, it is necessary that the behavior is both perceived as an influence attempt and that the perceived influence attempt is viewed as acceptable.

It is argued here that leadership is an *attribution* made about the intentions of others to influence members of a group and about the degree to which that influence attempt is successful. (p. 345, emphasis added)

Kracke, an English anthropologist, published his book on leadership in 1978. In it, he took a functional approach to leadership. His approach is basically group-oriented, but it has important differences from the mainstream group approach.

Leadership is an emotional relationship at least as much as it is a jural one; and it is a relationship, furthermore, which is an integral part of group dynamics. (pp. 3–4)

Leadership is not primarily a formal defined role, but an intrinsic part of group process. By "group" I mean a set of individuals who interact with one another over some time, with a degree of mutual recognition and openness to one another, some sense of common purpose or common destiny, and a sense of belonging together. Leadership is a set of functions related to the formation of such a group and to maintaining its continuity and coordination.

One such function, or set of functions, involves . . . the *commotive function* "which enables, and leads, a group of men to move together in the achievement of a common purpose" (Hocking, 1937, p. 107).

These functions need not be performed by a headman or by any formally recognized "head" or even always by the same individual; but it is usually expected that they will be carried out by the headman. Each of these functions, furthermore, can be performed by more than one person in concert. . . . Indeed, everyone taking part in a group is likely to make some contribution to adjustment and to the commotive process; but one or two people are apt to make the dominant contributions and coordinate the contributions of others, and they may be called leaders.

Leadership as I have defined it consists as much on the leader's effect on the group he leads as on his behavioral style. (pp. 84–85)

Two political scientists wrote important books on leadership in the 1970s. Paige (1977) makes the point that political scientists have not taken the subject of leadership seriously, and he calls for a new, interdisciplinary approach to studying leadership. He defined political leadership as "the behavior of persons in positions of political authority, their competitors, and these both in interaction with other members of society as manifested in the past, present, and probable future throughout the world" (p. 1). The last part of his definition strikes me as odd, since it does not seem to add any distinguishing elements to his concept of leadership. The definition also suffers from a lack of boundaries as to what behaviors are included in leadership. As the definition is worded, all behaviors that political authorities and their competitors in interaction with other members of society do each and every day are leadership. Thus, practically everything these people do is labeled leadership. But the inclusion of society members in the interaction was a nice touch, and that idea needs to be explored in studies of leadership.

Political scientists are wont to define political leadership instead of defining leadership as a generic process. (Educators and business people like to do the same thing—write about educational leadership and business leadership instead of writing about leadership.) Paige did that in his book, and Burns (1978) fell into the same pattern in constructing his definition. "Leadership is the reciprocal process of mobilizing by persons with certain motives and values, various economic, political and other resources, in a context of competition and conflict, in order to realize goals independently or mutually held by both leaders and followers" (p. 425). That definition has a certain political air about it, but it is nevertheless more generic than most. Perhaps it is more accurate to say that Burns took a political approach to leadership rather than to say that he defined political leadership. Be that as it may, Burns's definition suffers from being too long and including too many variables for either researchers or practitioners to handle in conceptualizing leadership. All that aside, his definition puts leadership into clear focus without confusing it with other social processes; it is straightforward and understandable; and it shows a new way to understand the nature of leadership. Burns's explication of leadership is the most important conceptual framework of leadership to have emerged in the 1970s. I will have more to say about his concept of leadership in future chapters.

Thus, the 1970s started with the blahs in leadership studies and ended with a serious challenge to the mainstream views of leadership. While the dominant paradigm remained firmly in control and the overwhelming majority of leadership scholars adhered to that framework, several scholars in various academic disciplines developed conceptual frameworks of leadership that challenged the organizational behaviorists and the psychologists. As a result, leadership studies would never be the same, and the 1980s saw an explosion of new ideas about the nature of leadership and its study.

REFERENCES

American college dictionary. (1953). New York: Harper & Brothers.

American Heritage dictionary of the English language. (1978). Boston: American Heritage and Houghton Mifflin. (Original edition published in 1969.)

American Heritage illustrated encyclopedic dictionary. (1987). Boston: Houghton Mifflin.

Burchfield, R. W. (1976). *A supplement to the Oxford English dictionary.* Oxford: Oxford University Press.

Candrey, R. (1604/1966). *A table alphabetical of hard English words: The first English dictionary.* Gainsville, FL: Scholars Facsimiles and Reprints. (Facsimile of the original version of the book.)

Century dictionary. (1889–1911). New York: Century.

Century dictionary and cyclopedia. (1906–1909). New York: Century.

Chamber's twentieth century dictionary of the English language. (1904). Philadelphia: Lippincott.

Cockeran H. *The English dictionary of 1623.* (1623/1930). New York: Huntington. (Facsimile of the original version of the book.)

Crabb, G. (1839). *English synonymes.* New York: Harper & Brothers.

Dictionary of American English on historical principles. (1942). Chicago: University of Chicago Press.

Fowler, H. W. (1982). *A dictionary of modern English usage* (2nd ed.). New York: Oxford University Press. (First edition published in 1926.)

Funk & Wagnalls. (1928). *New standard dictionary of the English language*. New York: Funk & Wagnalls.

Funk & Wagnalls (1962). *New practical standard dictionary of the English Language*. New York: Funk & Wagnalls.

Funk & Wagnalls, (1971/1982). *New comprehensive international dictionary of the English language*. Newark, NJ: Publishers International Press. (Original published in 1971.)

Hunter, R. (1979–1988). *The encyclopaedic dictionary*. New York: Cassell, Petter, Calpin.

Hunter, R., & Morris, C. (1898). *Universal dictionary of the English language*. New York: Peter Fenelon Collier.

Johnson, S. (1755/1967). *A dictionary of the English language*. London: Strahan. (Reprinted in New York by AMS Press in 1967.)

Johnson, S., & Walker, J. (1879). *The people's pronouncing and defining dictionary and exposition of the English language*. London: W. T. Amies.

Klein, E. (1966–1967). *A comprehensive etymological dictionary of the English language*. Amsterdam: Elsevier.

March, F. A., & March, F. A., Jr. (1925). *Thesaurus dictionary*. Philadelphia: Historical.

Miles, D. (1888). *A readable English dictionary, etymologically arranged*. London: n.p.

Murray, J.A.H. (1888–1928). *A new English dictionary based on historical principles*. Oxford: Clarendon Press.

New Britannica/Webster dictionary and reference guide. (1981). Chicago: Encyclopaedia Britannica.

New Century Dictionary (1927) New York: Century.

Onions, C. T. (Ed.). (1960). *The Oxford dictionary of English etymology*. Oxford: Oxford University Press.

Oxford English dictionary. (1933). Oxford: Oxford University Press.

Oxford English dictionary (2nd ed.). (1989). Oxford: Oxford University Press.

Partridge, E. (1958). *Origins: A short etymological dictionary of modern English*. New York: Macmillan.

Perry, W. (1788). *Royal standard English dictionary*. Worcester, MA: Isaiah Thomas.

Perry. W. (1805). *The synonymous, etymological, and pronouncing English dictionary*. London: John Walker.

Random House dictionary of the English language (2nd ed.). (1987). New York: Random House.

Richardson, C. (1844). *A new dictionary of the English language*. London: Charles Rich.

Skeat, W W. (1924). *An etymological dictionary of the English language*. Oxford: Clarendon Press.

Webster, N. (1828/1970). *An American dictionary of the English language*. New York: Johnson Reprint. (Reprint of the original version of the book.)

Webster, N. (1856). *An American dictionary of the English language*. (2nd ed.). Springfield, MA: Merriam.

Webster's collegiate dictionary (3rd ed.). (1927). Springfield, MA: Merriam.

Webster's new international dictionary of the English language. (1915). Springfield, MA: Merriam.

Webster's new international dictionary of the English language (2nd ed.). (1955). Springfield, MA: Merriam.

Webster's new twentieth century dictionary of the English language. (2nd ed.). (1956). New York: Publishers' Guild.

Webster's new world dictionary of the English language (3rd ed.). (1988). Springfield, MA: Merriam.

Websters third international dictionary of the English language (3rd ed.). (1965). Springfield, MA: Merriam.

Wedgewood, H. (1872). *A dictionary of English etymology* (2nd ed.). London: Trübner.

Weekley, E. (1921). *An etymological dictionary of modern English.* London: J. Murray.

Worchester, J. E. (1860). *Primary dictionary of the English language.* Boston: Brewer & Tileston.

World Book dictionary. (1976). Chicago: Field Enterprises Educational Corporation.

Wyld, H.C.K. (1939). *The universal dictionary of the English language.* Chicago: Standard American.

4

Leadership Definitions: The 1980s

The explosion of books and journal articles about leadership and the number of times the word appeared in newspaper headlines and magazine articles during the 1980s were incredible. In 1980–1983, there were on average six books on leadership published per year. The number grew to fourteen in 1984, twenty in 1986, and twenty-three in 1989. In all, there were 132 books on leadership published in the 1980s. Fifteen of these were edited books with ten chapters (on the average) written by different leadership scholars. Add to this the large volume of unpublished papers, reports, and dissertations, plus the numerous articles in popular magazines and daily newspapers, and the sheer volume of the 1980s literature on leadership is astounding. I doubt any other specialized subject in the behavioral or social sciences could equal the number of works devoted to the subject of leadership in the 1980s.

Such an explosion makes a comprehensive review and analysis of leadership definitions of the 1980s quite difficult. On the other hand, the explosion makes it all the more important to try to determine what leadership scholars thought about the nature of leadership in the 1980s. To do that, I have grouped the definitions into identifiable conceptual frameworks and, as with the analysis of previous decades, I hope this attempt to find patterns of thought helps to make sense out of what appear to be discrepant trains of thought about the nature of leadership.

I collected 110 definitions of leadership in the 312 books, chapters, and articles in the 1980s literature. There were 202 authors who did not give a definition of leadership in their work. Among that number are major leadership scholars. Even more than in previous decades, one gets the impression that many of these authors take one of two positions. The first position is basically a laissez-faire attitude; everyone knows what leadership is even though they may not be able to put the definition into words, so one doesn't need to define it. The second position comes down to one of fear and trepidation; no one knows what leadership really is, so there is no point in trying to define it. Some authors seem to fear that they are setting themselves up for failure, since no one will accept their definitions anyway.

Either way, the reality is that the 1980s saw more, not fewer, authors writing a book or chapter on a subject they chose not to define. Thus, the practice was more, not less, acceptable than it had been in previous decades, judging from both the number and the scholarly reputations of writers who did it. My own view, which should be obvious by now, is quite the opposite. Responsible scholarship requires that one clearly articulate the nature of leadership if one is going to expound on the subject.

Almost as bad as those who don't define leadership are those authors who do define the word and then ignore their definition in the body of their written work. Equally bad are those authors who give a definition that is so nondescript, general, or confused that readers cannot take it seriously. Both of these problems are not singular to the 1980s literature; they have been in evidence since at least the 1930s. But these problems have been getting worse, not better; and that is the bad news.

Be that as it may, there are 110 definitions to analyze. Contrary to the practice in analyzing the definitions of previous decades, some authors who did not provide their readers with a definition of leadership are included in this discussion.

Leadership as Do the Leader's Wishes

Topping the list of conceptual frameworks of leadership for the 1980s was one I call "do the leader's wishes." This group of leadership definitions delivers the message that leadership is basically doing what the leader wants done. This concept of leadership is extremely popular with many of the authors who do not define leadership and with the people in the media (newspapers, newsmagazines, and television news) who used the word *leadership* in the 1980s.

This view of leadership is a descendant of the great man/woman theory. Its ascendancy in popularity in the 1980s is quite surprising in many respects, since the theory has been, and still is, debunked by nearly all of the behaviorists in leadership studies, and the theory is quite antifeminist in its history. However, on second thought, such a view of leadership is not surprising, since the people of the Western world were surrounded by this idea of leadership in the three dominant personalities of the decade: Gorbachev, Reagan, and Thatcher, all of whom modeled this notion of leadership magnificently. And the decade ended with Bush playing the same role in the Panama invasion. In the business leadership literature, this concept of leadership was repeated over and over again in the stories of CEOs as told and analyzed within a leadership framework by Bennis and Nanus (1985), Donaldson and Lorsch (1983), Iacocca (1984), Kotter (1988), Levinson and Rosenthal (1984), Peters and Waterman (1982), Potts and Behr (1987), Ruch and Goodman (1983), Tichy and Devanna (1986), and Zaleznik (1989).

Another way to recognize this view of leadership in many of the popular books on the subject is to see if the author defines leadership by defining who a leader is. If the words *leadership* and *leader* are used interchangeably, there is a high probability that the author believes in this model of leadership. Burns (1978) fell into this trap to some extent because his notions of leadership were influenced by studying great presidents and prime ministers; thus some of the offshoots of his work in the 1980s reflect the do-the-leader's wishes model. And, finally, the considerable interest in charismatic leadership in the late 1980s is another significant indication that this model of leadership is very much alive and well.

Nicoll (1986) noted the pervasiveness of this model of leadership in his critique of it.

My basic concern is that we are ignoring the guts of our new paradigm. Our newest and best approaches to leadership—for example, those provided by James MacGregor Burns (1979 [*sic*]), Warren Bennis [and Burt Nanus] (1985) and Abraham Zaleznik (1977)—are still rooted in Newton's hierarchic, linear, and dualistic thinking, so much so that they do not provide us with completely satisfactory models for the world we face. To our detriment, we still see a leader as one person, sitting at the top of a hierarchy, determining for a group of loyal followers, the direction, pace, and outcome of everyone's efforts. (p. 30)

Bass accepted this view of leadership when he revised *Stodgill's Handbook of Leadership* in 1981: "For the purposes of this Handbook, leadership must be defined broadly. Leadership is an interaction between members of a group. Leaders are agents of change, persons whose acts affect other people more than other people's acts affect them. . . . Leadership occurs when one group member modifies the motivation or competencies of others in the group" (p. 16). Kanter (1983) defined leadership as "the existence of people with power to mobilize others and to set constraints" (p. 249). Misumi (1985) wrote: "Leadership is understood as the role behavior of a specific group member who, more than other members, exerts some kind of outstanding, lasting, and positive influence on fulfilling the group's functions of problem solving or goal achievement and group maintenance" (p. 8). Weiss (1986) really pinpointed the concept: "Leadership in this study refers to the top-level administrative executive and his/her dominant coalition of the organization, which is invested with the power, status, and resources to manipulate, interpret, and negotiate constraints and resources into policy" (p. 9).

Kellerman (1984a) adopted the do-the-leader's-wishes view in her definition: "Leadership is the process by which one individual consistently exerts more impact than others on the nature and direction of group activity" (p. 70). She then quotes McFarland (1969), who wrote that the leader is the one "who makes things happen that would not happen otherwise" (p. 155). Blondel, another political scientist and woman, gave a similar definition: "What, then, is political leadership? It is manifestly and essentially a phenomenon of power: it is power because it consists of the ability of the one or few who are at the top to make others do a number of things (positively or negatively) that they would not or at least might not have done" (p. 3).

Gardner (1986) waffled at the end of his definition by attaching the last phrase: "Leadership is the process of persuasion and example by which an individual (or team) induces a group to take action that is in accord with the leader's purposes or the shared purposes of all" (p. 6). In 1990, Gardner changed the words of his definition a bit, but none of the substantive meaning: "Leadership is the process of persuasion or example by which an individual (or leadership team) induces a group to pursue objectives held by the leader or shared by the leader and his or her followers" (p. 1).

Sergiovanni (1989), an influential leadership scholar in education, patterned his definition on Gardner's: "Leadership is the process of persuasion by which a leader or leadership group (such as the state) induce followers to act in a manner that enhances the leader's purposes or shared purposes" (p. 213). Sergiovanni gave a definition in 1984 that puts him in the next framework discussed (achieving organizational goals), and the content of his 1990 book (since there is no definition of leadership is that book) puts him in the excellence framework.

Military scholars have a certain penchant for the do-the-leader's-wishes definition of leadership. Sarkesian (1981) stated it bluntly: "Regardless of the complexities involved in the study of leadership, its meaning is relatively simple. Leadership means to inspire others to undertake some form of purposeful action as determined by the leader" (p. 243). Prince and Associates (1985) agreed: Leadership is "the process of influencing human behavior so as to accomplish the goals prescribed by the organizationally appointed leader" (p. 7). Two more recent books on leadership have been based on military leaders, and they promote the same understanding of leadership. Roberts (1989) developed his understanding of leadership by paraphrasing Attila the Hun's messages to his warriors and people; Ridge (1989) used General Patton as his model of a leader. Roberts did not provide a definition of leadership, but there can be little doubt that he accepts the do-the-leader's-wishes concept. (If you were a follower of Attila the Hun, would you not want to do his wishes?) Ridge quotes Patton for his definition: "Leadership is the thing that wins battles. It probably consists of what you want to do, and then doing it, and getting mad as hell if someone tries to get in your way" (1989, p. 35). Now, that is a really honest way of describing this understanding of leadership!

Bailey (1988), an anthropologist, is about as short and direct as one could be in a definition: "Leadership is the art of controlling followers" (p. 5). Tosi (1982) gives the traditional view of charismatic leadership (which he later critiques), and he summarizes this view well: "Leadership is the ability of one person to influence another to act in a way desired by the first" (p. 224). Finally, Schatz and Schatz (1986) summed up much of what this view of leadership represents: "Leadership is the total effect you have on the people and events around you. The effect is your influence" (p. 3). Leadership is, according to this conceptual framework, centered on the leader. She/he is the be-all and end-all of leadership. Do not let references to democracy confuse you about the real essence of leadership. Leadership is the leader's having his/her way. That sums up the essential message of the most popular understanding of leadership in the 1980s.

Zaleznik (1989), who has never defined leadership in any of his many publications on the subject, articulated this view of leadership:

Leadership is based on a compact that binds those who lead and those who follow into the same moral, intellectual, and emotional commitment. . . .

The leadership compact demands commitment to the organization. In the past this commitment was embodied in strong leaders such as Andrew Carnegie, Henry Ford, Pierre du Pont, Thomas Watson. In more recent times people such as Edwin Land, Walter Wriston, Kenneth Olsen, Ross Perot, An Wang and Steven Jobs represented it.

Sam Walton, the founder of the Wal-Mart retail chain, exemplifies the leadership compact. . . .

The legitimacy of the leadership compact arises either from tradition or from the personal qualities of the leader. Tradition operates in monarchies, the military, and religion. It is not as much a factor in purely secular and modern organizations. For a leader to secure commitment from subordinates in business and political organizations, he or she has to demonstrate extraordinary competence or other qualities that subordinates admire. If the leader fails to demonstrate these personal qualities and is not maintained in his or her role by tradition, the leadership compact begins to disintegrate.

Ronald Reagan's presidency provides an illuminating case. (pp. 15–16)

In the next chapter, Zaleznik sets up Neustadt's description of presidential leadership as the polar opposite of what leadership really is.

How many executives would agree that the following description of the job of the president of the United States should be taken as an accurate portrayal of a chief executive's job in American business? "In form all presidents are leaders nowadays. In fact this guarantees no more than that they will be clerks. . . . A President, these days, is an invaluable clerk. His influence, however, is a very different matter. Laws and customs tell us little about leadership in fact" (1960, p. 6).

The idea that a chief executive officer is a clerk and that his power stands in proportion to the need other people have of him for their goals may reflect the realities of election politics and bureaucratic continuity, but it is bizarre if applied to business. A chief executive officer in a modern corporation has enormous clout. This job, unlike that of the president of the United States, is less a problem of persuasion than of deciding what is the right thing to do. Once a course of action has been formed, it is relatively easy to persuade subordinates to work hard to get the job done. . . . (pp. 31–32)

Zaleznik's book is filled with hundreds of paragraphs reflecting the view that leadership is doing what the leader wishes. It is a fitting apologia for the John Wayneism that dominated leadership studies in the 1980s, and the fact that it was published at the end of the decade is doubly significant as a testament of what the 1980s were all about.

In contrast with the dominant, do-the-leader's-wishes view of leadership so vividly developed in Zaleznik's book, consider the introductory paragraphs of the preface in Manz and Sims's book, which was published in the closing months of 1989.

When people think of leadership, they think of one person doing something to another person. We call this "influence," and we think of a leader as one who has the ability to influence another. A classic leader—one whom everyone recognizes is a leader—is sometimes described as "charismatic" or "heroic." A popular current concept is the idea of a "transformational" leader, one who has the vision and dynamic personal attraction to generate total organizational change. The word *leader* itself conjures up visions of a striking figure on a rearing white horse, crying "follow me!" The leader is the one who has either power, authority, or charisma enough to command others. . . .

But is this heroic leadership figure the most appropriate image of the organizational leader of today? Is there another model? We believe there is. Well over ten years ago, we began our quest through empirical research for a sound theoretical conceptualization that effectively answers this question. What we discovered is that in many modern situations the most appropriate leader is the one who can lead others to lead themselves.

Our viewpoint represents a departure from the dominant, and we think incomplete, view of leadership. We begin with the position that true leadership comes mainly from within a person, not from outside. At its best, external leadership can provide a spark and support the flame of the powerful self-leadership that dwells within each person. At its worst, it disrupts this internal process, damaging the person and the constituencies he or she serves.

In this book, our focus is on a new form of leadership—one designed to facilitate the self-leadership energy within each person. This perspective suggests a new measure of leadership strength—the ability to maximize the contributions of others by helping them to effectively guide their own destinies, rather than the ability to bend the will of others to the leader's. (pp. xv–xvi)

I have many problems with the expressive individualism that is pervasive in Manz and Sims's concept of leadership, and the notion of self-leadership is a contradiction in terms that is totally incomprehensible. But that is not the point I want to make here. Forget all those substantive problems for the moment, and let the enormity of the 180-degree contrast in understandings of leadership sink in. Contrast Manz and Sims's view with Zaleznik's. What an incredible difference!

The dominant, do-the-leader's-wishes concept of leadership is alive and well and living in the Western world. Bennis and Nanus (1985) said it best: Leadership is leaders taking charge and doing the right thing. That overwhelming idea comes though even more strongly in Bennis's latest books (1989a, 1989b) and Nanus's book (1989), all of which focus on the leader and what he or she does as the essence of what leadership is all about, and on what the leader does not do as the lack of leadership.

Heifetz and Sinder (1988) critiqued what they called the "conventional wisdom" concerning leadership: "Leadership is again defined as having a vision or agenda of one's own, coupled with the ability to articulate one's message, gain support through transactional means, and bring one's own goals to fruition" (p. 180). The definitions reviewed above indicate that Heifetz and Sinder were correct. Doing the leader's wishes is what many scholars in the 1980s believed is the nature of leadership.

Despite Burns's dramatic attempt in 1978 to reformulate our understanding of leadership around an interactive process that achieves mutual purposes, despite the hundreds of times that Burns's ideas were quoted in the books and articles of the 1980s about leadership, we were left with the dominant paradigm of leadership in a stronger position than ever. At the end of the 1980s, leadership was still predominantly thought of as leaders getting followers to do the leader's wishes.

Leadership as Achieving Group or Organizational Goals

Among traditional leadership scholars (social psychologists and organizational behaviorists, in particular), leadership is still centered on the concept of achieving group or organizational goals. Hersey and Blanchard wrote in 1988 (as they had in previous editions of their book) that "a review of other writers reveals that most management writers agree that leadership is the process of influencing the activities of an individual or a group in efforts towards goal achievement in a given situation" (p. 86). That statement is as accurate for the 1980s as it was for the 1970s and the 1960s. I collected some seventeen definitions from the literature of the 1980s that fit into this framework; they came from different academic disciplines, all of which undoubtedly had been influenced by the social psychologists and organizational behaviorists.

This notion of leadership, of course, fits right into the do-the-leader's-wishes paradigm if one assumes, or if the information about any one group or organization indicates, that the leader's goals and the group's or organization's goals are the same. If they are the same, then this view of leadership is exactly the same as the previous view. However, that assumption is not necessarily made by some of the scholars represented in this literature, nor have studies revealed that such is actually the case in any number of groups and organizations that have been researched. Thus, this conceptual framework of leadership deserves a separate classification.

Hollander (1985) made it clear that the social psychologists and organizational behaviorists continue to favor this definition in his chapter on leadership in the *Handbook of Social Psychology*: "Leadership has been defined in many ways. The most consistent element noted is that leadership involves the process of *influence* between a leader and followers to attain group, organizational or societal goals" (p. 486). Jago (1982), in another review of the literature, concluded that "Leadership is a process and a property. The *process* of leadership is the use of noncoercive influence to direct and coordinate the activities of the members of an organized group toward the accomplishment of group objectives. As a *property*, leadership is a set of qualities or characteristics attributed to those who are perceived to successfully employ such influence" (p. 315). The second definition is, of course, a trait definition of leadership, the only one I could find in the literature of the 1980s. It does not fit into the goal achievement framework, but I included it for an accurate reflection of Jago's complete perspective. Adams and Yoder (1985), Rauch and Behling (1984), and Schriesheim, Tollivar, and Behling (1984) gave definitions in their works similar to Jago's process definition. So did Hart (1980) in a book on women and leadership: "Leadership is a process of influencing one or more people in a positive way so that the tasks determined by the goals and objectives of an organization are accomplished" (p. 16).

This framework expresses the thought of military scholars who are more organizationally oriented than Patton oriented. Segal (1981) wrote: "Leadership refers to interpersonal processes in social groups, through which some individuals assist and direct the group toward the completion of group goals" (p. 41). Montor et al. (1987) added the notion of willingness: "Leadership is the ability to influence people so that they willingly and enthusiastically strive toward the achievement of group goals" (p. 23).

The achievement of organizational goals definition is also quite common among leadership scholars in education. Smith, Mazzarella, and Piele (1981) gave this kind of definition: Leadership is "the activity of influencing people to strive willingly for group goals" (p. 5). Sergiovanni (1984) stated that "Leadership is broadly defined as achieving objectives effectively and efficiently" (pp. 105–106). Cuban (1988) wrote a perceptive discussion of the meaning of leadership and ended it by stating that leadership "refers to people who bend the motivations and actions of others to achieve certain goals" (p. 193).

Four political scientists accepted the goals achievement view of leadership, but they added a political touch. Rejai and Phillips (1988) used some of Heifetz and Sinder's (1988) thoughts in "reconceptualizing leadership as the mobilization of group resources towards solving group problems and achieving group objectives" (1988, p. 4).

As noted in the analysis of similar definitions in previous decades, this concept of leadership is quite inadequate as an explanation of what millions of people experience as leadership. Basically, the goal achievement notion of leadership reduces leadership to group facilitation and human relations skills of organizational development, all of which indicate an emphasis on style as a way of researching, explaining, and developing leadership. Leadership style continued to be the center of action in leadership studies in the 1980s. As evidence of that statement, check any review of the leadership literature (Bass, 1981; Bryman, 1986; Hollander, 1985; Immegart, 1988; Jago, 1982); you will immediately see how important personalistic styles in situational contexts were to leadership studies in the 1980s.

Second, the goal achievement view of leadership makes effectiveness a part of the definition of leadership instead of a quality of good leadership. In other words, it is impossible for leadership to happen in a group or organization where goals are not achieved. All leadership, then, has to be effective because leadership does not exist unless it is effective. It may be a nice idea of leadership, and it certainly puts leadership on a pedestal, but it does not square with what people experience in their daily lives. We all know of cases where leadership has been tried and found wanting, cases where leaders and followers tried to change an organization or society and failed. Leadership scholars need to get rid of the notion that leadership is the answer to all of our group, organizational, and societal problems. People who lead often do the wrong things in their attempt to solve problems.

Finally, equating leadership with achieving organizational goals causes insurmountable conceptual problems when relating leadership to management. Since the birth of management science in the nineteenth century, scholars and practitioners alike have agreed that it is the function of management to achieve organizational goals. Then leadership scholars came along and said, ''No, when organizational goals are accomplished, that is leadership!'' But management scholars continued to argue that the primary purpose of management is to co-ordinate human and material resources so as to achieve organizational goals. Thus, we have a problem. Leadership and management have been defined in such a way as to give them the same essential character. The nature of leadership is the same as the nature of management. That is similar to saying that AIDS is the same as hepatitis or, to use the proverbial analogy, that apples are the same as oranges.

If leadership is the same as management, then leadership is a useless concept, and scholars as well as practitioners ought to get rid of it. Most practitioners I know do not view leadership as the same as management. It is only when I read what scholars write about leadership that I encounter people who believe leadership and management are synonymous. And some of the most popular purveyors of this conceptual equation are the scholars who define leadership as achieving group or organizational goals.

Leadership as Management

Of course, there are numerous scholars who actually do define leadership as management, and so I have reserved a special category for them. The difference between the previous group of authors who hold that leadership is organizational goal achievement and this group of authors is that the goals achievement scholars do not explicitly state that leadership is management, whereas these scholars do.

I liked Kuhn and Beam's (1982) honest resignation:

The term *leadership* is already applied so widely to formal executives, officers, squad leaders, and the like that we will simply accept it and say that leadership is the performance of the sponsor, or managerial, function where the person who exercises it emerges from a more or less undifferentiated group or is placed in that position by formal appointment. (p. 381)

If everyone thinks that leadership is management, Kuhn and Beam argue, why fight it?

Kegan and Lahey (1984) are as direct as possible: "We define leadership as the exercise of authority" (p. 199). Dachler (1948), an Englishman, gave a definition of management and then gave a definition of leadership that is exactly the same except for one word. He did this, mind you, to solve our conceptual confusion! "*Management* from a social systems perspective is fundamentally an issue of *design, change, and development of, and giving directions to total social systems embedded in their environment. Leadership* is defined as the design, change, and development of, and giving directions to social *subsystems* embedded in their environment" (p. 102). I do not think this solves our leadership–management distinction problem.

Hunsaker and Hunsaker (1986) indicated that "Leadership involves *communicating* the what and how of job assignments to subordinates and *motivating* them to do the things necessary to achieve organizational objectives" (p. 37).

Fiedler has been famous for equating leadership with management since the mid-1960s, and he did not back down in his latest book (Fiedler & Garcia, 1987): "Our research thus far does not demonstrate the need for this distinction. Leadership, as we use the term, refers to that part of organizational management that deals with the direction and supervision of subordinates rather than, for example, inventory control, fiscal management, or customer relations" (p. 3).

Equally famous are J. G. Hunt and his associates (Baliga, Larson, Osborn, Schriesheim, Sekaran, and others), all of whom have had a very difficult time with the distinction between leadership and management. While they seem to recognize that the problem exists (Hunt, 1984c; and numerous introductions to symposia sections in the 1982, 1984, and 1988 books), they have been unwilling or unable to deal with this problem; thus the large body of their work must be placed in the leadership-as-management framework. In 1980, Hunt and Osborn gave this definition of leadership: "Leadership is the influence attempt a superior makes towards his subordinates as a group or on a one to one basis" (p. 49). In 1984, Hunt described "the *leadership process* as using power to obtain interpersonal influence" (1984a, p. 7). In what he called a refinement of that definition, he wrote: "Leadership is the use of personal-power bases (expert and referent) to influence group members. Supervision, then, is the use of position-power bases (reward, coercion, and legitimacy) to influence group members'' (p. 21). In 1985, Hunt and Blair indicated with approval that "the traditional notion of formal leadership is interpersonal superior–subordinate influence" (p. 76). In 1988, Baliga and Hunt wrote:

Managerial tasks are visualized as having an element of discretion which provides managers the opportunity to exercise leadership. Instances in which organizational members create and exercise discretion in tasks that have limited or no discretionary elements are also treated as "exercising leadership." . . . At the highest level of the organization, that is at the strategic apex, discretion can be so great and the leadership component of managerial roles can be so large that one can speak of the strategic apex manager(s) or organizational leaders in virtually synonymous terms. (p. 130)

Two other books, both published late in the decade, adopt a leadership-as-management framework. Smith and Peterson (1988) wrote: "Leadership which contributes to effective event management can be defined as *actions by a person which handle organizational problems as expressed in the events faced by others*" (p. 80). I am not sure I understand that definition, but what I do understand puts it into the leadership as management category. Yukl (1989), in the second edition of his popular textbook, defined leadership "broadly to include information processes involving determination of the group's or the organization's objectives, motivating tasking behavior in pursuit of these objectives, and influencing group maintenance and culture." He added, "The terms *leader* and *manager* are used interchangeably in this book" (p. 5). At least he was forthright.

The leadership as management perspective was pervasive not only in the 1980s but in previous decades as well. The melding of leadership and management shows the strong influence that management science has had on the study of leadership. But a number of scholars launched an attack on this view of leadership in the 1980s, and part of that attack was from scholars who equated leadership with influence, not with authority. Influence, as we have seen, is quite an old concept in the leadership literature, dating as far back as the 1930s. But the scholars of the 1980s gave the concept more clarity and strength.

Leadership as Influence

Influence is probably the word most often used in the leadership definitions of the 1980s. If there are few other unifying elements to our collective thought about leadership, the notion of leadership as influence is one that clearly stands out. Along with the definitions that follow in this section, many of those which emphasize the do-the-leader's-wishes and goal achievement views of leadership, given in previous sections, and those which view leadership as transformation, given in the next section, also include the idea of influence. Thus, the notion of influence transcends several conceptual frameworks of leadership. Influence is also a critical component in my definition, which is given in the next chapter.

Bryman (1986), an Englishman, reviewed a number of leadership definitions and then wrote the following statement: "The common elements in these definitions imply that leadership involves a social influence process in which a person steers members of the group towards a goal" (p. 2). Willner (1984), a political scientist and a woman, captured the concept of leadership as an influence relationship as well as anyone: "Leadership, in the general sense of the term in common usage, denotes a relatively sustained and asymmetric exercise of influence by one individual, the leader, over others, the followers. It is a patterned relationship of influence between one member of a group and its other members" (p. 5). Tucker (1981), another political scientist, equated leadership with politics by the end of his book. In the first chapter, he explained that "Leadership is a process of human interaction in which some individuals exert, or attempt to exert, a determining influence upon others" (p. 11). Notice how different these definitions are from those which require leaders to achieve goals.

Brittel (1984) reduced leadership to the basics: "Leadership is the ability to influence the actions of others" (p. 12). This definition is a bit too basic, since it doesn't distinguish leadership from other social processes that use influence. Blumberg and Greenfield (1986) deliberately chose to use the word *leading* rather than *leadership*, and then indicated that leading is "the principal exerting influence in a school setting" (p. 166). That definition is too limiting, of course, because it restricts leadership to principals and to school settings. It also fails to distinguish leadership from other social processes that use influence. Osborn, Morris, and Connor (1984) argued that the European view of leadership "is a 'patterning' over time, . . . a recognized consistency of the influence attempts made by those in leadership positions" (p. 360).

Graham (1988) added that the influence had to be noncoercive for the influence relationship to be labeled *leadership*.

Definitions of leader–follower relationships typically draw a distinction between voluntary acceptance of another's influence, on the one hand, and coerced compliance, on the other (Graham, 1982; Hunt, 1984; Jacobs, 1971 [*sic*]; Jago, 1982; Katz & Kahn, 1978). That distinction rests on the degree of free choice exercised by followers. Specific instances of obedience which stem from fear of punishment, the promise of rewards, or the desire to fulfill contractual obligations are examples not of voluntary followership but of subordination, and the range of free choice available to subordinates is relatively small. Appropriate labels for the person giving orders, monitoring compliance, and administering performance-contingency rewards and punishments include "supervisor" and "manager," but not "leader." (p. 74)

Naylor, Pritchard, and Ilgen (1980) qualified the type of influence used in leadership relationships.

Within the organizational context, leadership concerns focus upon the ability of those in higher status positions to influence those under them. Yet, every act of influence does not represent leadership. We side with Katz and Kahn (1978). . . . Supervision involves the routine application of procedures and practices bestowed upon the position in which the individual is placed. . . . Leadership, on the other hand, represents that influence over-and-above supervisory influence. Under these conditions, it is necessary to influence the subordinates to perform behaviors they technically would not have to do if they merely followed to the letter the procedures described in their positions. (pp. 230–231)

Popper (1989) made the same kind of argument, but the discussion may be somewhat difficult to follow because he uses a negative example and the A–B relationship.

But what is leadership? . . . It is enough to state that administrative control that obtains compliance to management decisions by means of a *coercive* capacity, that is the enforcement of bureaucratic rules and regulations, is by no stretch of the imagination an exercise of leadership. The *sine qua non* of leadership is followership; a condition that is not there when, in a formal interactive relationship, A controls the role behavior of B not because B is persuaded by the *influence* of A, but rather because A has an implicitly acknowledged right from B to use *authority* and, therefore, B grants compliance to administrative directives from A. (pp. 369–370)

Other authors did not use the word *influence* but put the concept of influence in their definitions. Kotter (1988) defined leadership as "the process of moving a group (or groups) of people in some direction through (mostly) noncoercive means" (p. 16). Parentheses in definitions bother me, so I have a problem with the word *mostly* in his definition. Betz (1981) used Bowen's definition of leadership: "Most comprehensible attempts to come to grips with the term *leadership* focus on the relational aspects of leadership. 'Leadership is an interpersonal relation in which others comply because they want to, not because they have to' (Bowen, 1974, p. 241)" (p. 7). Kouzes and Posner (1988) never gave a succinct and clear definition of leadership, except that on the first page of their book they stated that "Leadership is a relationship between leader and followers." That definition, of course, is fairly innocuous. In a discussion on the essence of leadership, however, they do indicate that they are in the influence camp: "To get a feel for the true essence of leadership assume that everyone who works for you is a volunteer" (p. 26). The only trouble with their essential concept is this: What if the people with whom you have a leadership relationship don't work for you? How do you get at the true essence of leadership then?

The leadership-as-influence conceptual framework is a vast improvement over the other frameworks analyzed above. For one thing, the definitions are fairly straightforward and workable, especially when they are not exclusively tied to an employer–employee relationship. Many of these scholars are still unable to divorce themselves from that kind of understanding, but this group of writers certainly has the potential for pointing us in the right direction.

Second, the scholars who have defined leadership as an influence relationship almost universally believe that there is a distinction between leadership and management, and the way to clear up the confusion between the two concepts is to insist that leadership is noncoercive influence. Again, that certainly is a step in the right direction, since there is nothing else on the horizon that helps us differentiate the two processes. I do not think the word *noncoercive* is the whole answer, but it is part of the answer.

Leadership as Traits

Traits as a way of understanding the nature of leadership made a big comeback in the 1980s after being disdained by scholars for decades. Actually, there have been trait theorists who have been popular in every decade, as has been indicated previously, but the leadership-as-excellence movement of the 1980s caused numerous researchers and writers to take a different and more exhaustive look at the issue of leader traits.

Peters and Waterman (1982), Peters and Austin (1985), and Peters (1987) all develop a trait theory of leadership. So do Badaracco and Ellsworth (1989), Bennis and Nanus (1985), Bennis (1989a, 1989b), Blanchard et al. (1985), Cribbin (1981), Cohen (1990), Conger (1989a), DePree (1989), Kouzes and Posner (1987), Levinson and Rosenthal (1984), Maccoby (1981), Manz and Sims (1989), Nanus (1989), Ridge (1989), Roberts (1989), Sergiovanni (1987a, 1990), and Waterman (1987).

As can easily be seen, these authors produced many of the most popular leadership books of the 1980s, and they are undoubtedly the source of many people's understanding of leadership. As a result, it does not take a very sophisticated analysis to assess why the traits view of leadership is so firmly entrenched in scholars' and practitioners' minds.

What is distressing is that most of these books were written by authors who have not articulated a clear, concise definition of leadership in their work. Those authors who did give a definition have, for the most part, not emphasized the concept of traits. Not one of the 312 definitions from the 1980s that were collected for this review articulated a traits concept of leadership. Yet, the leadership literature of the 1980s is littered with a traits orientation.

If nothing else, this contradiction points out in bold relief the problem of authors' not clearly defining leadership or, even worse, stating a definition and then ignoring it in the main body of the book or article. The traits mess in the 1980s literature shows dramatically that scholars who want to write books on leadership must think deeply about the nature of leadership, articulate their thoughts about what leadership is, and then be very consistent in their writing so that what they write flows from their definition.

Leadership as Transformation

Burns's basic definition of leadership was given in Chapter 3. Although his definition is not transformational, he introduced the notion of transformational leadership as one of two forms that leadership can take (the other being transactional), and he has become famous—and rightly so—for initiating a movement to reconceptualize leadership as a transformational process—"when one or more persons engage with others in such a way that leaders and followers raise one another to higher levels of motivation and morality" (1978, p. 20). This new, and some (Hunt, 1984) would say, radical view of leadership spawned numerous other definitions of leadership in the 1980s; some echo Burns's understanding, others expand it to different kinds of transformations besides those of motivation and morality, and others alter it to include transformations which lower as well as those which raise people's morality. In this section, I review many of these definitions that flowed out of Burns's attempt to reformulate our understanding of leadership around the notion of transformation.

Peters and Waterman (1982) never define leadership in their famous book, but the material on pages 81–86 indicates that they adopted Burns's view of transformational leadership. One sentence is particularly telling: "We are fairly sure that the culture of almost every excellent company that seems now to be meeting the needs of 'irrational man,' as described in this chapter, can be traced to transforming leadership somewhere in its history" (p. 82). Beyond their own subsequent books and articles, Peters and Waterman have spawned a movement in leadership studies that equates leadership with the process of transforming an organization to achieve excellence. Literally hundreds of books and articles have propagated this theme, but almost none of them include a definition of leadership (following the example of Peters and Waterman's original work). These works are almost all content based, focusing on how bad the situation is now, then articulating what excellence means, and finally pleading for some kind of transformational leadership to bring the organization (and, in the end, the United States) back to the nirvana of excellence.

Greenfield (1984) introduced the notion of social reconstruction into leadership definitions: "Leadership is a willful act where one person attempts to construct the social world for others" (p. 142). The definition suffers from being too personalistic and singular. Buckley and Steffy's (1986) definition was more organizationally oriented: "Leadership is being redefined as leaders are challenged to work within multiple dimensions of the organization in order to transform behavior, structures, and consciousness" (p. 233). The definition of Heifetz and Sinder (1988) also implies some social reconstruction: "Leadership is mobilizing the group's resources to face, define, and resolve its problems" (p. 195).

In Great Britain, Hosking and Morley (1988) defined leadership as "the process by which 'social order' is constructed and changed" (p. 90). Critical theorists, a significant voice now in educational administration, generally adopt the social reconstructionist view of leadership. Foster (1989) articulated that view well: "Leadership is and must be socially critical, it does not reside in an individual but in the relationship between individuals, and it is oriented towards social vision and change, not simply, or only, organizational goals" (p. 46). Two pages later, he repeated that understanding of leadership but added a fourth element: "We make the claim that leadership is fundamentally addressed to social change and human emancipation, that it is basically a display of social critique, and that its ultimate goal is the achievement and refinement of human community'' (p. 48). In summary, ''certain agents can emerge in transformative practices which change social structures and forms of community, and it is this that we label leadership'' (p. 49). Smyth (1989a), an Australian critical theorist, used the notions of Fay (an Englishman) about social change in his definition: ''Leadership becomes a form of enablement through which people 'can change their lives so that, having arrived at a new self-understanding, they may reduce their suffering by creating another way of life that is more fulfilling' (Fay, 1977, p. 204)'' (p. 182). Bates (1989), another Australian critical theorist, defined leadership by defining leaders: ''Leaders can be defined as those who articulate particular values within organizations and who negotiate those values into the organizational illusion that shapes, sustains, and justifies behavior'' (p. 137).

Bass (1985), suggesting that ''a shift in paradigm is in order'' (p. xiii), converted from a group notion of leadership to a transformational one, but he provided no clear definition of leadership. While differing significantly from Burns's definition (see Bass, 1985, pp. 20–22), Bass seemed to equate leadership with a leader who gets ''performance beyond expectations'' (to quote the title of his book) out of his/her employees. This definition comes through in the following statement: ''To sum up, we see the transformational leader as one who motivates us to do more than we originally expected'' (p. 20).

The performance-beyond-expectations view of transformational leadership was supported by Faris in a book on military leadership.

Leadership is best understood when disentangled from the context of formal organizational structure. It is clear that much of what persons who occupy chain-of-command positions do is not leadership (unless one subscribes to the vapid formulation that everything an incumbent of leadership position does is leadership); . . . Conversely, persons who do not occupy positions of formal authority can be effective leaders; . . .

Accordingly, the following definition is offered: Leadership is communication and other forms of behavior which elicit among peers or subordinates voluntaristic behaviors which are consonant with the intent of the leader and congruent with the manifest goals of the organization and which otherwise would not have occurred. (1981, p. 150)

Cronin's (1980) definition is simpler: ''Leadership is generally defined as the capacity to make things happen that would otherwise not happen'' (p. 372). So is that of Bryson and Kelly (1981): ''We define leadership as 'behavior that makes a difference in the purposeful behavior of others' (Karmel, 1978, p. 476)'' (p. 203). Cribbin (1981) used Burns's notion of mutual goals along with the idea of ''beyond organizational requirements'' in his definition: ''Leadership is the ability to gain consensus and commitment to common objectives, beyond organizational requirements, which are attained with the experience of contribution and satisfaction on the part of the work group'' (pp. 12–13). The last clause does not make much sense the way it is written, and it may be redundant in view of the "consensus and commitment" required in the first part of his definition.

Much of the literature of the 1980s stemming from Peters and Waterman (1982) has this notion of leadership—leaders getting people to do things over and above what is expected, so as to transform an organization according to some criteria of excellence. Excellence, evidently, demands that people do more than what is expected. The cynical wag, of course, would ask: What happens to leadership when the expectations are raised and become part of the regular requirements?

Bass was also responsible for equating transforming leadership with charismatic leadership, first in his 1981 *Handbook* and then more extensively in his 1985 book. Hunt (1984c) adopted that view, as did others, and so in the late 1980s another offshoot of the leadership-as-transformation concept developed as a renewed interest in charismatic leadership. House (1977), Tucker (1970), and Zaleznik and Ket de Vries (1975) provided the 1970s background for this movement, but it did not take off until the mid-1980s. Willner published her book on charismatic political leaders in 1984, Bass's book came in 1985, Conger and Kanungo's edited volume was delivered in 1988, and Conger followed with his book in 1989.

My own view is that the notion of leadership as charismatic is more consistent with the do-the-leader's-wishes conceptual framework than it is with the leadership-as-transformation framework. Doing the leader's wishes is what charismatic leadership is all about. There is no essential transformational quality to charismatic process as applied to leadership; the only requirement is to do what the leader wishes.

In 1986, Adams edited a book of readings on transforming leadership, and one would think that there would be considerable enlightenment in the different chapters on the nature of leadership as viewed from a transformational perspective. Unfortunately, the authors of only four chapters out of seventeen defined leadership. The four with the definitions are only minimally helpful, at best. Ritscher (1986), an organizational consultant, stated that "Leadership involves creating a vision that draws people toward a common desired reality" (p. 63). His chapter promoted leaders having a spiritual, value-oriented vision. Harman (1986), a futurist of some renown, equated leadership with "shared power" (p. 105) and later opined that "the function of a leader is to empower others to use their own creativity to accomplish goals that are emergent in the total situation" (p. 109). Owen (1986), an organizational development expert, gave a definition promoting leadership by indirection, which "means leading at the level of spirit. The essential tools are offered by the myths of the organization, and the process may be understood as the manipulation of the mythic structure in order to tune the dynamic field and thereby focus the spirit on the task or tasks at hand" (pp. 119–120). Finally, Fritz (1986) developed a definition of leadership as transformation: "Leadership in this new orientation is thus enabling strong individuals to join together in a collective creative act of bringing into the world what they all mostly deeply care about and want to see'' (p. 161).

In the introduction to the book, Adams and Spencer (1986) gave five ''operating premises of strategic leadership'' that ''guided the selection of the chapters for this collection of readings'' (p. 9). A reading of those premises and the accompanying paragraphs under each of them (see pp. 9–12) leaves one with the question: What do these premises have to do with transforming leadership, the title of the book? The answer is not obvious. That problem, along with the fact that Adams did not provide a definition of transforming leadership in the introduction, undoubtedly explains why thirteen authors were unable or unwilling to give a definition of leadership as transformation and why three of the four authors who did give a definition did not define leadership from a transformational perspective. It also explains why the book in toto lacked focus and was of little help to its readers, who wanted to grasp the difficult concept of transformational leadership.

Whitehead and Whitehead (1986), who are theologians, seem to have a view of leadership as transformational, but I had a hard time extracting a consistent concept of leadership from their book. They obviously want church people (lay and clerical) to transform the Roman Catholic Church, but their understanding of leadership as transformational is still fuzzy. Only an extended quotation will show the Whiteheads' concept of leadership.

The Scriptures authorize us to picture the Christian community as a body: a complex social system needing coordination if it is to perform gracefully. Leadership may then be imaged as these exercises of coordination: the internal ordering of the body's various strengths for purposes of graceful and effective action. . . .

This process of ''ordering'' has traditionally described the exercise of Christian leadership. The sacrament of ''Holy Orders'' celebrates the initiation of a new community leader. We ''ordain'' our leaders for service to the community. . . .

In a hierarchical vision of the body, we tend to picture leadership as the head ''giving orders to the rest of the body. . . . ''

A very different view of the body and its good order has begun to emerge, both in American culture and in Christian experience. We have begun to envision the body . . . not as a regal reason ordering the proletarian passions but as a consortium of powers. . . . The task of order is a mutual and corporate one. . . .

We have outlined here a more wholistic vision that is emerging within the church: plural powers within the body struggle together toward a unified and coordinated expression. . . . (pp. 66–68)

Leadership is not just the influence that one person (or even a small group of persons) has on the rest of us. Leadership is much more adequately seen as a *process of interaction*. This process includes everything that goes on in the group that contributes to its effectiveness. Leadership exists when group members deal with one another in ways that meet their needs and contribute to their goals. Understood in this way, leadership includes all those elements in a group's life that *lead to* its survival and growth. (pp. 74–75)

Understood that way, leadership is the same as management. From time immemorial "the elements in a group's life that lead to its survival and growth" is exactly what management scholars have been proclaiming is management. If one leaves survival and growth out of organizational management, what else is there? Survival and growth are precisely what the Whiteheads argue, in other parts of their splendid book, are wrong with the Catholic Church; yet, there it is as a definition of leadership.

Hagberg (1984), writing from a feminist perspective, adopted Burns's transformational model in viewing leadership as a form of power. She did not give a definition of leadership, but it is clear from her text that she equated leadership with empowerment born out of the leader's integrity. Tichy and Devanna (1986) also do not give a definition of leadership, but the title of their book, *The Transformational Leader*, and the notion of leadership as a transformational drama (see pp. 27–33) indicate that their personalistic view of leadership falls within this conceptual framework. Nanus (1989) also concentrates on the leader who is visionary and futuristic, but he does provide a definition that is somewhat transformational in connotation: "Leadership is making people into effective collaborators in the important work of organizations, institutions, and society" (pp. 51–52). I have trouble with definitions of leadership that want to make people into something. They smack much more of the do-the-leader's-wishes framework, but in this case I have given Nanus the benefit of the doubt by inserting ideas from other parts of his book into the "important work" that these "collaborators" do through leadership. More explicitly transformational in its chosen words is Griffiths' (1986) definition: "Leadership is to set new goals and bring about 'some change of direction or some improvement in performance' " (p. 46, quoting Clark Kerr). Perhaps that is a good definition on which to end this section.

What can be said about the fate of transformational leadership in the 1980s? My overall impression is that Burns's model of transformational leadership has been badly mishandled by most of the leadership scholars of the 1980s. From Peters and Waterman's (1982) equation of transformation with excellence to Bass's (1985) and Conger's (1989a) equation of transformation with charisma, leadership as transformation has been watered down, bottom-lined, denuded of its moral essence, emotionalized, and to some extent overidealized. After finishing a yearlong study of a transformational leadership, Freiberg (1987) told me that his biggest problem with the concept and its application was that it seemed too goody-goody. No matter how Freiberg wrote up the story, the leader and the leadership relationships he had with thousands of people appeared unreal, too ideal, too otherwordly (K. Freiberg, personal communication, June 1987). Having read his study, I agree with his assessment, but the fact is that real transformational leadership, wherein leaders and followers raise one another to higher levels of morally purposeful action, really does happen.

Transformation leadership happened in Eastern Europe in 1989–1990, but to many of us it seemed totally unreal, too good to be true. The problem with the "transformational" leadership literature of the 1980s is that the authors did not take the concept seriously. As a result, one looks in vain for some explanation of the events in Eastern Europe in the "transformational" leadership literature. There is very little, if anything, in the Adams (1986) book that explains the transformation occurring in the Soviet Union and Eastern Europe. What good is this book if it and others like it on transforming leadership do not help us make sense of transformational leadership when we witness it happening before our very eyes?

We will never understand the nature of leadership from a transformational perspective until scholars and practitioners stop trivializing the concept. The 1980s saw the concept remade into everything that it was never meant to be. In the end, transformation in the 1980s meant doing the leader's wishes as the transformational leader took charge and did the right thing. That notion is only one-fourth (if that much) of what transformational leadership is all about, and we haven't even begun to seriously consider the other three-fourths. Only the social reconstructionists and critical theorists, a small band of brave souls bucking the dominant paradigm, have articulated a conceptual framework of leadership that is anywhere close to being transformational. While I have significant problems with their emphasis on the content of leadership and their consequent neglect of the nature of leadership as a relationship and process, I applaud their insistence that the transformation in transformational leadership be real, that it be substantive and substantial.

Burns's transformational leadership framework has serious conceptual problems. I do not mean to minimize them. My point is that we should get on with the job of dealing with them, and the leadership scholars of the 1980s did not do that job.

Miscellaneous Definitions

There are several definitions of leadership from the 1980s that do not fit into any of the five conceptual frameworks above. They are discussed in this section.

Smircich and Morgan wrote a perceptive piece in 1982 that has attracted considerable attention. Their definition and framework come from a phenomenological perspective in which reality is understood as socially constructed by people in specific contexts.

Leadership is realized in the process whereby one or more individuals succeeds [*sic*] in attempting to frame and define the reality of others. Indeed, leadership situations may be conceived as those in which there exists an *obligation* or a perceived *right* on the part of certain individuals to define the reality of others. . . .

Leadership, like other social phenomena, is socially constructed through interaction (Berger & Luckmann, 1966), emerging as a result of the constructions and actions of both leaders and led. It involves a complicity or process of negotiation through which certain individuals, implicitly or explicitly, surrender their power to define the nature of their experience to others. . . . (p. 258)

A focus on the way meaning in organized settings is created, sustained, and changed provides a powerful means of understanding the fundamental nature of leadership as a social process. . . . This process can be most easily conceptualized in terms of a relationship between figure and ground. Leadership action involves a moving figures—a flow of actions and utterances (i.e., what leaders do) within the context of a moving ground—the actions, utterances, and general flow of experience that constitute the situation being managed. Leadership as a phenomenon is identifiable within its wider context as a form of action that seeks to shape that context.

Leadership works by influencing the relationship between figure and ground, and hence the meaning and definition of the context as a whole. (p. 261)

Smircich and Morgan's concept of leadership is, perhaps, a more sophisticated version of attribution theory, and as such it makes sense only to those who want to discuss whether leadership as a process is real. I think they would have a hard time convincing Bill and Barbara that their framework is serving them (see Mintzberg, 1982). Nevertheless, the Smircich and Morgan article is a thoughtful piece that articulates an alternative view of leadership, and any fresh ideas about leadership are a welcome relief from the standard material in the literature.

In a definition based on Smircich and Morgan's framework, Watkins (1989) referred to leadership as "a social construction of reality which involves an ongoing interaction" (p. 27). This definition helps us not one bit, since it fails to distinguish leadership from any other social construction of reality.

In another perceptive chapter, this one in Kellerman's (1984b) book on multidisciplinary perspectives of leadership, Grob (1984) looked at philosophical approaches to leadership and settled on a Socratic view: "Leadership [is] understood as a dialogical activity" (p. 275). As much as I am impressed with Grob's chapter (and I have used it repeatedly in my classes), the definition is meaningless because it is obvious that there are many dialogic human processes besides the leadership process. It is, as a result, of no help in understanding what leadership is in contradistinction to what other human processes are. As a statement of how leaders *should* interact with other leaders and followers, the chapter is a superb and thoughtful piece. As a statement of what philosophers believe the nature of leadership is, it cannot stand up to even the simplest critical analysis.

Also in the Kellerman book, Carroll's (1984) chapter is representative of the views of a number of feminists who equate leadership with empowerment. She also equates leadership with the effective leader, a conceptual inconsistency of no small proportion when one wants to emphasize empowerment. "What does such a reconception of power suggest about the nature of leadership? An effective leader is one who empowers others to act in their own interests rather than one who induces others to behave in a manner consistent with the goals and desires of the leader" (p. 142). Besides equating leadership with the person of the leader, Carroll's definition reflects the therapeutic background assumptions of expressive individualism (Bellah et al., 1985). There is no concept of shared purpose in that definition, a lack that reduces leadership and empowerment to little more than me-tooism.

My nomination for the classic nondefinition of leadership goes to Immegart

(1988), who reviewed the research of leadership in educational administration literature.

A loose rather than a precise definition of leadership was adopted in selecting pieces to review. It was simply assumed that, regardless of conceptualization or operational definitions, those engaged in the study of leadership and leader behavior were, more or less, directing their efforts toward the same kind of phenomenon. (This can be debated, but the fact remains that although operational definitions for theoretical or research purposes may vary a great deal, there is general agreement on what is commonly meant by the term or the concept *leadership*.) (p. 260)

Loose definition, indeed! Do we need to wonder why the concept of leadership is confused when recognized leadership scholars engage in that kind of reductionism?

Some Concluding Comments on the 1980s

I am a professor of leadership studies who teaches in a master's program in educational administration and a doctoral program in leadership. Prior to writing this book, I had studied more than 300 books, chapters, and articles about leadership. I thought I knew the history and the current state of the leadership literature in the English language. In preparation for this book, I read another 300 books, chapters, and articles about leadership. A large part of those 300 books, chapters, and articles had been written since 1965 and particularly in the 1980s. Every time I went to libraries and bookstores in southern California and in several cities in other parts of the United States, I unearthed books, chapters, and articles about leadership that I had never seen before. I was constantly amazed that there was yet another piece of the leadership literature that I had not seen. I am sure there are other books, chapters, and articles that I have not discovered. Time, of course, is a major problem, but so is the ability to find relevant materials in unfamiliar academic disciplines.

The point of relating this tale of my never-ending quest to conquer the Mt. Everest of leadership literature is this. I had a rather strongly held view of where leadership studies was in the 1980s, and that view—simply stated—was that Burns had begun the process of reformulating our understanding of leadership, and that by the mid-1980s leadership studies as an academic discipline was in the midst of a paradigm shift. The evidence used to support this conclusion was the number of leadership scholars who appeared to be moving to a new understanding of leadership. By 1988 I had begun to reevaluate my position as doubts surfaced that these authors were actually articulating a new concept of leadership. In 1989, my once strongly held view was slowly, but surely, wiped out as I confronted the mountain of evidence that did not support it. As a result, I no longer hold that view.

The 110 definitions of leadership collected from the 1980s, as well as the lack of leadership definitions in the remaining works of 202 authors, provide over-whelming evidence that a new paradigm of leadership did not take hold in the 1980s. On the contrary, if any conclusion as to the 1980s' concept of leadership is warranted, it would be that that concept reflected the conservative and indi-vidualistic Yuppie character of Western society and in the end articulated an updated version of the industrial view of leadership paradigm. Taking its cue from the past, the 1980s saw *leadership recast as great men and women with certain preferred traits influencing followers to do what the leaders wish in order to achieve group/organizational goals that reflect excellence defined as some kind of higher-level effectiveness.* The influence of the industrial paradigm on leadership theory and practice has been monumental and pervasive.

If some analysts or commentators have a problem with this conclusion and, as evidence of a contrary view, point to the respect and influence that Burns's model of transformational leadership has had on leadership studies as a discipline and on the concept of leadership that practitioners have used in Western societies, my response would be straightforward and strong. The evidence provided in this chapter indicates that Burns' conceptual framework has been co-opted. Trans-formational leadership has been redesigned to make it amenable to the industrial paradigm and all that it represents. Knowingly or unwittingly, the authors of some of the most popular books on leadership in the 1980s have dressed up Burns's major ideas of leadership in designer outfits that appeal to *Fortune* 1000 companies and those to whom they deliver their goods and services. What we have at the beginning of the 1990s is clearly old wine in new bottles; great man/woman, trait, group, organizational, and management theories of leadership that look new because they bespeak excellence, charisma, culture, quality, vision, values, peak performance, and even empowerment. It's a snow job, not a new paradigm.

And, mind you, I was taken in, just like everyone else.

THE INDUSTRIAL SCHOOL OF LEADERSHIP

Many leadership scholars and practitioners see the leadership literature since about 1910 as confusing, discrepant, disorganized, and unintegrated. Burns (1978) lamented the lack of a school of leadership. Argyris (1979) and Hosking and Morley (1988) castigated the literature for not adding up. Practitioners see the literature as irrelevant (see the Bill and Barbara test in Mintzberg, 1982) because it does not deliver a consistent message that is meaningful to them. The conventional wisdom about the leadership literature is that, in toto, it does not make sense. Many people are so disgusted by the mess they see in the literature that they consider leadership studies as an academic discipline to be bad joke. Leadership studies, in their view, is not worthy of the name "academic disci-pline."

I have expressed some of these views in classes, speeches, and various papers written in the 1980s. Part of what I have been trying to do as an academic is to clean up some of this mess.

On the surface, this view of the leadership literature—that it is in disarray— is perfectly accurate. The *words* that scholars have used to define leadership are contradictory. The *models* that leadership scholars have developed are discrepant. The *emphasis on periphery and content*, as opposed to the essential nature of leadership, does make for highly personalistic and unidisciplinary views of leadership that do not cross over to other persons and disciplines. The *confusion of leadership with management* and the *equation of leaders with leadership* do cause serious conceptual problems that are hard to reconcile in the real world. And, finally, the *exploitation of the concept* of leadership in terms of symbolic mythmaking (for instance, as the savior of organizations, communities, and societies that have somehow lost "it") and in terms of the *almost sexual appeal* that has been attached to the word by some advertisers, trainers, program developers, and authors has clearly indicated that the concept has lost its moorings, if not its essential character.

But, when one looks at the literature at its most fundamental level, which is the basic understanding of leadership that the literature as a whole articulates, a surprising revelation emerges. Discovering what is fundamental, the absolutely basic understanding of a concept or a phenomenon, is what is meant by the word *paradigm*, and this kind of investigation into fundamental meanings is what Thomas Kuhn (1970) did in his celebrated book, *The Structure of Scientific Revolutions*, from which the notion of paradigm shifts has come.

In order to deal with a paradigm, one has to investigate basic meanings of a fundamental concept, and this is exactly what I have done in researching the definitions of leadership that make up the leadership literature of the twentieth century. One cannot get any more fundamental than investigating the word *leadership* in attempting to understand the literature of leadership. But paying attention to the denotations of the words in leadership definitions and models is not enough. That conclusion is obvious from the first-cut analysis of these definitions as presented in the last two chapters. Even some attempt at a second-cut analysis, as has been done several times in those chapters, reveals a literature that has some patterns of development but is basically still in disarray.

It is only when a third cut is done and one looks at the background assumptions (Gouldner, 1970) embedded in the definitions and models, when one looks at the meanings behind the words and investigates what the definitions and models really say, as well as what they do not say, that the revelation comes. And then the leadership literature begins to make sense.

I first hit upon this possibility—that there was, indeed, a school of leadership in the leadership literature since about 1910—in the summer of 1988. I was in the throes of rethinking my view of Burns's definition of leadership. In the midst of constructing the definition explicated in this book, which required that I admit to myself that a new paradigm of leadership had to be articulated, I suddenly came upon the elemental notion that the scholars and practitioners I thought had confused leadership with management were actually not confusing the two. They were reflecting their reality as they saw it. Their perception of leadership as management was the reality they perceived in the industrial era in which they lived and worked. They did not distinguish between leadership and management because in their minds there was no need to do so. They were one phenomenon. Leadership was management, and management was leadership. Their perception of leadership as management was the reality that they saw, practiced, propagated, and dealt with in their everyday world of work and play.

In putting their perceptions to work, the scholars wrote about leadership in a way that mirrored the reality they saw. They used the two words interchangeably in their books, chapters, and articles; and their definitions of leadership reflect that fact. Their definitions of leadership were, in fact, definitions of management; and since they viewed leadership and management as the same thing, they saw no need to give a definition of leadership that clearly distinguished it from management.

The fact that many of these authors recognized that they used the words *leadership* and *management*, or *leader* and *manager*, as synonymous terms and clearly did not think they were doing anything erroneous is a significant clue to what was happening in their minds. Leadership and management, leader and manager were synonymous; leadership and management were the same processes; leaders and managers were the same people. Nothing else makes sense of the data that are abundantly—overwhelmingly—evident in text after text, book after book, author after author, for decades—indeed, for almost a century. The data are massive and point in one direction—leadership and management are the same. The number of authors who wrote differently about leadership and management up until, roughly, the 1980s can be counted on one hand. Or, at the very most, two. Despite all the different words in the definitions of leadership; despite all the different leadership models; despite all the different disciplines from which the leadership scholars came; despite all the different organizations in different countries in which leadership was practiced and studied; despite the differences in epistemological perspectives and and research methodologies of the scholars; despite two world wars, severe economic depression, Communist revolutions, nuclear energy, and landing on the moon (momentous events that could easily shake any entrenched paradigm), there was unanimity among all these scholars about one fact: Leadership is management.

But synthesizing the school of leadership into "leadership is management" still did not ring true to me. And doing the research in preparation for this book did not help. There were too many discordant notes in the symphony of leadership studies as it had been played in the twentieth century. Much of the literature of the late 1970s and the 1980s, particularly, seemed to be playing a different tune. So I did a fourth cut. What began to make more and more sense to me was that leadership scholars and practitioners were playing an industrial tune (to continue the analogy); the melody they sang was "Ode to Industrialism," wherein the central theme was the leader as good manager. Leadership is not just management. That was too confusing and, deep down, the equation didn't make sense.

Everyone knows that what passes for management in many organizations is not leadership. *Leadership is good management.* The basic distinction between just plain management and good management does it. It fits. This fundamental view of leadership fits the literature and makes sense to scholars and practitioners alike, not to mention more common folk, all of whom understand leadership as having a saviorlike essence in a world that constantly needs saving. It also preserves the notion that management is an essential part of leadership. If just any management will not do, it is comforting to know that good management will. Leadership as good management is what the twentieth-century school of leadership is all about. Leadership as good management is the twentieth century's paradigm of leadership.

This school of leadership is not the exclusive property of any one academic discipline. Rather, the same basic understanding of leadership is embedded in the leadership definitions emanating from all the disciplines that have something to say about leadership: anthropology, history, political science, psychology, sociology, theology, and such applied sciences as business, educational, health, military, and public administration.

Leadership as good management is a perfect summary of what leadership has meant in the industrial era. Good management is the apex of industrial organizations, the epitome of an industrial society, the consummate embodiment of an industrial culture. Industrialism is unthinkable without good management, and understanding leadership as good management makes perfect sense in an industrial economy. Thus, the twentieth-century school of leadership takes on a title, a name that fits naturally and easily. *Leadership as good management is the industrial paradigm of leadership.*

Leadership as good management articulates a paradigm of leadership that fits the descriptors scholars have given to the more widespread industrial paradigm (since it is embedded in the entire society and culture). Analyzed individually and in toto, the leadership definitions reviewed in these chapters reveal a fundamental understanding of leadership that is rational, management oriented, male, technocratic, quantitative, goal dominated, cost-benefit driven, personalistic, hierarchical, short term, pragmatic, and materialistic. If there are any humanistic, emotional, qualitative, high-touch characteristics embedded in this model of leadership, and I believe there are, they boil down to a therapeutic, expressive individualism that has become part of the industrial culture since the 1960s. These expressive characteristics soothe the existential realities of living in a democratic culture wherein people believe that a high standard of living is their birthright but the realities do not quite match the promise. These expressive characteristics also help to enculturate women into what is essentially a male model of leadership. They also explain why this concept of leadership has the support of millions of people of all races, religions, genders, economic and social statuses, and sexual orientation. Leadership as good management, when seen through colored lenses of expressive individualism, says, in so many words, ''Yes, Virginia, there is a Santa Claus.'' And Santa Claus looks remarkably like those great men and women with certain preferred traits who influence followers to do what the leaders wish in order to achieve group/organizational goals that reflect excellence defined as some kind of higher-order effectiveness.

5

The Nature of Leadership

DEFINING LEADERSHIP

Beyond all the difficulties scholars have had with definitions of leadership that were expressed in the two previous chapters, we have the constant misuse of the term in the daily press, on television, and in advertisements. Leadership has become a "hot" word, and there is no better proof of that than its use in advertisements.

In San Diego, people can see a magazine advertisement or a mailer proclaiming "LEADERSHIP, COMMITMENT, AND VISION." Under that banner, they read: "For more than a hundred years, Great American First Savings Bank has been helping the West grow. We're proud of all the communities we serve. And our leadership role in their continuing success."

In the *San Diego Union* and on the local television Channel 10, there is a picture of three men and two women with the words "LEADERSHIP: 10 NEWS" printed across the picture.

In *Fortune* magazine there is a full page ad about "ASTRA Leadership . . . by design."

In the *Chronicle of Higher Education* there is an advertisement recruiting for a "Director of Leadership Gifts Development & Alumni Affairs" by Skidmore College.

I decided to go to one of my favorite fish restaurants in San Diego, and when I sat down at the table, there were place mats on the table proclaiming "SEA-FOOD LEADERSHIP, ANTHONY'S FISH GROTTOS."

The usage in these advertisements reflects the excellence theory of leadership. Leadership is being number one, leadership is producing excellence.

A second use of the word *leadership* is as a substitute for "the collective leaders who are in office" or "the leaders in an administration." Headline writers for daily newspapers constantly use the word this way. Some examples from the *New York Times* in 1989 will give the flavor. (The same kind of usage of the word *leadership* can be found in major daily newspapers throughout the country.) "Interim Rumanian Leadership Is Named"; "Where Mayors Lead With the Left: The leadership is new, but the agenda is much the same"; "Leadership: An Aristocrat Among the Revolutionaries"; "Worried Chinese Leadership Says Gorbachev Subverts Communism." This usage is much beyond the century-old meaning of the word commonly found in dictionaries: "The office or position of a leader."

A third popular notion of leadership is that of one person directing other people. Thus, a conductor exerts leadership over an orchestra, a director over a choir, a coach over a sports team, a captain over a platoon, a chairperson over a committee, a manager over a business firm, a principal over a school, and so on. Leadership is equated with what one person *does to* a group of people who make up an organization. This is the Pied Piper of Hamlin idea of leadership. An updated version would be the John Wayne or the Patton view of leadership. This notion of leadership has been very popular since the 1930s. It was more popular in the 1980s than in the 1960s and 1970s, so its currency is on the rise, not suffering.

All three of these meanings of leadership—being number one, the collectivity of leaders in an organization, and one person in charge of a group of people—are legitimate uses of the term because they reflect the dominant characteristics of the industrial paradigm as people have experienced it for the past century or more. These notions of leadership do not come out of thin air; they come out of the lived experience of the people in the United States and other Western societies. They are part of our mythology, the folklore that people use to make sense out of life. Being number one, putting top officials into a collective unit, and having one person in charge are how people have made sense of the word in the industrial era. These notions of leadership are simplistic, but the nature of mythology is to reduce complex realities to simple explanations.

However, if scholars want to study leadership, a more sophisticated definition of leadership is needed to make sense of the data that scholars gather both to generate and to prove theories of human behavior. The same is true for practitioners of leadership. Leaders and followers who use mythological understandings of leadership are at a distinct disadvantage in practicing leadership. The reality that leaders and followers face in their organizations and societies is much more complex than the simplistic notions of leadership handed down in the mythology would have us believe.

In an effort to capture some of that complexity, leadership scholars and practitioners since about 1910 (perhaps longer) have tried to develop a reality-based understanding of leadership in groups, organizations, and societies. There has been a great deal of fumbling, as the detailed story of defining leadership presented in the last two chapters has made abundantly clear. On the surface, these attempts to define leadership have been confusing, varied, disorganized, idiosyncratic, muddled, and, according to conventional wisdom, quite unrewarding. These scholars have not provided a definition of leadership that is (1) clear, (2) concise, (3) understandable by scholars and practitioners, (4) researchable, (5) practically relevant, and (6) persuasive. Most, if not all, analysts have concluded that the leadership literature since about 1910 has not generated a school of leadership. We have had, according to this view, no consensus on the meaning of leadership, no generally accepted understanding of what leadership is.

I have presented an alternative view. A more penetrating analysis—one that looks under the surface for background assumptions and takes a more holistic view of the literature over the long haul—suggests that despite all the apparent confusion of the hundreds of definitions and dozens of models, leadership has consistently been understood since the 1930s as good management. In a culture that has been managerial at its core, the scholars and practitioners in that culture could do no less than give the coveted and new concept of leadership a definition that equated it not with just management but with good management.

If that analysis is at all accurate, we have to reject the conclusion that there has been no school of leadership in the twentieth century. On the contrary, there has been a pervasive and powerful school of leadership, one that I believe should be called the industrial school of leadership. This school of leadership helped people imbued with the industrial paradigm make sense out of the concept because they already had a more or less sophisticated sense of what good management was. And the mythology of leadership—being number one, putting top officials into a collective unit, and having one person take charge—makes sense when leadership is understood as good management.

The problem today is that this school of leadership is no longer accepted by some scholars and practitioners of leadership. The consensus that leadership is good management has, to some degree, broken down. In an effort to make sense of the world they see, some leadership scholars and practitioners have defined leadership in a way that significantly challenges the dominant school of leadership. Many of these scholars and practitioners no longer see leadership and good management as the same. In issuing such challenges, these people are calling for a new school of leadership. They are involved in a paradigm shift which changes our understanding of leadership so that it makes sense in a postindustrial world.

LEADERSHIP AND THE LARGER TRANSFORMATION OF SOCIETY

Futurists and other commentators are virtually unanimous in their belief that a new era is rapidly approaching and that the Western world (and perhaps the whole world) is presently going through a radical transformation which is changing the basic values upon which the present, industrial era has been based. Futurists have not settled on a name for this new era, but many have called it *postindustrial*. The word *postindustrial* doesn't tell us much about the central beliefs of the new era and paradigm. It does tell us, however, that it will not be like the industrial era, since *postindustrial* denotes that the new era is beyond, or more than, or different from the present, industrial era.

The message that futurists keep sending over and over again is that the Western world is at present in a state of transition, a fundamental or paradigmatic transition wherein the values of the industrial paradigm are being transmuted in ways that eventually will produce a new paradigm, a postindustrial paradigm. This new paradigm will presumably become the mainstream paradigm sometime in the twenty-first century, and at that point the new era and paradigm will be firmly entrenched. Some people argue that the new paradigm and era are already upon us, and what we have now is a cultural lag—a period in which the mainstream culture catches up with the new reality that is already present. (I do not accept that view, but that is another issue.) Whether we are in transition or are already in a new era, there is a pervasive sense that our values are changing radically, and that the values built into the industrial paradigm are not going to be the ones that support a transformed Western civilization in the postindustrial world.

Leadership is one such value, and it, too, is being transformed. However, the definitions of leadership from the 1980s analyzed in Chapter 4 clearly show that the mainstream leadership literature is overwhelmingly industrial in its concept of leadership, demonstrating that the transformation of leadership thought to a postindustrial framework has barely begun.

If this analysis is accurate—if our thought and practice about leadership in the 1990 still express the dominant values of the industrial era—then a profound transformation of leadership thought and practice must take place in the 1990s if the needs of the people living in this decade and the twenty-first century are to be well served. Indeed, it could be argued that during this time of transition, the crisis in leadership is not that we in the United States and the Western world lack good leaders or that the leaders lack a vision of what is needed in the 1990s, but that our school of leadership is still caught up in the industrial paradigm while much of our thought and practice in other aspects of life have undergone considerable transformation to a postindustrial paradigm. We will not resolve that crisis in leadership until scholars and practitioners begin to think radically new thoughts about leadership, until they begin to make quantum leaps in leadership theory, until they develop a new school of leadership that is serviceable to the coming era. When that happens, the new school of leadership can be used to train and develop the thousands—indeed, hundreds of thousands—of local, regional, national, and international leaders who will help propel Western societies into the postindustrial era and who will help shape the future of our civilization and the quality of life of future generations.

In short, if a transformation to a postindustrial era is to happen in the 1990s, we need leaders who are imbued with a postindustrial model of leadership that guides the choices, behaviors, and thoughts of leaders and followers—which, in turn, molds their relationships with other followers and leaders. The crisis of leadership which people in the Western world are facing today is that they have not developed such a postindustrial school of leadership and that the leaders and followers—with rare exception—are still acting, choosing, and thinking on the basis of an industrialized leadership paradigm. While the industrialized model of leadership has served the people of the United States well since the late 1800s, it increasingly ill serves our needs as we approach the twenty-first century. While I know less about other Western nations, I would guess that the same statement could be made for them. Certainly, the events in Eastern Europe dramatically suggest that the old paradigms of change (and thus of leadership) ill served the needs of those people. Perhaps the revolutions of Eastern Europe are the cataclysmic events that were needed to help leadership scholars and practitioners understand the importance of dealing explicitly with the need for a paradigm shift in leadership studies.

WHAT IS LEADERSHIP?

The purpose of this chapter is to explicate a postindustrial definition of leadership. Before developing this definition of leadership, I had been using Burns's definition (1978, p. 18 or p. 425). Over a period of five years and with the help of many of the doctoral candidates in leadership studies at the University of San Diego, I found several significant inconsistencies between the reality that I researched and knew from daily experience and Burns's definition of leadership. For instance, there is an inconsistency between his definition of leadership and the concept of transformational leadership that he favored (rightly, I believe) in the final three chapters of his book. That inconsistency posed the question: What is Burns's *real* definition of leadership? Many scholars and practitioners who have read Burns's book think that his *real* definition of leadership is his definition of transformational leadership.

As a result of this and other conceptual problems, I set about trying to construct a definition that dealt with these inconsistencies and yet remained somewhat faithful to Burns's thought, which is much more forward-looking than the traditional conceptual frameworks of leadership. Thus, I view this definition as a development of Burns's thought. This definition of leadership could not have been constructed without repeatedly and thoroughly studying his concept of leadership as developed in his 1978 book. I read and reread, discussed and rediscussed, that book, often with doctoral candidates and graduates of the leadership program at USD, more than I have done with any other book. Studying Burns's book is like having scales fall off your eyes; you can never view leadership as you did before.

As a development of Burns's model of leadership, however, it is important to understand from the beginning that this definition and the conceptual framework embedded therein are significantly different from his concept of leadership in ways that will be very clear as the definition is analyzed in this chapter. It is an attempt to begin a new school of leadership that consistently and consciously accepts postindustrial assumptions and values. There is considerable textual evidence in Burns's book that in 1978 he was still under the influence of the industrial paradigm. In 1990, I have the advantage of twelve years' further experience that includes the 1980s with all its Yuppie characteristics, the new ideas about leadership, and the momentous events of 1989–1990. And I have the advantage of being only a decade away from the twenty-first century. Even more, it is hard to ignore the paradigm-shattering events in Eastern Europe during the fall and winter of 1989–1990. As suggested earlier, the industrial leadership paradigm doesn't explain the history-making events of 1989–1990. A new school of leadership that articulates a postindustrial concept of leadership is more and more imperative. While this definition may not be the last word on the subject, it may be the first, and that is where both scholars and practitioners have to start when paradigm leaps are in the making.

The definition of leadership is this: *Leadership is an influence relationship among leaders and followers who intend real changes that reflect their mutual purposes.* Every word in that definition was carefully selected to convey very specific meanings that contain certain assumptions and values which are necessary to a transformed, postindustrial model of leadership.

What follows in the remainder of this chapter is, first, an outline of the four essential elements of leadership and their various parts; second, a listing of the four essential elements of leadership that are contained in the definition and a short discussion of what a definition means and how it is useful to scholars and practitioners alike; and, third, an extended discussion of each of the four elements and the various parts of each element. The chapter ends with some concluding comments on the definition as a powerful expression of the postindustrial paradigm.

A DEFINITION OF LEADERSHIP: AN OUTLINE

Leadership is an influence relationship among leaders and followers who intend real changes that reflect their mutual purposes.

From this definition, there are four essential elements that must be present if leadership exists or is occurring:

1. The relationship is based on influence.

   a. The influence relationship is multidirectional.

   b. The influence behaviors are noncoercive.

2. Leaders and followers are the people in this relationship.

    a. The followers are active.

    b. There must be more than one follower, and there is typically more than one leader in the relationship.

    c. The relationship is inherently unequal because the influence patterns are unequal.

3. Leaders and followers intend real changes.

    a. *Intend* means that the leaders and followers purposefully desire certain changes.

    b. *Real* means that the changes the leaders and followers intend must be substantive and transforming.

    c. Leaders and followers do not have to produce changes in order for leadership to occur. They intend changes in the present; the changes take place in the future if they take place at all.

    d. Leaders and followers intend several changes at once.

4. Leaders and followers develop mutual purposes.

    a. The mutuality of these purposes is forged in the noncoercive influence relationship.

    b. Leaders and followers develop purposes, not goals.

    c. The intended changes reflect, not realize, their purposes.

    d. The mutual purposes become common purposes.

THE ESSENTIAL ELEMENTS OF LEADERSHIP

Definitions have been problematic in the behavioral and social sciences. And, generally speaking, the definitions themselves have not been well served (if I could be excused an anthropomorphic reference in this instance) because the scholars in these disciplines, in contradistinction to those in the hard sciences, have not paid enough attention to them in the form of serious, prolonged thought, nor have they reaped the rewards that accurate definitions would bring to their disciplines. The kinds of sloppy definitions of leadership that were documented in the last two chapters could be repeated in every behavioral and social science concerning very important words in those sciences. So leadership studies is hardly alone in this problem.

Definitions should have several properties in order to be useful to scholars and practitioners. Without going into an extended discussion on this subject, those properties will be explained. Then the readers can evaluate whether I have fulfilled my own criteria in constructing the postindustrial definition of leadership.

A definition must be clearly worded to communicate very specific messages as to what constitutes the reality being defined.

A definition must state specific criteria for people to use in separating one reality from similar realities. In other words, for a definition to be serviceable, it must say that these criteria must be fulfilled for this phenomenon to be called what is being defined. These criteria take the form of essential elements. A phenomenon must include all the essential elements if it is to be called the reality that is being defined.

A definition must be usable by practitioners as well as by scholars. If the definition is unusable in the real world by people who live and work in that world, it is useless in any research that scholars may want to conduct to understand that world.

A definition must be usable in the here and now, giving the user the power to do an analysis of a particular phenomenon immediately after gathering data. How much data must be gathered of course depends on the complexity of the phenomenon. Good definitions limit the data gathering necessary and shorten the analysis needed; poor definitions do the opposite. For example, any definition of leadership that requires the user to wait a month or a year to find out if such and such resulted from a phenomenon is unacceptable. People in the real world will not wait for extended periods, suspending judgment of people and events, to determine what that phenomenon was. Ordinarily, definitions must give people the ability to make decisions about determining the nature of something in a matter of minutes, if not seconds. There are exceptions, of course. Many scholarly definitions require that scholars and practitioners take long periods of time to gather and analyze data to determine the nature of some phenomenon. And some definitions make such a determination impossible, no matter the amount of data collected and analyzed and the amount of time elapsed.

The definition of leadership given above includes four essential elements:

1. The relationship is based on influence.
2. Leaders and followers are the people in this relationship.
3. Leaders and followers intend real changes.
4. Leaders and followers develop mutual purposes.

All four of these elements must be present if any relationship is to be called leadership. Three out of four are not sufficient. All that people need to do to establish if leadership is happening is to determine if these four essential elements are present. If they are present, the phenomenon is leadership.

Scholars and practitioners should be able to use these four elements to distinguish leadership from other relationships they have as human beings, and to do so in a matter of several seconds or a minute, not hours or days or months or years. Once a person understands these four elements, they are easily used as criteria in analyses of whether some phenomenon is leadership. The elements are clear and simple, they are expressed in words that people use in everyday English, and they are very easy to remember. Judgments that these four criteria require are well within the scope of the thousands of similar assessments people make daily in their professional and personal lives.

A discussion of these elements will clarify the exact meaning of each element and give some rationale for why each, and all four together, are essential in defining leadership from a postindustrial perspective. Each element has several parts, which are delineated by a subheading. Under each subheading there is explication of the element as a whole, followed by an extended analysis of each part of the element, and then a summary.

This kind of discussion is necessary at this time because (1) these essential elements are significantly different from those contained in other definitions, so they have to be justified or rationalized in order to persuade other people that they are necessary, and (2) people need help to understand this new definition of leadership because it is so radically different from previous definitions. Once they understand it, it will be part of their thinking patterns.

Influence Relationship

The relationship that is leadership must be based on influence. Influence is defined with Bell (1975) as the process of using persuasion to have an impact on other people in a relationship.

Persuasion, as Neustadt (1980) has so cogently reminded us, "amounts to more than the charm of reasoned argument" (p. 27). Along with rational discourse, influence as persuasion involves reputation, prestige, personality, purpose, status, content of the message, interpersonal and group skills, give-and-take behaviors, authority or lack of it, symbolic interaction, perception, motivation, gender, race, religion, and choices, among countless other things. I call these things *power resources*. Influence does not come out of thin air. It comes from people using these power resources to persuade.

If we conceive of leadership as an influence relationship and influence is persuasion, then two consequences follow.

Multidirectional Relationship

First, the leadership relationship is multidirectional. The relationship involves interactions that are vertical, horizontal, diagonal, and circular. This means that (1) anyone can be a leader and/or a follower; (2) followers persuade leaders and other followers, as do leaders; (3) leaders and followers may change places (I do not like the word *roles* because it has heavy industrial paradigm connotations) in the relationship; and (4) there are many different relationships that can make up the overall relationship that is leadership. These relationships can be small and large groups, departmental, organizational, societal, or global, and can be based on race, gender, ethnicity, family relations, clubs, political parties, and friendships, among other things. These relationships are often subsumed under or component parts of a leadership relationship. If a relationship is one-sided, unidirectional, and one-on-one, those are clear signs that the relationship is not leadership.

Noncoercive Relationship

Second, leadership as an influence relationship means that the behaviors used to persuade other people must be noncoercive. If the behaviors are coercive, the relationship becomes one of authority or power, or one that is dictatorial.

Authority is a contractual (written, spoken, or implied) relationship wherein people accept superordinate or subordinate responsibilities in an organization. Power is a relationship wherein certain people control other people by rewards and/or punishments. Both authority and power relationships can be coercive, although they need not be. In such relationships, people can be forced to behave in certain ways if they want to remain in the relationship. Coercion is not only an acceptable behavior in authority and power relationships, it is often essential if the relationship is going to be productive or effective. For instance, our system of highways and streets is fundamentally based on coercive authority relationships. Obey the traffic laws or get caught and be punished. Freedom is not essential in authority or power relationships, although a limited notion of freedom is often a part of authority and power relationships as they are practiced today in many business organizations. Freedom can also be used to get out of some authority and power relationships. People are free to change jobs, for example, in order to get out of an authority relationship. Or people can move to rural areas to avoid having to obey so many traffic laws. Other such relationships are practically impossible to get out of, short of total isolation from society or death or significant risk to one's personal welfare.

Dictatorial relationships are what Burns (1978) termed *power wielding*, though again his use of the term is inconsistent. Such relationships rely on physical and psychological abuse that one person or several persons use to control other people absolutely. Dictatorial relationships use people as objects, not as persons; keep people in subservient roles, not just subordinate ones; and are often life threatening in the extent of the abusive actions taken to control people. Obviously, dictatorial relationships are coercive at their core. Ceausescu in Romania, Noriega in Panama, and the drug lords in Colombia and other countries are obvious cases. Examples closer to home may be street gangs, godfathers in organized crime, party bosses, church officials, and employers or labor union officers who are abusive of their employees or members.

Coercion is antithetical to influence relationships. People in influence relationships can refuse to behave in prescribed ways and still remain on good terms with other people in the relationship. Freedom is essential to influence relationships. Of course, one can exercise so much freedom that one loses much of the influence one could have. Freedom is never absolute, and in influence relationships people can lose influence by exercising freedom of thought and action. The point is that people are free to influence or not influence, to drop out of one influence relationship and join another, or to drop out of all influence relationships. Passivity is not ruled out of the postindustrial paradigm.

There are more descriptions of coercive and noncoercive behaviors in Chapter 7. Coercion and noncoercion have implications for the essential nature of leadership (which is the topic here) and for the ethics of leadership. Deciding what is coercive or not coercive is a bit more tricky than deciding whether the relationship is multidirectional. The key word is *influence*, so concentrate on a clear understanding of influence as the basis for a relationship. If influence is what makes the relationship tick, then it is leadership. If not, some other relationship is happening.

Summary

To summarize the first essential element of leadership, it is a relationship based on influence, which is defined as using persuasion to have an impact on other people in a relationship. Leadership as an influence relationship has two characteristics: (1) it is multidirectional, in that influence flows in all directions and not just from the top down; and (2) it is noncoercive, meaning that it is not based on authority, power, or dictatorial actions but is based on persuasive behaviors, thus allowing anyone in the relationship to freely agree or disagree and ultimately to drop into or out of the relationship.

Leaders and Followers Are the People in This Relationship

The second essential element flowing from the definition of leadership is that the people involved in this relationship are leaders and followers. This sounds rather innocuous, but there are several important points to be gained from examining this element, especially the meaning of the word *followers*.

Active Followers

I have no trouble with the word *followers*, but it does bother a number of other scholars and practitioners, who view the word as condescending. Gardner (1986, 1990), for instance, has rejected the word in favor of *constituents*. That word is problematic, however, because it has strong political connotations. People don't speak about constituents in small groups or clubs, business or religious organizations, and the like. The word is mostly used in political organizations and as a result is unsatisfactory for a model of leadership that applies to all organizations and groups. Ford (1990) used the word *participants*, which has much more generalizability to different organizations. Gardner and Ford are two of quite a number of leadership scholars who want to get rid of the word *followers* for mostly egalitarian reasons.

My view is that the problem is not with the word, but with the passive meaning given to the concept of followers by people who lived and worked and wrote in the industrial era. Followers, as a concept, connoted a group of people who were (1) part of the sweaty masses and therefore separated from the elites, (2) not able to act intelligently without the guidance and control of other, (3) willing to let other people (elites) take control of their lives, and (4) unproductive unless directed by others. In the leadership literature since the 1930s, therefore, followers were considered to be subordinates who were submissive and passive, and leaders were considered to be managers who were directive and active. Since leaders were managers, followers had to be the subordinate people in an organization. There is no other logical equation.

In a postindustrial frame, leaders are not equated with managers, so followers are not equated with subordinates. Since leaders can be anyone, followers can be anyone. That does not mean that leaders and followers are equal. No amount of egalitarian idealism will change the fact that there will be followers as long as human beings inhabit this planet. Only the meaning of the word *followers* will change, not the existence of human beings who are followers.

A distinction between leaders and followers remains crucial to the concept of leadership. Since leadership is a relationship, leaders must interact with other people. If all the people with whom leaders interacted were other leaders, leadership as a meaningful construct would not make much sense.

For one thing, leadership would be quite an elitist or exclusive group of people, since there are and will be many people who are not motivated to be leaders, who do not have the personal development needed to be leaders in a sophisticated and complex society, or who are not willing to use the power resources at their command to exercise significant influence through persuasion. I think we need to reject any elitist notion of leadership in spelling out who can participate in the relationship that is leadership.

One could argue that if all people were leaders, the notion of leadership would not be elitist. I agree. But everyone being leader is not consistent with what we know of human nature, even if we do not equate leadership with good management. Our human nature is not going to change all that much in the postindustrial era.

A second difficulty with the notion that we are all leaders is the complexity of our times and that of the postindustrial era. Active people may be involved in a dozen or more leadership relationships at any one time, and it is conceptually impossible to conceive of them being leaders in all of these influence relationships. Scholars tend to think of people being in only one leadership relationship, but that is not the way people live their lives. Even people who are less active may have several leadership relationships going on at any one time. The only possible way for people to cope with such multiple relationships is for them to be leaders in some relationships and followers in others. If one examines the many other relationships in which these active people are involved (love, friendship, professional, work, religious, etc.), the complexity of their lives becomes clear. Time restraints alone require that people be followers in some leadership relationships.

Realistically, we know from past experience that some people choose to be followers all the time and that many other people choose not be involved in any leadership relationships. The complexity of life and our understanding of human nature based on centuries of experience would suggest that these two groups of people will continue to exist in the postindustrial era.

Thus, followers are part of the leadership relationship in a new paradigm of leadership. What is different about the emerging view of followers is the substantive meaning attached to the word and the clarity given to that understanding. The following five points give the concept of followers substance and clarity.

First, only people who are active in the leadership process are followers.

Passive people are not in a relationship. They have chosen not to be involved. They cannot have influence. Passive people are not followers.

Second, active people can fall anywhere on a continuum of activity from highly active to minimally active, and their influence in the leadership process is, in large part, based on their activity, their willingness to get involved, their use of the power resources they have at their command to influence other people. Some followers are very active; others are not so active. Some followers are very active at certain times and not so active at other times.

Third, followers can become leaders and leaders can become followers in any one leadership relationship. People are not stuck in one or the other for the whole time the relationship exists. Followers may be leaders for a while, and leaders may be followers for a while. Followers do not have to be managers to be leaders. This ability to change places without changing organizational positions gives followers considerable influence and mobility.

Fourth, in one group or organization people can be leaders. In other groups and organizations they can be followers. Followers are not always followers in all leadership relationships.

Fifth, and most important, followers do not do followership, they do leadership. Both leaders and followers form one relationship that is leadership. There is no such thing as followership in the new school of leadership. Followership makes sense only in the industrial leadership paradigm, where leadership is good management. Since followers who are subordinates could not do management (since they were not managers), they had to do followership. No wonder followership connoted subordination, submissiveness, and passivity. *In the new paradigm, followers and leaders do leadership.* They are in the leadership relationship together. They are the ones who intend real changes that reflect their mutual purposes. Metaphorically, their activities are two sides of the same coin, the two it takes to tango, the composer and musicians making music, the female and male generating new life, the yin and the yang. Followers and leaders develop a relationship wherein they influence one another as well as the organization and society, and that is leadership. They do not do the same things in the relationship, just as the composers and musicians do not do the same thing in making music, but they are both essential to leadership.

Numbers of Leaders and Followers in the Relationship

The next point to be made concerning the people involved in the leadership relationship has to do with the number of people in the relationship. The question boils down to this: Can dyadic relationships be leadership? Typical dyadic relationships are wife-husband, parent-child, employee-employer, teacher-student, client-therapist, doctor-patient, buyer-seller, and so on.

Industrial era models of leadership have been unanimous in viewing dyadic relationships as leadership. Such models show how much humanistic psychology had been infused into the leadership paradigm. The human relations movement in organizational behavior has had a large impact on leadership thought and practice. The apex of such thought is Hersey and Blanchard's (1988) situational leadership theory, which reduces leadership to one manager and one employee fitting into one of four style boxes based on the maturity of the employee. Blanchard et al.'s (1985) one-minute manager and leadership model reduces situational theory to one manager and one employee spending one minute together practicing leadership. The *Blanchard Training and Development Catalog* for the winter/spring of 1990 proclaims that "Situational Leadership II is the cutting edge of leadership training."

Despite the popularity of reducing leadership to pop psychology and equating leadership with styles of human relations, leadership scholars and practitioners would do well to exclude dyadic relationships from their concept of leadership. Those relationships are much better categorized as parental, educational, love, friendship, therapeutic, counseling, or management relationships. Leadership is better thought of as larger, more complex, and less intimate than a dyadic relationship typically is. The changes that leaders and followers intend are usually more involved than changing one or two persons. The mutual purposes that feed leadership relationships rarely, if ever, are limited to two people.

Many people feel they have to ennoble relationships by calling them leadership. A more natural view is that these relationships are already exalted in the very essence of what they are. The teacher-student relationship is a wonderful, highly elevated relationship on its own. Teachers do not have to lead their students to ennoble their calling; teachers educating their students are noble enough. The same can be said of other dyadic relationships: parent-child, wife-husband, counselor-client, doctor-patient, and so on. Why do people think they have to infuse these inherently exalted relationships with leadership in order to make them more appealing, more workable, more developmental, and/or more interesting and exciting?

From the point of view of a leadership expert, such practices only add confusion to our already confused understanding of the nature of leadership. There is no other way of getting a handle on the meaning of leadership except by limiting the concept to some restricted describable phenomena. Eliminating dyadic relationships from our notion of what leadership is would help greatly.

Eliminating dyadic relationships from the definition of leadership means that people do not call a single husband and wife relationship *leadership*. That does not mean, of course, that a wife and husband may not be part of a leadership relationship. They may, but the operative words are that they are *part of* that relationship, not the whole relationship. The husband and wife may be part of an environmental movement to save the ocean from pollution. The teacher and student may be part of a movement to reform education by emphasizing critical thinking. The doctor and patient may be part of a movement to stop the medical practitioners in a certain hospital from keeping terminally ill people alive by artificial means. The manager and subordinate may be part of a movement to upgrade the quality of product made in their department. And so on. Notice that the leadership relationship adds a new dimension to the nature of the dyadic relationship. The wife and husband do not just want to love one another and raise children (the very noble and exalted purposes of the husband-wife relationship); they want to help save the ocean environment, and to achieve that purpose they join with other people in a leadership relationship. Saving the ocean environment is not inherently necessary to a loving wife-husband relationship, but it is absolutely necessary to the leadership relationship in this instance.

These one-on-one relationships are important within the overall leadership relationship because, for one thing, they are the source of tremendous power resources that people use to persuade others of the righteousness of their cause and to form coalitions and other types of connections. However, these dyadic relationships individually considered are not the relationship that is leadership. Leadership is the sum total of all the interactions among all the leaders and followers in that relationship, not the individual interactions between one leader and one follower in that relationship.

With considerable enlightenment and cogency, Foster (1989) stated:

The idea that leadership occurs within a community suggests that ultimately leadership resides in the community itself. To further differentiate leadership from management, we could suggest that leadership is a communal relationship, that is, one that occurs within a community of believers. Leadership, then, is not a function of position but rather represents a conjunction of ideas where leadership is shared and transferred between leaders and followers, each only a temporary designation. Indeed, history will identify an individual as the leader, but in reality the job is one in which various members of the community contribute. Leaders and followers become interchangeable. (p. 49)

This view of leadership as community is a larger notion than is being developed here, but Foster's point is very well taken. We must learn to think of leadership as a "communal relationship," as a "community of believers," which is something larger than one leader and one follower, and even more than a number of loosely connected dyadic relationships.

For a leadership relationship to exist, there must be more than one follower, and there typically is more than one leader. I say *typically* because the norm in the postindustrial era will be for leadership relationships to have more than one leader. However, more than one leader is not absolutely essential. Much depends on the size of the community of believers, to use Foster's phrase. Think of a small group organized to change something. Is it possible to conceive of a small group with only one leader? I think it is, and such small group leadership relationships will continue to exist in the postindustrial era. Of course, a small group organized to change something, a leadership relationship, also can have more than one leader.

The conclusion is that one leader is possible in a leadership relationship. The trend, however, is quite clearly toward shared or collaborative leadership. As the postindustrial paradigm becomes more and more accepted in mainstream thought and practice, leadership will lose its Lone Ranger or Pied Piper of Hamlin image—the idea that there is one person who is out in front taking charge, and everyone else is following, more or less blindly, toward leader-initiated goals. As the new school of leadership takes hold, we will be less willing to agree that Lee Iacocca single-handedly turned Chrysler around or that Peter Ueberroth single-handedly took charge of the summer Olympic Games in Los Angeles and made them the rousing success that they were. Such leadership relationships— those involving one leader and numerous followers—become less and less possible and more and more improbable as we move to a postindustrial era.

Unequal Relationship

The third and final point that flows from leaders and followers being the people in the leadership relationship is this: The relationship is inherently unequal because the influence patterns are unequal. Typically, leaders have more influence because they are willing to commit more of the power resources they possess to the relationship, and they are more skilled at putting those power resources to work to influence others in the relationship.

However, there are times when followers may exert more influence than leaders, times when they seize the initiative, and times when their purposes drive the relationship. If one or a few followers cause this influence pattern to develop, the followers then become leaders. If this influence pattern develops from a larger number of people, I think analysts should see this as followers being more active in the relationship but still being followers. These fluctuating patterns of influence are normal and developmental, as viewed from a postindustrial school of leadership. The industrial paradigm of leadership saw/sees these fluctuations as abnormal, an aberration of the real leadership process, and counterproductive to the attainment of goals—which is the purpose of leadership. Such a view is no longer acceptable as followers take an increasingly active part in the leadership process. Again, followers do leadership, not followership. And, while followers sometimes change places and become leaders, they do not have to be leaders to exert influence, to use power resources to persuade others of their position. In sum, followers are active agents in the leadership relationship, not passive recipients of the leader's influence. That is the new meaning of the word *followers* in a postindustrial model of leadership.

Summary

Leaders and followers are the people in the influence relationship called leadership. A distinction between leaders and followers is crucial in the new school of leadership, but the concept of followers takes on new meaning as we move to the postindustrial era. Followers are active, not passive, in the relationship. They do leadership, not followership. There is typically more than one leader, and there must be more than one follower. And, finally, the influence patterns in the relationship are inherently unequal because leaders typically exert more influence than do followers.

Leaders and Followers Intend Real Changes

The third essential ingredient of leadership that flows from the definition of leadership is the notion that leaders and followers intend real changes. This concept comes from Burns's (1978) model of transformational leadership, but a postindustrial school of leadership would take the concept much further than Burns took it.

Burns did not include the concept of real, intended change in his definition of leadership on page 18 or page 425. His definition is different from his concept of transformational leadership, which he defines on page 20 and elsewhere. The centrality of real, intended change was never prominent in Burns's model of leadership, which he explicated in the first five chapters of his book. Real, intended change was rather like an afterthought that he emphasized in the last three chapters of his book, wherein he discarded transactional leadership (for the most part) and wrote eloquently and persuasively about transformational leadership.

On pages 413–461, Burns stated and reiterated that the test of leadership is real, intended change. "The leadership process," he wrote, "must be defined, in short, as carrying through from decision-making stages to the point of concrete changes in people's lives, attitudes, behaviors, institutions. . . . Leadership brings about real change that leaders intend, under our definition" (p. 414). In the end, Burns stated that "the test [of leadership] is purpose and intent, drawn from values and goals, of leaders, high and low, resulting in policy decisions and real, intended change" (p. 415). On the next-to-last page of his book, Burns concluded with considerable force: "*The ultimate test of practical leadership is the realization of intended, real change that meets people's enduring needs*" (p. 461).

Beyond the problem of having to wade through 400-plus pages to come to the conclusion that leadership is intended, real change, the fact is that the conclusion is not consistent with Burns's definition of leadership that he reiterates as late as page 425: "Leadership is the reciprocal process of mobilizing, by persons with certain motives and values, various economic, political and other resources, in a context of competition and conflict, in order to realize goals independently or mutually held by both leaders and followers." (The notion of "independently . . . held" also contradicts his definition on page 18, but that is another issue.) In the definition just quoted, there is no requirement for intended, real change. The "goals independently or mutually held by both leaders and followers" in Burns's definition could be status quo goals that change nothing. Much of his concept of transactional leadership can be interpreted in that fashion. Transactional leadership is an exchange of valued things, and as we know from real life, such bargains often promote the status quo. In summary, Burns's notion of real, intended change is consistent only with his transformational model of leadership, not with his overarching definition of leadership.

The way out of this conceptual confusion is both easy and clear. The way out is to put the concept of intended, real change into the definition of leadership and make it essential for any human relationship to be called leadership. That is what I have done. The definition articulated in this book states that leadership is a relationship wherein leaders and followers intend real changes. Thus, a relationship wherein leaders and followers do not intend real changes is not leadership.

Leaders and Followers Intend Changes

The word *intend* means that the leaders and followers purposefully desire certain changes in an organization and/or in the society. The desire is not accidental or developed by chance. The intention is deliberate and initiated on purpose.

Since the leaders and followers intend the changes *now*, while they are in a relationship with one another, the intention is in the present and is part of the leadership relationship. The changes, if they take place, are in the future, defined as any time beyond the present, and are not necessarily part of the leadership relationship. They may result from the leadership relationship, or they may result from other factors beyond the leadership relationship. Establishing cause and effect in situations where leadership and change are the variables is very difficult to do, and this definition of leadership frees us as practitioners and scholars from getting caught up in that problem.

This view points up a major difference between Burns's model of leadership and this postindustrial school of leadership. Burns's test of leadership (real, intended change) is in the past tense. It is primarily a test for analysts (leadership researchers and practitioners) who want to look back on a series of events and decide whether leadership took place. To reiterate, Burns did not place this requirement in his definition of leadership. Since it is now an essential element in the postindustrial definition of leadership, the criterion must be framed in the present tense: "leaders and followers who intend real changes." The present tense allows leaders and followers to recognize leadership as it is happening—to distinguish leadership from other human relationships in the here and now—and it allows leadership scholars and commentators (as well as leadership watchers) to do the same. This definition also allows analysts to look back on a process of change to evaluate whether it was a leadership relationship. Thus, this definition allows people to assess leadership relationships as they are happening, but it still allows analysts to evaluate situations that happened in the past.

Intention must be demonstrated by action. People cannot analyze the minds of leaders and followers to determine what they are intending. Persons typically evaluate the intentions of others by their words and actions. The same is true with the leaders and followers in a leadership relationship. They cannot interact and influence one another unless they show their intentions by communicating through speaking, writing, and doing. To make the leadership process work, the followers and leaders must show their intentions—that they intend certain changes—through their words and actions. They must try to influence others in the relationship by using power resources to persuade others. In their acts of persuading, leaders and followers reveal their intentions.

Real Changes

The word *real* means that the changes the leaders and followers intend must be substantive and transforming. *Real* means that leaders and followers intend changes in people's lives, attitudes, behaviors, and basic assumptions, as well as in the groups, organizations, societies, and civilizations they are trying to lead.

How does one decide if the changes the leaders and followers intend are real or if they are spurious or pseudo changes? The problem is quite difficult, and I do not have a good answer. One answer may be that in the beginning people will take the words and actions of the leaders and followers at face value. As the relationship continues, people make judgments concerning the intentions of the leaders and followers. Some of those judgments have to do with whether the intentions of the leaders and followers are perceived as serious after they have had some time to work on the proposed changes, or whether the leaders and followers show that they mean what they say by backing up their words with actions, or whether their intentions are sham and posturing because the leaders and followers do not follow through when crucial decisions about the changes they intend are made.

These judgments are made by people in and out of the leadership relationship. Followers make judgments about the leaders and other followers; leaders make judgments about the followers and other leaders; people in other leadership relationships that, for instance, might be opposed to the changes the leaders and followers intend, make judgments about the leaders and followers; and leadership watchers and commentators make judgments about the leaders and followers.

Even though the analysis is difficult, a definition of leadership must include the concept of *real* change in it. That concept must be included to be both logical and consistent with the other elements of the definition. If the definition allowed leaders and followers to intend pseudo changes, it would sink into the morass of confusion for which other definitions of leadership have been justly criticized. Change is the most distinguishing element of leadership, and if the integrity of that word is not preserved, people cannot possibly distinguish leadership from other social processes. Preserving the integrity of the word *change* is accomplished in this definition by modifying it with the word *real*. Intending pseudo changes will not qualify. Make-believe, sham, fakery, pretense, posturing, masquerading, hypocrisy, simulation, and other dishonest behaviors that suggest the leaders and followers are not serious about intending real changes are unacceptable in applying this definition. Only when leaders and followers actually intend real changes is a leadership relationship possible.

Do Leaders and Followers Have to Produce Changes?

Another difference between the postindustrial definition of leadership and Burns's leadership model is that this definition eliminates the notion that leadership has to result in a product—a change that is real and was intended. Burns's view is quite product-oriented, and to that extent his model still articulates an industrial concept of leadership. "By social change, I mean here *real change*—that is, a transformation to a marked degree in the attitudes, norms, institutions, and behaviors that structure our daily lives" (Burns, 1978, p. 414). On the same page Burns wrote: "The leadership process, in short, must be defined as carrying through from the decision stages to a point of concrete changes in people's lives, attitudes, behaviors and institutions." On page 461, he stated: "Political leadership, however, can be defined only in terms of, and to the extent of the realization of, purposeful, substantive change in the conditions of people's lives." Note the emphasis on "transformation to a marked degree," "carrying through . . . of concrete change," and "realization of [,] purposeful, substantive change." All these statements define leadership in terms of intended change that has been achieved—a product. Leadership can be leadership only when the relationship is effective, that is, when it produces what it intended to produce.

In the 1980s, a new group of leadership scholars took their cue from Burns, as well as from a long tradition of leadership researchers of the industrial paradigm who predated Burns, and developed a new twist on the effectiveness orientation to leadership. In earlier chapters I have labeled this conceptual framework the "excellence theory of leadership" because these scholars define leadership as people achieving excellence in outcomes.

The fundamental concept of the excellence leadership framework can be stated very concisely. Leadership is that which is done by excellent managers, and management is that which is done by average managers. Leadership delivers excellent organizations, excellent products and services, and excellent people in the organization. The major result, of course, is an excellent bottom line. In sum, leadership is excellent management. People (leaders, followers, leadership watchers and commentators) evaluate whether leadership happened by the excellent results, by the effectiveness of the leader's behavior on the organization and on the employees of the organization in terms of excellence. If the results add up to excellence, leadership happened. If not, leadership did not happen.

The postindustrial school of leadership proposed here is process oriented. The definition states: "Leadership is an influence relationship among leaders and followers who intend real changes that reflect their mutual purposes." Leadership is not limited to relationships that achieve results, the real changes that the leaders intended. Leadership happens when leaders and followers enter into a relationship that intends real changes. Effectiveness or whatever synonym is used—achievement, results, excellence, products, success, peak performance—is not an essential element of leadership. A relationship wherein leaders and followers intend real changes but are unsuccessful or ineffective, or achieve only minimum changes, is still leadership. Leaders and followers can fail to achieve real changes and still be in a relationship called leadership.

As indicated earlier, this definition puts the intention to change in the present and makes it an essential element in a leadership relationship. The changes that may result from the leadership relationship are in the future (defined as any time beyond the present), and the changes themselves are not essential elements of the relationship that is leadership. One obvious reason for this distinction is that the leadership relationship may (and often does) dissolve before the intended changes are actually achieved. To make achieving changes part of the definition means that people could not decide whether a leadership relationship existed until after the changes were in place. As a result, leadership is always a process that was in the past; it can never be taking place in the present. Such a criterion is unacceptable because it makes leadership analysis and practice unattainable in the here and now.

Changes

A third difference from Burns's model of leadership is that the word *change* has been pluralized in this definition, in contrast with the singular form that Burns used. Leaders and followers rarely, if ever, intend one change; ordinarily they intend several changes at any one time. The plural allows for several important ideas to be included in the new, postindustrial framework. First, *changes* means that different people in the relationship can emphasize different but related purposes. Second, *changes* indicates that most leadership relationships have a long-term focus; when one change is actually accomplished, the relationship need not break up, because those involved in the relationship ordinarily have other changes they intend. Third, *changes* suggests that leaders and followers can rarely focus on only one change if they seriously intend real change; real change rarely comes in the singular. Fourth, *changes* connotes that the intentions regarding one or several changes may themselves change—develop maturity, be reassessed, undergo revision, even disappear—as time passes. Events impact on the relationship, words and actions take on new meanings, different networks or coalitions are formed, and the people in the relationship grow and develop. As a result, the people in the relationship reformulate their intentions.

Summary

The third essential element of leadership is that the leaders and followers intend real changes. *Intend* means that the changes are purposeful and are in the future. The intention is in the present, and the leaders and followers give solid evidence of their intention by their words and actions. The intention is part of the glue that holds the relationship together. *Real* means that the changes the leaders and followers intend are substantive and transforming, not pseudo changes or sham. To be leadership, the intention to change is all that is required. Leadership does not require the leaders and followers actually to accomplish the changes. Finally, leaders and followers ordinarily intend more than one change at any one time, so the word is pluralized in the definition to *changes*.

From all of these statements, it is clear that the third element of this definition of leadership places the postindustrial school of leadership squarely against the notion prominent in the industrial paradigm of leadership: that leadership must be effective to be leadership; that leadership must produce excellence, achievement, success, or results; that leadership is good management. Leadership is a relationship of leaders and followers who *intend* real changes, not who *produce* real changes. Changes may, indeed, be produced as a result of a leadership relationship, but they are not essential to it. Leadership can still be leadership when the relationship fails to produce results.

Leaders and Followers Develop Mutual Purposes

The fourth essential element of leadership that flows from the definition of leadership is the concept of mutual purposes. The changes the leaders and followers intend reflect their mutual purposes.

Mutual Purposes

If the purposes are mutual, the changes cannot reflect only what the leaders want or only what the followers want. They must reflect what the leaders and followers have come to understand from numerous interactions as the mutual purposes of the leaders and followers. Notice that I did not say the mutual purposes of all the leaders and followers. That is too high a standard, and it is unrealistic from any point of view. How would the leaders or followers know if the mutual purposes encompassed every single person in the relationship? How would analysts know? One of the reasons the word *purposes* is pluralized is to alleviate this problem. When leaders and followers have several purposes, the likelihood of mutuality is enhanced because different leaders and followers can emphasize related purposes and still achieve some mutuality. It also means that there are several purposes around which different followers and leaders can build a common vision or mission.

Purposes, Not Goals

The concept of mutual goals is very strong in Burns's model of leadership (1978, pp. 18–20). He used the word *goals*, which reflects the influence that the industrial model of leadership had on him and the obsession that leadership scholars before him had with the products and results of leadership. The goal concept of leadership has had a long and illustrious history among leadership scholars of the industrial era, as even a short perusal of *Stogdill's Handbook on Leadership* (Stogdill, 1974; Bass, 1981) makes abundantly clear.

Burns did not seem to make a distinction between goals and purposes. At times he suggested that leaders initiate a purpose to which the followers respond on the basis of their individual, personal goals. At other times he treated the words as synonyms. "*Leadership is morally purposeful*. All leadership is goal-oriented. The failure to set goals is a sign of faltering leadership. . . . Both leaders and followers are drawn into the shaping of purpose" (p. 455; the first sentence is a heading, not an emphasis).

There may not be any difference between purposes and goals, but I tend to think there is. Purposes are broader, more holistic or integrated, more oriented to what people ordinarily think of as a vision or mission. Purposes are often stated in qualitative terms. Goals, on the other hand, are usually quite specific, more segmental and often prioritized, and more oriented to what people ordinarily think of as objectives. Goals are often stated in quantitative terms.

Be that as it may, I deliberately chose the word *purposes* in this definition rather than the word *goals* to get away from the industrial and managerial perspective of leadership and to shift to a postindustrial one; to suggest a long-range frame of reference instead of a short-range one; to indicate that leadership has more to do with who we are than with what we do, with the culture of the organization than with its effectiveness, and with how leaders and followers integrate into the community or society than with how they get their needs and wants met as individuals or a group.

Foster (1989) reflected the same idea in what he called a critical practice of leadership:

It is an enduring feature of human life to search for community; to attempt to establish patterns of living based on mutual need and affection, development and protection. But this communitarian impulse is never 'accomplished'; rather it is an ongoing and creative enterprise in which actors or agents continually re-create social structure, and it is this which allows us to identify "communities". . . .

Certain agents can engage in transformative practices which change social structures and forms of community, and it is this that we label leadership. But for leadership to exist in this capacity requires that it be critical of current social arrangements and that this critique be aimed at more emancipatory types of relationships; any other type of "leadership" is basically oriented toward the accumulation of power and, while this is certainly a feature of all relationships within social structures, such accumulation indicates a personal rather than communitarian impulse. Emancipation, it should be stressed, does not mean total freedom; rather, the concept as it is used here means the gradual development of freedoms, from economic problems, racial oppression, ethnic domination, the oppression of women and so on. (pp. 48–49)

Reflect, Not Realize

Burns used the word *realize* in his definition: " . . . in order to realize goals mutually held by both leaders and followers" (p. 18). Realizing goals is a necessary element of leadership if one conceives of leadership as producing results. The concept of realizing goals is—as indicated above—embedded in the industrial paradigm of leadership as good management. Under that framework, it is very logical to expect the manager–subordinate relationship to produce good results and then call it leadership. With that theme so dominant in the literature, it is little wonder that Burns wanted the leadership process to "realize goals mutually held by both leaders and followers."

In constructing a postindustrial school of leadership, the notion of realizing goals has to go. It is essential that it be eliminated if we define leadership as an influence relationship among leaders and followers who intend real changes that reflect their mutual purposes. A concept of leadership so defined cannot include the notion of realizing goals.

I chose the word *reflect* not only to eliminate the results and effectiveness dimensions of the industrial approach to leadership but also to soften the linear and exchange notions built into the idea of "realizing goals mutually held by both leaders and followers." *Reflecting* the mutual purposes suggests that there is no $2 + 2 = 4$ view of the changes that the leaders and followers intend. *Reflects* suggests ambiguity and fluidity in the intentions; it suggests development (progressive change) in the purposes of the leaders and followers rather than fixed, stable positions on what often are complicated and rapidly changing issues.

Reflects is meant to eliminate the hierarchical notions built into the industrial leadership paradigm: the background assumptions (1) that leaders and followers resemble a hierarchical chain of command; (2) that leaders announce the goals they have for a group or organization and followers more or less automatically accept those goals and then set about achieving them; (3) that leadership is primarily a one-way communication process which involves telling and selling when ordering is not feasible; (4) that leaders have the right answers and thus lead the parade of followers. A postindustrial school of leadership must put aside such linear views of leadership. These notions were acceptable when leadership was equated with good management. They are unacceptable when leadership is distinguished from management.

Mutual Purposes Are Common Purposes

Neither do we want to think of leadership as exchange theorists would have us view it. Purposes are not mutual just because exchanges are made, because leaders and followers have bargained one thing for another or traded valued objects. This kind of cost-benefit, interest group approach to leadership may "realize goals independently or mutually held by both leaders and followers" (Burns, 1978, p. 425), but it does not *reflect* the mutual purposes of leaders and followers.

To reflect their mutual purposes, leaders and followers must come to some agreement about their purposes. That agreement must be consciously achieved by the interaction of leaders and followers. It must be developed using non-coercive methods. It must be forged in the relationship that leaders and followers have, one which allows followers to influence leaders (and other followers) as well as leaders to influence followers (and other leaders).

The concept of mutuality has been deeply eroded by two of the central strands of American culture called utilitarian individualism and expressive individualism. These, along with the biblical and republican strands, were eloquently described by Bellah et al. (1985) in their perceptive and popular book, *Habits of the Heart*.

Utilitarian individualism applies "a basically economic understanding of human existence" to a society wherein human life is seen as "an effort by individuals to maximize their self-interest" relative to the basic goals of life (p. 336).

Expressive individualism holds that each person has a unique core of feelings and intuition that should unfold or be expressed if individuality is to be realized. This core, though unique, is not necessarily alien to other persons or to nature. Under certain conditions, the expressive individualist may find it possible through intuitive feelings to "merge" with other persons, with nature, or with the cosmos as a whole. (pp. 333–334)

Burns reflected both of the individualistic strands of the United States culture in his definition of leadership: " . . . in order to realize goals independently or mutually held by both leaders and followers" (p. 425). The word *independently* speaks for the utilitarian individualists and the word *mutually* speaks for the expressive individualists.

Burns's transactional leadership model is made to order for both kinds of individualists. This conclusion is easily documented in his descriptions of trans-actional leadership. There are many examples of cost-benefit analyses, exchange processes, what's-in-it-for-me, and self-interest politics (all of which articulate utilitarian individualism) in his model of transactional leadership. There are also many examples of Maslovian self-actualization, personal fulfillment by getting one's wants and needs met, interpersonal and group dynamics, and therapeutic psychology (all of which represent expressive individualism) in Burns's thought on transactional leadership.

It is not until Burns finally settles on his transformational model of leadership in the last three chapters of his book that his readers gain a view of leadership that speaks to the biblical and republican strands of the United States culture.

The biblical tradition "originates in biblical religion and, though widely dif-fused in American culture, is carried primarily by Jewish and Christian religious communities" (Bellah et al., 1985, p. 333). The core of this tradition is a belief in God and in human redemption.

The republican tradition originated in Greece and Rome, was expressed in medieval and modern Europe, and contributed to the development of modern Western democracies. "It presumes that the citizens of a republic are motivated by civic virtue as well as self-interest. It views public participation as a form of moral education and sees its purposes as the attainment of *justice and the public good*" (Bellah et al., 1985, p. 335).

Burns, in describing transformational leadership, consistently developed the notions that leaders "shape and alter and elevate the motives and values and goals of followers through the vital teaching role of leadership" (p. 425); that "transformational leadership is more concerned with end-values such as liberty, justice, equality" (p. 425); and that "transforming leaders 'raise' their followers up through levels of morality" (p. 425). "Leaders and followers," he wrote, "are engaged in a common enterprise; they are dependent on each other, their fortunes rise and fall together" (p. 426). Or, again, "There is nothing so power-full [*sic*], nothing so effective, nothing so causal as common purpose if that purpose informs all levels of a political system. Leadership *mobilizes*, naked power *coerces*. . . . Moreover, unity of purpose and congruence of motivation foster causal influence far down the line. Nothing can substitute for common purpose, focused by competition and combat, and aided by time'' (p. 439). And on the next-to-last page of his book, he summed up his concept of leadership: ''The function of leadership is to *engage* followers, not merely to activate them, to commingle needs and aspirations and goals in a common enterprise, and in the process make better citizens of both leaders and followers'' (p. 461). He concluded his book with this sentence: ''That people can be lifted *into* their better selves is the secret of transforming leadership and the moral and practical theme of this work'' (p. 462).

Such grand and eloquent statements (and others that could be cited) are Burns's finest hour, making it abundantly clear that the biblical and republican strands of the United States culture dominate Burns's view of transformational leadership. This basic thrust probably accounts for the widely popular and enthusiastic reception accorded the book by academics and practitioners alike. I love and respect the book immensely for the same reason. It was, as they say, a breath of fresh air in the polluted libraries of leadership books. It is this theme from Burns's transformational leadership that I want to pick up and infuse into this postindustrial school of leadership by insisting on a proper understanding of the words *mutual purposes*.

The changes that leaders and followers intend must reflect their mutual purposes. Mutual purposes are common purposes, not only because they are forged from the influence relationship, which is inherently noncoercive, not only because they develop over time from the multidirectional nature of the relationship, *but because the followers and leaders together do leadership*. Leadership is their common enterprise, the essence of the relationship, the process by which they exert influence. If leadership is the common enterprise of the leaders and followers, it cannot be done without commonality of purposes. Independent goals mutually held, a concept pervasive in Burns's overarching model of leadership that includes transactional as well as transformational leadership, are not enough because they are not common purposes.

The mutual purposes have an impact on the changes that the leaders and followers intend. The intention changes when the mutual purposes grow and develop. The changes that are intended themselves change when the mutual purposes grow and develop. When the mutual purposes become more common among the leaders and followers, leadership takes on new meaning as a communal relationship, a community of believers (Foster, 1989). At that point, leaders and followers can articulate the second language about which Bellah and his associates (1985) wrote: a mode of public, moral discourse that springs out of the biblical and republican traditions, a language that speaks to the habits of the heart because it deals with public virtue and the common good. At that point, leaders and followers will have come to the understanding that putting their own good as individuals, groups, or organizations ahead of the common good of the community or society is not leadership, because that kind of understanding does not reflect mutual purposes, only independent goals mutually held. In leadership writ large, the mutual purposes are the common good.

Using the second language, mutual purposes go to the heart of what Burns called *end values*: liberty and equality, freedom and justice, equity and care, peace and security. These are the values that serve as standards, representing the most comprehensive and highest of universal human goods. When leaders and followers reflect true mutual purposes, leadership expresses the common good: (1) a common striving for a community wherein public discourse about end values is commonplace, (2) a common commitment to a social ecology wherein public discourse addresses the issue of how living things, including human beings, can exist in relationship with one another in their common habitat, (3) a common mission to transform our culture and our society so as to reconstitute the social world (Bellah et al., 1985, pp. 283–290).

Summary

Leaders and followers develop mutual purposes.

1. The mutuality of these purposes is forged through the noncoercive, influence relationship.
2. These are purposes, not goals. Purposes are more overarching and holistic than goals, and they are less oriented to quantification. Purposes allow for the development of more mutuality; goals tend to be more fixed and rigid.
3. The leaders and followers reflect, not realize, their purposes.
4. Mutual purposes become common purposes because followers and leaders engage in leadership together. Independent goals mutually held do not qualify for what is meant here as mutual purposes. Mutual purposes are common purposes held by a community of believers.

TRANSFORMATION AND LEADERSHIP

Leadership is about transformation. Burns said it, but he failed to follow through as well as he could have throughout his penetrating book. In this attempt at a new paradigm of leadership for the postindustrial age, I want to say it, and I want transformation to be the cornerstone of the postindustrial school of leadership. Real transformation involves active people, engaging in influence relationships based on persuasion, intending real changes to happen, and insisting that those changes reflect their mutual purposes. The definition of leadership offered herein includes all four of those essential elements.

Transformation is done by active people. A definition of leadership that states only active people are able to do leadership and a definition that insists the followers—as well as the leaders—be active is a concept of leadership that engenders transformation. Passive people are rarely transformed by ordinary human processes. Calamities may transform them, but not leadership. Leadership helps to transform people in organizations who engage themselves in the relationship that is leadership. In the process, organizations and societies may also be transformed.

Transformation is about influence relationships based on persuasion, not coercion. A definition that states that leadership is a multidirectional influence relationship of people who use persuasion to make an impact is a paradigm that articulates what transformation is all about. People, groups, and organizations that are persuaded to change may be transformed; those that are coerced to change are rarely transformed.

Transformation is about people intending real changes to happen. A definition of leadership that encompasses only those relationships of people who intend real changes and that excludes those relationships of people who intend the status quo or pseudochanges, is a conceptual framework that takes transformation seriously. When real, substantive changes are intended, transformation is possible and even likely. When pseudochanges are intended, transformation is quite unlikely.

Transformation is insisting that the changes reflect the mutual purposes of the people engaged in the transformation. A definition of leadership which requires that the changes the leaders and followers intend reflect their mutual purposes is a model of leadership which explicates the nature of transformation. Changes that realize mutually held independent goals may have some impact, but they will not often engender transformation. Transformation happens in groups, organizations, and societies when people develop common purposes. In leadership writ large, mutual purposes help people work for the common good, help people build community.

A second point that should be made about leadership and transformation is this: Including a moral requirement in either the definition of leadership or an understanding of transformation is too limiting, and thus unacceptable.

There are no moral criteria in the postindustrial definition of leadership. An influence relationship among leaders and followers who intend real changes that reflect their mutual purposes can be moral or immoral. While there is a requirement that the process of leadership be ethical (noncoercive, multidirectional, influence-oriented, real, and mutual), the changes that the leaders and followers intend can fall along a continuum of morality. Thus, it is possible to have an influence relationship among leaders and followers who intend abortion upon demand as a public policy in the United States, as that position reflects their mutual purposes, and to have another influence relationship among leaders and followers who intend a public policy centered on the right to life, as that position reflects their mutual purposes. Some people believe that the pro-abortion position is immoral; other people believe that the anti-abortion position is immoral. If morality is a requirement for leadership, neither of these influence relationships could be labeled leadership, since each of them is considered immoral by a large portion of the population.

The same can be said about the concept of transformation. To limit the notion of transformation to those changes that take the higher moral ground (to use Jesse Jackson's phrase) is unacceptable because in many situations and for many issues there is no consensus as to what the higher moral ground is. Capital punishment is a good example. Many people passionately insist that capital punishment is the higher moral ground and that they want our society (and the world) transformed to punish convicted murderers so that other people will not be murderers. Other people just as vehemently say that life in prison without parole is the higher moral ground and that they want our society (and the world) transformed so as to eliminate the possibility of states (nations) killing prisoners as a punishment for their crime. If morality is a requirement for transformation, neither of these changes could be labeled a transformation because each of them is immoral according to a large portion of the population.

Burns's notion of transformational leadership is that "leaders and followers raise one another to higher levels of motivation and morality" (p. 20). Toward the end of his work, he is even stronger. "*Transforming leadership is elevating. It is moral but not moralistic. Leaders engage with followers, but from higher levels of morality; in the enmeshing of goals and values both leaders and followers are raised to more principled levels of judgment*" (p. 455; the first sentence is a heading, not an emphasis).

Burns based his concept of transformational leadership on *only* the moral development of the leaders and followers. This requirement means that the real intended changes inherent in transformational leadership must be of the kind that raise leaders and followers to higher levels of morality. The raising of groups, organizations, societies to higher levels of morality was not emphasized by Burns, although the idea could be implied from his model of transformational leadership. One could make the argument that if leaders and followers raised their levels of morality, the morality of the groups, organizations, and societies to which they belonged would also be raised. There is considerable controversy concerning that view of moral development. Moreover, the question of what critical mass of morally raised individuals it takes to have an impact on a group, organization, or society is, at this point, unanswerable. That an organization or society is better because of individuals who raise their morality is unquestioned. Whether that organization or society is itself raised to a higher level of morality by such individual actions is an issue about which we do not have a clear understanding or a satisfactory answer.

Having a moral requirement for transformational leadership may be acceptable if the overall definition of leadership does not include that moral requirement (which Burns's definition does not) and there is another kind of leadership that allows for what some people would consider immoral changes (as Burns does in his model of transactional leadership). But the problem is that the large majority of people reading Burns's book have not paid attention to the overall definition of leadership and have deliberately ignored or rejected transactional leadership as leadership; thus they are left with the inevitable conclusion that Burns's concept of leadership is transformational with the moral requirement included. Such an understanding of leadership is scientifically impossible to accept because it does not account for many human relationships that practically everyone labels leadership. The facts do not support such a definition. Such an understanding of leadership is conceptually unacceptable because it does not make sense. It makes it impossible for analysts to agree on what leadership is, since that is dependent upon what they believe is moral. We have more than enough trouble untangling the confusion about what leadership is without linking the concept of leadership to some notion of moral development.

Since two forms of leadership that allow for one form of leadership to be immoral and the other to be moral, have not been included in the postindustrial paradigm of leadership, and since the purpose here is to focus on a single definition that takes into account all possible situations with extremely diverse phenomena involved, a moral requirement cannot be included in the postindustrial definition of leadership.

The same is true of the concept of transformation. Stated bluntly, there are more transformations that people and organizations go through than those which raise them to higher levels of morality. In my view, transformation can take place in many aspects of our personal, professional, and moral lives as well as in many aspects of the groups, organizations, communities, and societies in which we live and work. These transformations can be physical, intellectual, aesthetic, psychological, social, civic, ecological, transcendental, moral, spiritual, and holistic. A leadership paradigm that is serious about transformation must take into account all of these transformations, not exclude all of them except one. A definition of leadership that requires leaders and followers to intend real changes must take the notion of transformation seriously, not limit it to certain kinds of changes. Changes come in all shapes, sizes, qualities, and moral perspectives; so do transformations. The facts of life are that some transformations are good and others are bad; some may be good for a while and not so good after some time elapses; some are considered good by one portion of the people and mediocre or bad by another portion. Leadership and transformation, properly conceived, must deal with the reality of human existence as it is lived, wherein changes are variously evaluated and desired. Leadership, properly defined, is about transformation, all kinds of transformations.

CONCLUSION

I have tried to put together a consistent, coherent, workable, and accurate model of leadership that is easily understood by both academics and practitioners. This new model is not more of the same; it is an attempt to start a new school of leadership, a school that is radically different from the industrial school of leadership, which articulates an understanding of leadership as good management. This new school of leadership presents a substantial paradigm shift toward a model of leadership that is postindustrial in its basic background assumptions and in its definition. That this paradigm shift is massive is immediately evident from the complete separation of leadership from management inherent in the definition and the seriousness with which that distinction is taken. Other telltale signs are in the four essential elements of leadership that flow from the definition: (1) a relationship based on influence, (2) leaders and followers develop that relationship, (3) they intend real changes, and (4) they have mutual purposes. These four elements are radically different from any set of essential elements which are presently found in the industrial paradigm of leadership that does not distinguish leadership from good management. These elements are, as we have seen, quite different from Burns's definition of leadership, which is viewed as a transitional model from the industrial to the postindustrial paradigms of leadership.

While a moral definition of leadership has been rejected, I have insisted that the ethics of leadership be included in the definition. The ethics of leadership has to do with the process of leadership—the relationship that is leadership—and not with the content of leadership, not with the question of whether such and such changes that certain leaders and followers intend are morally uplifting. While such questions are obviously very important to the people who do leadership—and I am one of those people—they do not deal with the nature of leadership, which is what this chapter is all about.

The ethics of leadership is a subject just now taking hold. Leadership scholars and practitioners must pay increasing attention to the subject. Professional development workshops and seminars must be developed to deal with the subject. But leaders and followers should not confuse the nature of leadership with what they think good leadership is. The two are not the same. What leaders and followers, as well as leadership watchers and commentators, need to know about the ethics of leadership is the centrality of influence in the leadership process and the essentiality of mutual purposes as common purposes. When they have learned that, they can then talk about and encourage good leadership—that which will, according to their moral standards, generate people, groups, organizations, and societies that exude a higher moral purpose.

There are exciting times ahead. Change is so rapid that the people living today are the first generation who can participate in a massive paradigm shift and know that they are going through it. The shift to a postindustrial paradigm certainly involves many significant changes in our lives and in our background assumptions. Ferguson (1980) and others have already documented the extensive changes many people have experienced in this monumental swing to the twenty-first century, and these authors have also predicted some of the transformations the postindustrial era has in store for us in practically every aspect of life. Leadership is one of the concepts and practices that will be transformed as Western societies move from an industrial to a postindustrial paradigm. Indeed, leadership may be crucial to a peaceful and orderly process as people individually and collectively struggle with that paradigm shift. But leaders and followers are not up to that job unless leadership scholars and practitioners begin now to move toward model of leadership that is more attuned to the postindustrial era. What our organizations and communities need are leadership relationships based on a postindustrial model of leadership. Such relationships will facilitate the transition to the postindustrial era. But they will not become widespread until scholars and practitioners build a new school of leadership.

6

Leadership and Management

Confusing leadership and management and treating the words as if they were synonymous have a long and illustrious history in leadership studies. The practice is pervasive in the mainstream literature of leadership. It is pervasive in all academic disciplines where one can find the literature on leadership. As has been shown in the discussion of the definitions of leadership since the 1930s, leadership scholars instilled the values from the industrial paradigm into their understanding of leadership and equated leadership with good management. Many scholars and practitioners went even further and equated leadership with management.

Some scholars, including myself, have had serious conceptual problems with using leadership and management as synonymous words. These authors have written books, chapters, and articles in which they have argued that leadership is not the same as management, but these works have had little impact on the mainstream of literature or practice of leadership. The melding of these concepts and understanding leadership as good management still dominated leadership studies at the end of the 1980s (see Badaracco & Ellsworth, 1989; Bennis, 1989a, 1989b; Cohen, 1990; Conger, 1989a; DePree, 1989; Hunt, Baliga, Dachler & Schriesheim, 1988; Immegart, 1988; Janis, 1989; Kotter, 1988; Muriel, 1989; Nanus, 1989; Ridge, 1989; Sergiovanni, 1990; Smith & Peterson, 1988; Yuki, 1989; Zaleznik, 1989). The industrial paradigm of leadership is still holding strong.

A postindustrial school of leadership must come to terms with this issue, and that is the purpose of this chapter. After some discussion of previous attempts to distinguish between leadership and management, most of which have not been successful, I propose a new framework that uses the essential elements of the definitions of leadership and management to make a clear separation between the two concepts.

SOME ATTEMPTS TO DISTINGUISH BETWEEN LEADERSHIP AND MANAGEMENT

There were only a few serious attempts to deal with the leadership is management syndrome prior to 1978, when Burns rethought the concept of leadership, and the 1980s, when a number of scholars called for a different approach to understanding leadership.

The first such attempt I have found was by Selznick (1957) in his marvelous little book *Leadership in Administration*. He wrote:

Leadership is not equivalent to office-holding or high prestige or authority or decision-making. It is not helpful to identify leadership with whatever is done by people in high places. The activities we have in mind may or may not be engaged in by those who are formally in positions of authority. This is inescapable if we are to develop a theory that will be useful in diagnosing cases of inadequate leadership on the part of persons in authority. If this view is correct, it means that only some (and sometimes none) of the activities of decision-makers are leadership activities. Here again, understanding leadership requires understanding of a broader social process. If some types of decisions are more closely related to leadership activities than others, we should learn what they are. To this end in this analysis let us make a distinction between "routine" and "critical" decision-making. (p. 24).

Selznick devoted an entire chapter in the book to fleshing out the distinction between routine and critical decision making, between management and leadership.

Jacobs (1970), in a very thoughtful book that was not widely read but should have been, devoted considerable space to distinguishing between leadership and management. Toward the end of the book, he wrote: "Perhaps the most important conclusion reached in this work is the importance of distinguishing between the concepts of leadership, power, and authority, and of identifying superordinate role behaviors that constitute each" (p. 341). Jacobs gave one-sentence definitions of each of the three terms, and they contained discrete elements that an analyst could use to distinguish among them. "Authority [management] resides in the relationships between positions in an organization, and is derived from consensually validated role expectations for the position incumbents involved" (p. 231). "Leadership is taken as an interaction between persons in which one presents information of a sort and in such a manner that the other becomes convinced that his outcomes (benefits/costs ratio) will be improved if he behaves in the manner suggested or desired'' (p. 232). ''Power is defined . . . as the capacity to deprive another needed satisfactions or benefits, or to inflict 'costs' on him for noncompliance with an influence attempt'' (p. 230).

Katz and Kahn (1966/1978) articulated a distinction between leadership and management that has had some currency among leadership scholars, especially psychologists: ''One common approach to the definition of leadership is to equate it with the differential exertion of influence. . . . We maintain . . . that every act of influence on a matter of organizational relevance is to some degree an act of leadership. . . . We consider the essence of organizational leadership to be the influential increment over and above mechanical compliance with routine directives of the organization'' (pp. 302–303). Management, obviously, is the mechanical compliance of people in organizations with routine directives. A variation on this theme is that leadership is the use of influence and management is the use of authority. In the 1970s, quite a few authors actually used this distinction in their works, but they often failed to remain true to their definitions in their research and in their discussions of leadership after the definitions were given.

Graham (1988) followed up on this distinction.

Definitions of leader-follower relationships typically draw a distinction between voluntary acceptance of another's influence, on the one hand, and coerced compliance, on the other (Graham, 1982; Hunt, 1984; Jacobs, 1971 [*sic*]; Jago, 1982; Katz & Kahn, 1978). That distinction rests on the degree of free choice exercised by followers. Specific instances of obedience which stem from fear of punishments, the promises of rewards, or the desire to fulfill contractual obligations are examples not of voluntary followership but of subordination, and the range of free choice available to subordinates is relatively small. Appropriate labels for the person giving orders, monitoring compliance, and administering performance-contingency rewards and punishments include ''supervisor'' and ''manager,'' but *not* ''leader.'' (p. 74)

Zaleznik (1977) attempted to distinguish between leaders and managers in a celebrated article published in the *Harvard Business Review*. In that article as well as his 1989 book, he equates management with managers and leadership with leaders, so his distinction between management and leadership is based on the personality differences of managers and leaders. ''Managers and leaders differ fundamentally in their world views. The dimensions for assessing these differences include managers' and leaders' orientations toward their goals, their work, their human relations, and their selves'' (1977, p. 69). Using William James's two basic personality types, Zaleznik suggested that managers are ''once-born'' and leaders are ''twice-born.'' He used a trait approach to distinguish between leaders and managers, and consequently between leadership and management.

There are contextual indications in Burns (1978) that he did distinguish between leadership and management, but they are more or less hidden in the text. The index in his book does not contain an item labeled ''management'' or one labeled "leadership and management." There is a section titled "Bureaucracy Versus Leadership" (pp. 295–302), but the material in those pages is not helpful in trying to distinguish between leadership and management (or authority, as Burns called it).

Several commentators, including myself, have reinterpreted Burns's model of leadership to be, in reality, a model of management *and* leadership. This reinterpretation states quite simply that Burns's transactional leadership is management, and his transformational leadership is leadership, and the difference between the two is the distinction between leadership and management. Enochs (1981), in a very popular article in the *Phi Delta Kappan*, stated this reinterpretation very well: "Transactional leadership is managerial and custodial; it is competent but uninspired care-taking for a quiet time. Transformational leadership is a more lofty undertaking. It is not a trade-off for survival between leader and followers during good times, but rather a process for achieving fundamental changes in hard times" (p. 177).

The same point was made in a reaction paper by Jill Graham (1988) to Avolio and Bass's presentation on transformational leadership and charisma at a leadership symposium:

The distinction between transactional and transformational leadership in the Avolio & Bass chapter bears a striking resemblance to what is now a well-established difference between supervision and leadership. Certainly, a transactional leaders' use of contingent reinforcements is nothing more than supervision. Research on supervision, moreover, is in the same conceptual category as theories of organizational control and the operant paradigm for employee motivation (Jago, 1982, 330). Only transformational leadership occupies a conceptual category that is independent of those topics, that is, leadership standing alone. (pp. 74–75)

In personal conversations with Burns in 1989, he made it very clear to me that he does not agree with this reinterpretation of his conceptual framework of leadership. He has continued to hold the view that transactional leadership is leadership, not management, and his views on that subject are quite strongly held.

Dubin wrote a stinging critique of leadership research in 1979 that to some extent dealt with the distinction between leadership and management.

Another observation: 3) the ease with which the concept of *leadership* is treated as a synonym for *management* and *supervision*. This is amazing. My knowledge of organizational behavior has led me to the conclusion that effective organizations can be managed and supervised and *not* led, while some ineffective organizations can be led into their difficulties without the benefit of management and supervision. . . .

This leads to my first conclusion. Leadership is a rare phenomenon, not a common one in organizational behavior. Those who proposed to *observe* leadership behavior as their methodology for study to gain knowledge (an orientation I applaud), will find that tracking managers to record their every behavior will produce relatively little data on leadership. . . . The first cut at such data mass will consist of sorting it into two piles: the small stack of leadership acts, and the very large pile of acts of managing and supervising.

...In my view, the central problem has to do with the reluctance, or inability, to specify the dimensionality of the leadership phenomena. We have even succeeded in confusing "leadership" with other social behaviors as my predecessor in this "overview" role, Miner, did when he boldly proposed to substitute "control" for the concept of leadership (Miner, 1975). We have failed in handling the dimensionality problem by focusing on some of the wrong dimensions of leadership and ignoring others.

One major problem that has preoccupied American social science has been the formulation of leadership as an interpersonal phenomenon. This has been a major shortcoming in the study of leadership.... There are face-to-face relations between a leader and followers. But it should also be evident that there are situations of leadership which do not involve face-to-face relations with followers. In the modern world these are by far the most frequent leadership situations. Furthermore, there are many face-to-face relations between superiors and subordinates that *do not* involve leadership in the ongoing interaction....

I believe that the primary emphasis of the work in this volume is on leadership in face-to-face relationships. I will boldly propose: There may be many significant findings among the studies [in this book], but in the broad span of human affairs, they are largely trivial findings because they fail to address leadership *of* organizations. (pp. 225–227)

Tucker (1981) used the Selznick dichotomy to distinguish between leadership and management. Defining a political leader as "one who gives direction, or meaningfully participates in the giving of direction, to the activities of a political community" (p. 15), Tucker suggested that "One might argue that even in ordinary, day-to-day group life, when no great uncertainties exist, groups are in need of being directed. But such routine direction might better be described as *management*, reserving the term *leadership* for the directing of a group at times of choice, change, and decision, times when deliberation and authoritative decision occur, followed by steps to implement decisions reached" (p. 16).

Bennis has long held that leadership is different from management. In 1977 he wrote: "Leading does not mean managing; the difference between the two is crucial. I know many institutions that are very well managed and very poorly led" (p. 3). Similar statements appear in many of his other articles and books. In their 1985 book, Bennis and Nanus wrote:

The problem with many organizations, and especially the ones that are failing, is that they tend to be overmanaged and underled.... They may excel in the ability to handle the daily routine, yet never question whether the routine should be done at all. There is a profound difference between management and leadership, and both are important. "To manage" means "to bring about, to accomplish, to have charge of or responsibility for, to conduct." "Leading" is "influencing, guiding in direction, course, action, opinion." The distinction is crucial. *Managers are people who do things right and leaders are people who do the right thing.* The difference may be summarized as activities of vision and judgment—*effectiveness* versus activities of mastering routines—*efficiency*. (p. 21)

Other paragraphs on other pages in the book deliver essentially the same message.

A persistent theme of the 1980s literature on leadership is an attempt to label

as leadership those management possesses which produce excellence in organizational outcomes and which leave the meaning of management to include all
the other management processes that produce less than excellent outcomes. Leadership is excellence management; management is doing anything less than excellence. This distinction, of course, is simply a restatement of the industrial
paradigm of leadership that upgrades good management to excellent management.

AN EVALUATION OF THE ATTEMPTS TO DISTINGUISH
LEADERSHIP FROM MANAGEMENT

While the attempts to distinguish between leadership and management listed
in the last section are admirable, and while a few scholars actually get at substantive differences, the attempts are as a whole more or less weak in giving
scholars and practitioners the conceptual ability to make such a distinction.
Generally, the distinctions are prefunctory and poorly constructed, and the criteria
given to make the distinction are often too general and too ambiguous for people
to use with any accuracy in real life or in research. Another problem is that
many of the distinctions given by scholars are distinctions of personality traits
and behaviors of leaders and managers, not differences in the processes or
relationships that get at the nature of leadership and management. There is a
pervasive tendency among these scholars to equate leadership with leaders,
confusing a process with a person, which, in the end, doubles the confusion
present in the use of the words *leadership* and *management* as synonyms.

The other problem, of course, is that these scholars were swimming against
the tide of the mainstream concept of leadership as embedded in the industrial
paradigm: Leadership is good management. These authors had a very difficult
time making their case. They were generally ignored, and so the distinctions
were not pursued and developed. They had a difficult time gaining collaborators.
And, it is important to remember that leadership as a field of study was often a
sideline for these scholars; their main scholarly interest was more connected to
their primary academic discipline.

Worse yet is that most of the authors mentioned above paid little attention to
their own distinctions. It was not uncommon for an author to make the distinction
in an early chapter and then ignore it in the other chapters of the book. Using
Argyris's (1976) framework to make sense of such inconsistencies, one could
state that these authors developed theories of leadership that espoused a difference
between leadership and management, but their theories-in-use reflected the industrial paradigm, which equated leadership with good management. Selznick
and Jacobs are the major exceptions; they were able to use the words *leadership*
and *management* consistently throughout their books.

Bryman (1986) noted the same tendency, and he criticized leadership scholars
for not paying attention to the distinction.

It would seem important to maintain a distinction between a leader who is in a leadership
position and who has power and authority vested in his or her office, and leadership as

an influence process which is more than the exercise of power and authority. . . . However, . . . a great deal of leadership research rides roughshod over these distinctions. Studies abound on the subject of the behavior of leaders in which the strategy involves discerning the activities of people in positions of leadership, with little reference to how these activities might be indicative of leadership *per se* as distinct from the exercise of power and authority. (p. 4)

Unfortunately, Bryman ignored his own critique: "It is necessary to hold many of these terminological difficulties in abeyance and the remainder of the book will focus on what, in the author's view, is generally taken to be the study of leadership in organizations" (p. 16).

Wilpert (1982) did the same kind of turnaround in response to three papers at a leadership symposium.

What should be noted right at the outset . . . is the terminological uncertainty in all three contributions [papers presented at the symposium] with respect to the use of the terms "leader" and "manager." Although some difference of kind is even implied in the titles of two of the presentations (Steward; Lombardo & McCall), not one of the three contributions elaborate [*sic*] the distinctions, in fact, all use the two terms synonymously. So I will follow suit and assume for purposes of discussion that managers always perform some leadership function due to their organizational position. (pp. 68–69)

Schon (1984) did exactly the same thing in his presentation at another symposium. "Leadership and management are not synonymous terms, one can be a leader without being a manager. . . . Conversely, one can manage without leading. . . . Nevertheless, we generally expect managers to lead, and criticize them if they fail to do so. Hence, for the purposes of this essay, I shall treat management and leadership as though they were one" (p. 36).

Lombardo and McCall (1982) show how much the industrial concept of leadership has penetrated even highly sophisticated centers on leadership. They worked at the Center for Creative Leadership in Greensboro, North Carolina during the 1980s. (McCall left the Center in the late 1980s.) The Center is a multimillion-dollar operation that employs some 100 professional researchers and trainers "to encourage and develop creative leadership and effective management for the good of society overall" (from the Center's mission statement).

In the early 1980s, Lombardo and McCall produced an elaborate simulation called "Looking Glass, Inc.," which has been one of the cornerstones of the Center's leadership/management training programs. The authors made a presentation at the 1982 leadership symposium in which they stated:

This chapter is based on a day in the life of a glass manufacturing company and the 20 leaders who run it. . . .

It was with this inherent belief—that management or leadership only makes sense when viewed in its entirety—that a complex simulation was designed for use in leadership research. Its goals were both clear and fuzzy: to mirror as realistically as possible the demands of a typical managerial job in a complex organization, to have actual managers run the simulated company as they chose, and to bring multiple methods to bear on learning something new about leadership. By watching a day in the life of managers dealing with the complexity and chaos of organizations, we hoped to develop some more pertinent questions to guide future research on what leadership is, and how and when it matters. (pp. 50–51)

Notice the equation of leaders with managers, and the equation of leadership with what managers do. Lombardo and McCall clearly state that if a person studies a day (or several days) in the life of a manager (or several managers), he/she will certainly understand leadership better. The industrial concept of leadership has seldom been articulated more forcefully.

Actually, the brochures from the Center for Creative Leadership publicizing the Looking Glass simulation are considerably more accurate in describing the simulation.

Looking Glass, a robust simulation of managerial action, is beginning its second decade and gaining worldwide use for one critical reason: It teaches the lessons that matter. What lessons? How managers react to constantly changing environments. How they make decisions, set priorities, network and communicate to get the job done. . . . Looking Glass puts managers in the middle of the chaos of managerial life and lets them . . . examine how well they did and how they might do better. (Center for Creative Leadership, n.d., p. 1)

Notice that the words *leader* and *leadership* are never used in the description.

The same cannot be said about the trainers who use Looking Glass in the Center-sponsored workshops. I attended a one-day, introductory session of the Looking Glass simulation in 1989, and the equation of management and leadership was pervasive. The simulation as I experienced it on that day had almost nothing to do with leadership as I define the word. The whole thing was relatively straightforward, and the simulation delivered exactly what the brochure promised: insights into enlightened management. However, the trainers had a different view entirely. They thought that they were delivering insights into enlightened leadership (since they were imbued with the industrial view that leadership is good management), and they definitely wanted the workshop participants to take home the idea that the Looking Glass simulation was about leadership.

Allison (1984) took another strategy in articulating the industrial view of leadership. He rejected outright the notion that scholars need to distinguish leadership from management and then proceeded to ignore any definitional problems that position might have on his understanding of leadership. After discussing five ''leadership'' authors who claimed to have discovered ''the essence of the concept'' of leadership, Allison opined that ''one might conclude that 'administrative leadership' is, in fact, and oxymoron—a contradiction in terms'' (p. 215). Then, he concluded: ''I find the claims of these authors to have isolated the 'real thing' ultimately unpersuasive'' (p. 217). So what does Allison do?

For the purpose of this discussion, I cannot hope to surmount these formidable obstacles [definitional problems]. Thus, this paper will attempt to circumvent them by taking a less abstract, more simplistically empirical path: focusing on people playing lead roles in administrative settings. . . . Following Webster I will use the term "lead" to mean "to show the way by going in advance; to conduct, escort, or direct." Those who lead in administrative settings, I will call managers. Again, following Webster, I will use the term "management" to mean the "purposive organization and direction of resources to achieve a desired outcome." (p. 218)

The upshot of these approaches to the concepts of leadership and management is a cultural acceptance in the research community (and ultimately in the popular press and among practitioners) of sloppy scholarship and practice, which produce conceptual frameworks that use different terms interchangeably. In a very real sense, the culture of permissiveness goes like this: "Since other scholars and practitioners confuse leadership and management, since other scholars have not come up with a definition of leadership that distinguishes it from management, I am free to do the same thing. I will also use the words *leadership* and *management*, *leader* and *manager*, as synonymous terms. I will also equate *leadership* with *leader* and *management* with *manager*, so there are four terms that I will equate with one another."

Some scholars defend this practice by calling it diversity of thought or academic freedom. I once challenged Fiedler at an Academy of Management conference about his view that leaders and managers are the same, a view he has consistently held since the 1960s. I asked: "How can you be sure that the managers you study in your research are actually leaders?" His answer went something like this: "My definition of a leader is as good as your definition or that of any other researcher. I believe that managers are leaders and so the managers in my studies are leaders."

Schriesheim, Hunt, and Sekaran (1982) ended the leadership symposium of that year with a ringing defense of definitional diversity. "We cherish diversity and see it as needed for our collective endeavor. . . . Our values and beliefs suggest that . . . if we are to advance the field . . . we should . . . encourage diversity. . . . We want to be able to enjoy our enterprise and, at the same time, to serve constituencies of our own choosing, with products compatible with their own needs and ours" (pp. 297–298). While this statement is a stirring defense of the free market of ideas, scholarship brings with it the responsibility to critically analyze the ideas in the free market. It seems that Schriesheim, Hunt, and Sekaran want to be able to use the words *leadership* and *management* interchangeably so as to serve the self-esteem needs of the corporate manager, who, they seem to think, need to view themselves as leaders simply because they are managers. Such a position is equivalent to accepting the age-old assumption undergirding the free market framework: Let the buyer beware. I believe that scholars have more responsibility than that.

So do practitioners. Burack (1979) summarized the interviews he had with four executives, and the interviews indicate they had some of the same difficulties with leadership research.

Past SIU symposia, whatever their academic and intellectual merits, have been so far removed from the pressure on the practitioner as to be useless to anyone running training programs or to anyone in leadership positions. (p. 27)

The implications of this observation [given in previous paragraphs, that only 25 percent of the people in any group have leadership skills] should be quite clear by now. . . . It leads to Moses' Commandment which is . . . "Thou shalt study leaders who are first *accurately identified* as leaders before attempting to build theories of leadership behavior."

. . . much of our "research" is based on available (translate that to mean the easiest to obtain) measures. . . . There does not seem to have been a serious effort to obtain adequate samples of leaders in most of the research studies purporting to be evaluating leaders. Rather, one studies what is available. Sometimes these are college sophomores, sometimes these are managers—rarely however, are the subjects of intensive analysis evaluated to determine if they have the skills we are trying to study. (p. 32)

The leadership research reported in the 1982 symposium did not pass the Bill and Barbara test developed by Mintzberg (1982) from the feedback of two practitioner colleagues. What bothered Barbara the most, she wrote, "was the gnawing suspicion that the research was being carried out as an end in itself. Hence relevance was really a side issue." Bill concluded that the researchers "seemed more interested in studying the subtleties of a particular research approach—or even worse, studying other studies—than they are in contributing to a real understanding of leadership itself" (p. 243).

Evidently Barbara and Bill, as well as the four executives on whom Burack reported, thought that leadership researchers had a professional responsibility which included more than enjoying themselves and serving their own self-interests. At the same time, they stated very strongly that the products of these researchers did not meet their needs, which goes to the heart of the argument Schriesheim, Hunt, and Sekaran (1982) used to support the free market of ideas approach to leadership studies.

Hosking and Hunt (1982) delivered a stinging critique of leadership literature at the end of the symposium. "A pervasive . . . theme [of the speakers at the symposium] concerned the meaning of the terms 'leaders' and 'leadership.' It was very apparent that people used them to mean totally different things but on the whole . . . did not seem to see this as a problem. Indeed we saw little evidence of any desire to develop a common language." On the other hand, a few other speakers "felt it was essential to distinguish clearly different aspects of leadership and between such related terms as leadership and management" (p. 280).

Later in the chapter, Hosking and Hunt summarized the approaches of U.S. scholars to the study of leadership. First, "there seems very little interest in developing models or theories of leadership. . . . Second, when theoretical propositions are tested, they are typically concerned with the distribution of control and decision-making authority within organizations, little or no reference being made to 'leadership.' Third, . . . there is relatively little concern with getting down to definitional problems: by not studying leaders and leadership it is possible to focus on members of organizations (usually appointed officials)'' (p. 288). The coauthor of these words is the same Hunt who argued for diversity in leadership studies in the concluding chapter of the same book (Schriesheim, Hunt, and Sekaran, 1982) wherein leadership studies is likened to an ice cream manufacturer who serves up different flavors of ice cream to satisfy the varied needs of the customers. The only trouble with the metaphor is this: Ice cream manufacturers know the differences between ice cream and sherbet or frozen yogurt, but I see no evidence, even by 1990, that leadership researchers know the differences between leadership and management. The differences are in the natures of the processes (such as the differences in the natures of ice cream, sherbet, and frozen yogurt) and not in the people—their traits, styles, and be-haviors—who do the processes (not in the colors and flavors of the ice cream, sherbet, and frozen yogurt).

Increasingly, however, scholars have insisted that the old order is not good enough. Foster (1986b) flatly stated that "Leadership is a construct which must be dismantled and rebuilt. The dismantling is necessary because it would appear that the future of leadership studies in social science research is bleak" (p. 3). In another book, Foster (1986a) wrote: "The concept of leadership often receives poor treatment from scholars and educators alike. Often, it is mistaken for the ability to manage small groups in accomplishing tasks; at other times, as a means for improving production. We shall argue that both views adopt a fundamentally mistaken approach to leadership insofar as they identify leadership with aspects of management" (p. 169).

Two British researchers have taken the bull by the horns, so to speak. Hosking and Morley (1988) made a serious attempt to reconstruct the concept of lead-ership, as Foster insisted we must do:

Our opening argument was for taking the concept of leadership seriously. This requires an explicit definition that can be employed to interpret existing literature and to direct subse-quent research and theory. We argue for a definition of leaders as those who consistently contribute certain kinds of acts to leadership processes. More precisely, we define partici-pants as leaders when they (1) consistently make effective contributions to social order and (2) are both expected and perceived to do so by fellow participants. . . . This conceptualization has three general and important implications. The first is that we prefer *not* to follow the common practice of using the terms *leader* and *manager* interchangeably. . . . In our view, studies of managerial behavior should not be assumed necessarily to inform our under-standing of leadership. Of course they may; however, it is always necessary to establish that the managers concerned were also leaders in the sense the term is used here. . . .

The second and related point is that the only sure means of identifying leaders is through the analysis of leadership processes. The reason, quite simply, is that leaders achieve their status as a result of their contributions, and the ways these are received, relative to the contributions of others. . . . In other words, to study leaders must be to study leadership, that is, the process by which "social order" is constructed and changed.

Third, and last, our conceptualization recognizes that significant leadership contributions may come from a minority, including a minority of one; equally, they may be expected and contributed by the majority. (p. 90)

By our definition, it is necessary to study the processes by which particular acts come to be perceived as contributions to social order, and therefore come to be perceived as leadership acts. . . . Our conceptualization implies that these processes are endemic to leadership whether or not there are appointed managers involved. In other words, the position taken here is that leadership, properly conceived, is emergent. (p. 91)

The entire chapter must be read by anyone interested in reconstructing leadership by taking it out of its industrial moorings. This short quotation shows how differently leadership can be conceptualized when one takes the concept seriously by distinguishing between leadership and management and then putting that distinction to work consistently in a conceptual framework of leadership.

DENIGRATING MANAGEMENT TO ENNOBLE LEADERSHIP

In 1985 I wrote a paper (Rost, 1985) called ''Distinguishing Leadership and Management: A New Consensus,'' in which I suggested that there was a new consensus among the leadership scholars of the 1980s, namely, that leadership is fundamentally different from management and that the two words should not be used synonymously. Then I explicated a conceptual model that contrasted leadership and management according to twelve different criteria. In each case, I suggested that there is a fundamental difference between the two processes.

I presented the paper for the first time at the Organizational Development Network National Conference in 1985, and I received a largely positive response from an overflow crowd. I gave the paper at several other national conventions, and I received the same positive response. I also used it in my leadership classes, and the doctoral students generally approved of the model, many of them using it in their own training activities in various organizations.

Unfortunately, the paper was problematic on both of its major points. As the 1980s wore on and the leadership literature continued to pour off the presses, it became increasingly obvious that the predictive force of the paper was in error. A new consensus was not developing around the reinterpretation of Burns's model of leadership (transactional leadership is really management and transformational leadership is leadership). If anything, as suggested in Chapter 4, the 1980s' consensus developed around a very old idea of leadership, the great man/ woman theory of leadership (do the leader's wishes), and not a reconstructed notion of leadership as transformation.

Second—and the leadership doctoral students were the first to identify this problem—the twelve differences between leadership and management developed in the paper were different more in degree than in fundamental nature. Several of the twelve contrasting elements did hit upon essential elements of each process, but the overall model gave the impression that the people practicing leadership were the "good guys in white hats" and the people practicing management were the mediocre types bungling the job, the "bad guys in black hats." (*Guys* is a slang expression that in common parlance is used to refer to both women and men.)

The model had a third problem. Traits and behaviors were used to explain some of the differences between leadership and management. I was very conscious of using them in writing the piece. While I didn't like using them, I didn't know of any way around that problem. This feature of the model, however, did not bother the large majority of those who read the paper because traits and behaviors were what they were used to reading about in leadership books and articles.

The good guy/bad guy scenario, however, did bother some thoughtful critics a great deal, and in the end it caused me to completely rethink the model and eventually to reject it. I had written the piece with the express purpose of not raising up leadership and putting down management, but the paper ended up giving that impression anyway, mostly in covert ways. Such is the nature of deeply held background assumptions, even when a person expresses the opposite view to him/herself and consciously believes the opposite view.

Indeed, the good guy/bad guy view of leadership/management is pervasive in the 1980s literature on leadership. The most recent and overtly stated example of this view is in Zaleznik's (1989) book. The title of the book states the point succinctly: *The Managerial Mystique: Restoring Leadership in Business.* The managerial mystique is the bad guy, the cause of U.S. business problems in the 1980s. Leadership is the good guy, and restoring leadership is the solution to the United States' business problems. Zaleznik's book is only the most recent of such tracts. Leadership was consistently viewed as excellent management in the 1980s. That, in a nutshell, is what the excellence movement is all about.

United Technologies struck a responsive chord with an advertisement published in numerous magazines in 1984. It was titled: "Let's Get Rid of Management," and its message was that "people don't want to be managed, they want to be led." (The advertisement was reprinted in Bennis & Nanus, 1985, p. 22.) H. Ross Perot is quoted in Kouzes and Posner (1987, p. xv) as expressing the same thought: "People cannot be managed. Inventories can be managed, but people must be led." The view of leadership and management presented in the advertisement and in the Perot quotation are great for symbolic mythmaking, but as a conceptual framework for understanding both leadership and management, it is dead wrong.

First of all, the universal human experience, at least in the Western world in the last few centuries, is that people do like to be managed—as long as management is not equated with dictatorship. If you want to find out how much people love management, try these simple strategies:

• Deliver the payroll checks late.
• Decrease the supplies people need to do their jobs.

- Stop any utility service people need to live or work.
- Have the buses, trains, airplanes run late.
- Eliminate stop lights on city streets.
- Deliver unworkable products to consumers.
- Tie promotions or salary raises to idiosyncratic criteria such as pleasing the whims of a supervisor.

The list could go on to include thousands of items that people have come to expect from being managed. We literally live in a managed society; management is what the industrial era is all about, and much of it is not going to change in the postindustrial era. Our civilization is so complex, it has to be managed. We have no other choice. As the saying goes, "We want our trains to run on time." And that epitomizes what managers and subordinates do when they manage.

Effective managers are a joy to behold and a pleasure to work with in any organization. People love to work for well-organized managers who facilitate getting the job done by coordinating the work of various people, and they hate to work for managers who are ineffective, uncoordinated, or incompetent. Most human beings crave order, stability, well-run programs, coordinated activity, patterned behavior, goal achievement, and the successful operation of an organization. They take pride in their ability to produce and deliver quality goods and services to consumers, and they are generally unhappy when the opposite conditions prevail. People generally like some predictability in their lives concerning the basic elements of living. That is the attraction of having the trains run on time. On the other hand, people become frustrated when they encounter poor or ineffective management, when the proverbial trains do not run on time. They vent their frustrations in many ways, from passivity and anomie to sabotage and revolution.

An example of this frustration with poor management can be seen in the revolutions in Eastern Europe in 1989–1990. The major causes of these revolutions will probably be debated for years to come. I heard a persuasive argument recently that the root cause of all the yearning for democracy was ethnic unrest. The Eastern European nations under Communist rule have never succeeded, this professor suggested, in gaining a real commitment to national unity from the various ethnic groups through some kind of melting pot strategy. The peoples in these countries identify with their ethnic group first and with their nation second. The cry for democracy has been a cry for ethnic freedom.

Another explanation may be just as persuasive. Despite, or maybe because of, the Communist belief in a planned economy and centralized (even dictatorial) control of society and business organizations, the Eastern bloc countries were badly managed. As a result, quality goods and services wanted and needed by the people were not delivered by the state. Some of the goods and services were not delivered at all. Thus, the revolution against the Communist system could be interpreted as a revolt against bad management and the effects that it has on people's lives and work. Under the Communist system, the people had no alternatives, since every-thing was strictly controlled by a few people at the top. Thus, they could not re-place bad managers with good managers, nor could they replace a bad system of management with a good one. The cry for freedom, then, was a cry for the freedom to select, among other things, the managers and the system of management that would provide them with the basic goods and services they had come to expect from life (and that they could easily see on television that the people of neighboring countries enjoyed). With freedom came the ability to choose one management sys-tem over another, rather than being forced to accept a management system that ob-viously has not been working.

If that analysis is even somewhat accurate, it shows that effective management is highly valued by people. If people are willing to risk life and limb to get rid of bad management; if people believe that the ability to obtain wanted goods and services from the effective management of business and governmental or-ganizations in their societies is essential to the good life; and if they engineer revolutions, in part, to throw out bad managers and a bad management system and to have the freedom to replace them with good managers and a better management system, then management is indeed a powerful process in our societies. Management is a process highly valued by people who do not have it operating effectively and do not have the power to change either the managers or the management system. Effective management is so widely expected as the normal operating procedure in highly developed countries that it is often taken for granted. The people in Eastern Europe found they could not take it for granted.

It is time to stop the denigration of management and begin to rethink the nature of management and its necessity to the operation of our complex societies and the organizations that help make these societies function. The view that management is less than satisfactory if it is not infused with leadership is un-acceptable as a conceptual framework to understand either management or lead-ership. That view contributes to the confusion over what leadership is and what management is. If we cannot manage effectively without leading, then certainly there is no fundamental distinction between leadership and management.

Scholars do not have to glamorize the concept of management by equating it (or good management) with the more popular concept of leadership. Manage-ment, pure and simple, is necessary and essential to the good life as we have come to experience it, and as such it has as much going for it as leadership does. It should be highly valued for what it is, not for what some authors want to make of it. Devaluing management in favor of leadership has disastrous effects in the everyday world of work and play. Human beings depend on the effective and efficient management of organizations hundreds of times every day, and that basic fact of life alone should make us want to understand the essential nature of management so as to promote and foster its widespread use in operating our organizations effectively and efficiently. Down with management and up with leadership is a bad idea.

Thus, I want to say quite forcefully that I reject the following views of leadership and management.

1. Management is ineffective unless it is equated with or infused with leadership.

2. Management is bad; leadership is good.

3. Management is a necessary but inadequate process in operating organizations. Leadership is needed at all times to operate any organization effectively.

4. Management is okay, but leadership is what makes the world go round.

5. Management is what got the United States into the mess that it is in vis-à-vis Japan and Germany and other international go-getters. Leadership is what will get the United States out of the mess. Or, management is what got the federal government into the mess that it is in with regard to the budget deficit, and leadership is what will get the federal government out of the mess. Or, management is what got the public schools into the mess they are in regarding low student learning, dropouts, and so on, and leadership is what will get the public schools out of the mess. And so on.

The difficulty with all of these statements is that they, one and all, denigrate management and ennoble leadership. Leadership is not the answer to all the ills of our societies or their institutions and organizations. Leadership may, in some cases, be part of the answers. (Note the plural!) But management, properly understood, is also part of the answers. Any concept of leadership that dignifies leadership at the expense of management has to be defective. Exalting leadership by casting aspersions on management is an inherently flawed approach to understanding the nature of either concept.

The second problem with these statements is that they assume leadership is always good, effective, and helpful. There is, according to this view, no such thing as bad or ineffective leadership. Bad leadership is an oxymoron. Again, this approach to leadership may be adequate for symbolic mythmaking, but it does not square with the lived experience of human beings since the word *leadership* came into common usage. Including an effectiveness dimension in our understanding of leadership creates all kinds of conceptual and practical problems in any attempt to come to terms with the nature of leadership. The same is true of management, except that most people do not automatically equate management with being good or effective. In both the scholarly and the popular press and among practitioners, there *is* a notion of bad management. There is no similar notion of bad leadership in most of the leadership literature and among practitioners, especially in the 1980s.

The practical results of requiring leadership to be effective or good are readily apparent. It does not work when we try to make sense out of the distinction between leadership and management. The conceptual result of such a view is that either (1) management cannot be effective, since whenever it becomes effective, it turns into leadership, or (2) leadership must include management because leadership is management that is good. At the very least, management becomes a necessary but inadequate element in defining leadership. What, then, happens to the definition when people experience leadership in a relationship wherein no one is a manager and the process of management is not occurring? The definition quickly loses its validity.

The practical result of such a view is to require every manager to be a leader because leaders are an absolutely essential element in all notions of leadership. Being only a manager means that one is relegated to being an ineffective professional person. Thus, being a leader becomes essential to the self-concept of every manager, clearly an impossible task, if not an inhuman requirement, for many people.

Finally, such a view in effect makes leadership as a concept redundant. If leadership is good management, the concept of leadership is superfluous because management as a construct had a lengthy and illustrious linguistic history long before people started talking and writing about leadership. As we have seen, leadership as a concept is relatively new, whereas the concept of authority or management is ages old. There must be something more to leadership as a concept than redundancy.

DEFINING MANAGEMENT

If leadership is an influence relationship among leaders and followers who intend real changes that reflect their mutual purposes, what is management? Taking a cue from the four essential elements of the definition of leadership, I would like to suggest a corresponding definition of management. *Management is an authority relationship between at least one manager and one subordinate who coordinate their activities to produce and sell particular goods and/or services.*

From this definition, a person can identify four essential elements for a phenomenon to be labeled management:

1. Management is an authority relationship.
2. The people in this relationship include at least one manager and one subordinate.
3. The manager(s) and subordinate(s) coordinate their activities.
4. The manager(s) and subordinate(s) produce and sell particular goods and/or services.

Some discussion of each of these essential elements follows. Since my purpose is to explicate the difference between leadership and management, not to explicate a full-blown model of management, the discussion is limited to what is necessary to distinguish between leadership and management.

Authority Relationship

The first element is that management is a relationship based on authority. This element contains two points.

Management is a relationship. Many management scholars do not view management as a relationship but conceive of it as either (1) a manager doing certain behaviors, such as organizing, planning, staffing, communicating, motivating, controlling, and decision making, or (2) the process whereby a manager gets the job (whatever that job is) done efficiently and effectively. In both of these models of management, as well as others that could be cited, management is what the manager does. Management is not what both the manager and subordinate do, only what the manager does.

The behavior of managers is a necessary but insufficient explanation of the nature of management as a concept. The behaviors of managers make no sense without the corresponding behaviors of subordinates, and so I view management as a relationship.

The distinguishing feature of this relationship is that it is based on authority. Authority is a contractual (written, spoken, or implied) relationship wherein people accept superordinate or subordinate responsibilities in an organization. By its very nature, authority includes the use of both coercive and noncoercive actions. The contract allows the managers to tell the subordinates what to do, and some of this telling is coercive. Management as a concept is built on such telling: "Sell this product for $3.95"; "Put a half-inch nut on this bolt on this part of the product"; "Do these five problems for homework tonight"; "Be at work at 7:30 A.M."; "Stop at all stop lights when they are red"; "Pay a percentage of your income for Social Security"; "Take this patient to the lab for an X-ray"; "Enter the name of the product in these 25 spaces on the bill of sale"; and so on.

Not all the behaviors in any management relationship are coercive. The point is that many of them are (while many of them may not be), and the second point is that coercive behaviors are perfectly acceptable to both managers and subordinates. While subordinates may resent some coercive behaviors—for instance, a police officer giving a person a ticket for running a red light—most subordinates accept the general pattern of coercive action in the management of organizations—for instance, a law requiring everyone to stop at red lights and police officers to enforce the law.

Manager and Subordinate

The people in the relationship called management are at least one manager and one subordinate. This is the second essential element in the definition.

Both words are in the singular because it takes at least two people to have a relationship, and we know from information readily available to anyone who looks for it that some organizations are actually managed by only two people, one being a manager and the other being a subordinate. Such organizations are not very typical any more, but they are a reality. If management actually happens in such organizations, and I believe it does, the definition must be worded to include them.

Generally speaking, however, most management relationships include one manager and several subordinates or, even more typical, numerous managers and even more numerous subordinates.

Both of these words (manager and subordinate) indicate positions within an organization. It is easy to identify who is a manager and who is a subordinate in an organization because they are positions identified on the organization chart or in a contract. A manager is a person who is contracted to manage an organization or some part of one; a subordinate is a person who reports to the manager and is contractually required to obey the manager. To make things complicated, some people are both managers and subordinates in an organization. Teachers, for instance, are subordinates in relationship to the principal or superintendent, but they are managers in relationship to the students.

If both the manager and the subordinate are part of the relationship called management, it follows that they both are involved in management. A relationship cannot exist unless both parties contribute to it.

The contributions, however, are not necessarily equal. In fact, in management the component parts of the relationship are inherently unequal, with the manager having the dominant part and the subordinate—as the name indicates—having the subordinate part. Management is a two-way relationship that is primarily top-down as to the directives given and bottom-up as to the responses given. In more democratic or flat organizations, the two-way relationship may be more horizontal than hierarchical.

Coordination of Activities

The third essential element in the definition of management is that the manager and subordinate coordinate their activities. The coordination of activities is necessary if the relationship is to achieve its purpose—the production and sale of goods and/or services. Coordinating their activities is the means whereby the manager(s) and subordinate(s) achieve their goal. Without some coordination, goods or services could not be produced or sold. The goods and/or services are the result of the coordinated activities of the manager(s) and subordinate(s) who enter into the authority relationship.

Production and Sale of Particular Goods and/or Services

The manager and subordinate are in a relationship to produce and sell particular goods and/or services.

Producing and selling are the raison d'être of management. They are the heart of the relationship called management. Both are essential. Producing is the expense, and selling is the income. While some people in public organizations may think that selling is not part of the management of their organizations, since many clients or consumers might not pay for the services specifically rendered to them, such a view of public management is inaccurate. Public management involves the selling of services to the public because income to cover the expenses of the services is required for the organization not only to exist but also to prosper.

Producing and selling are the purpose of the relationship that is management. They are why people enter into the relationship. They are what the people in the relationship do. They identify what the relationship is all about. Management is a relationship established in organizations so that people can produce and sell particular goods and/or services.

Goods and/or services are also what the people in the relationship produce by their coordinated activities. Management is essential to their production. However, the relationship goes further than just production. The people in the relationship also sell these goods and/or services because they understand that focusing only on production will get them nowhere. Thus, the relationship is incomplete unless the products are sold.

The word *particular* precedes goods and/or services in the definition because the manager(s) and subordinate(s) coordinate their activities to produce and sell only certain goods and/or services, not any or all goods and services.

And/or is used in the definition because I am not certain that all managerial relationships involve both goods and services. Its use allows for some managerial relationships to produce and sell one or the other, not both. My guess is that the large majority of managerial relationships involve both.

LEADERSHIP AND MANAGEMENT

The definition given above does not require management to be effective or ineffective, good or bad, efficient or inefficient, excellent or mediocre, and so on. All of these words are adjectives that people can apply to particular managerial relationships when they evaluate the management of an organization according to stated criteria. These evaluative criteria are different from the essential elements analysts should use as criteria to determine if the phenomenon is management. Thus, there is a two-step process. First, one must determine if the phenomenon is management. Second, the analyst can then determine if the relationship that is management is effective or ineffective, good or bad, efficient or inefficient, excellent or mediocre.

The same statement can be made about leadership. The definition of leadership given in Chapter 5 does not require leadership to be effective or ineffective, good or bad, efficient or inefficient, excellent or mediocre, and so on. All of these words are adjectives that people can apply to a particular relationship that is determined to be leadership when they evaluate that relationship according to predetermined criteria. That evaluation comes after the analyst determines if the phenomenon is actually leadership. The two-step process is the same as that for evaluating management.

The essential nature of management as a relationship and that of leadership as a relationship are neutral to all such evaluative criteria. Management that is

Table 6.1
Distinguishing Leadership from Management

LEADERSHIP	MANAGEMENT
Influence relationship	Authority relationship
Leaders and followers	Managers and subordinates
Intend real changes	Produce and sell goods and/or services
Intended changes reflect mutual purposes	Goods/Services result from coordinated activities

ineffective, bad, inefficient, or mediocre is still management. Leadership that is ineffective, bad, inefficient, or mediocre is still leadership. Management that is effective, good, efficient, or excellent is still management. These qualities do not transform management into leadership. The idea that good management is leadership destroys any possible clear definition of both leadership and management. Leadership as good management mixes both management and leadership into a mishmash of conceptual confusion. Out of that confusion comes our inability to distinguish leadership from management (and vice versa) and our inability to intelligently understand either concept.

DISTINGUISHING BETWEEN MANAGEMENT AND LEADERSHIP

Using the essential elements of the two definitions, four substantive differences between leadership and management can be ascertained. The first three are clear and distinct, and scholars and practitioners can easily use them to distinguish between leadership and management. The last difference is perhaps less distinctive and is, therefore, more difficult to use in distinguishing leadership from management.

Table 6.1 presents the four differences between leadership and management in short statements. A discussion of each of these differences follows.

Influence vs. Authority Relationship

The difference is that leadership is an influence relationship and management is an authority relationship. The differences in these two kinds of relationships have to do with (1) use of coercion and (2) directionality of the attempts to impact on people.

Influence requires that coercion not be used, at least as a regular and patterned form of behavior. Authority allows the use of coercion as a regular and patterned form of behavior.

Attempts to influence other people in a leadership relationship are multidirectional. Leaders influence other leaders and followers while followers influence other followers and leaders. Attempts to use authority in a managerial relationship are unidirectional and top-down. Managers use authority to impact on subordinates, who then respond to the authoritative directive, producing the two-way relationship. While there may be more democratic relationships between managers and subordinates these days, the basic and fundamental relationship remains top-down.

Leaders and Followers vs. Managers and Subordinates

Leaders and followers are the people involved in a leadership relationship. Subordinates can be leaders, as can managers. Managers can be followers, as can subordinates. Leaders and followers can have a relationship that includes no managers and no subordinates.

Managers and subordinates are the people involved in a managerial relationship. Followers can be managers, as can subordinates. Leaders can be subordinates, as can followers. Managers and subordinates can be involved in a relationship that includes no leaders and no followers.

The two sets of words are not synonymous. Leaders are not the same as managers. Followers are not the same as subordinates. Managers may be leaders, but if they are leaders, they are involved in a relationship different from management. Subordinates may be followers, but if they are followers, they are involved in a relationship different from management. Leaders need not be managers to be leaders. Followers need not be subordinates to be followers.

People in authority positions—presidents, governors, mayors, CEOs, superintendents, principals, administrators, supervisors, department heads, and so on—are not automatically leaders by virtue of their holding a position of authority. Being a leader must not be equated with being in a position of authority. The definition of a leader cannot include a requirement that the person be in a position of authority. Such a definition of a leader is totally inconsistent with the definition of leadership given in Chapter 5.

On the other hand, people in authority positions are automatically managers because that is the definition of a manager: a person who holds a position of authority. Being a manager must not be equated with being a leader. The definition of a manager cannot include a requirement that the person be a leader. Such a definition of a manager is totally inconsistent with both the definition of leadership presented in Chapter 5 and the definition of management given above.

A distinction between leadership and management requires that the words *leader* and *manager*, *follower* and *subordinate*, be defined differently. The two sets of words cannot be used interchangeably.

Intending Real Changes vs. Producing and Selling Goods and/or Services

Leaders and followers intend real changes, while managers and subordinates produce and sell goods and/or services.

Leadership involves an intention on the part of leaders and followers. Management involves the production and sale on the part of managers and subordinates. Intending is very different from producing and selling.

Leadership involves (intending) real changes. Management involves (producing and selling) goods and services. Leaders and followers join forces to attempt to really change something. Managers and subordinates join forces to produce and sell goods and/or services. When managers and subordinates join forces to really change the ways they produce and sell their goods/services, or really change the kind of goods/services they produce and sell, those managers and subordinates may have transformed their managerial relationship into a leadership relationship. (I say *may* because the three other essential elements must be present for there to be leadership.)

Mutual Purpose vs. Coordinated Activities

The intended changes must reflect the mutual purposes of the leaders and followers. The goods and/or services result from the coordinated activities of the managers and subordinates.

There is nothing in the definition of management about mutual purposes, so when one sees mutual purposes being forged in a relationship, that is a cue that leadership is happening. (Again, the three other essential elements have to be present.) Mutual purposes are more than independent goals mutually held. They are common purposes developed over time as followers and leaders interact in a noncoercive relationship about the changes they intend. Leaders and followers are constantly in the process of developing mutual purposes, and their commitment to that development makes the leadership relationship different from the management relationship.

Coordinated activities, on the other hand, allow for independent goals mutually agreed upon by managers and subordinates in order to get the job done, in order to produce and sell particular goods and/or services. Coordinated activities include negotiated agreements, exchanges, transactional accommodations, and compromises. They also include telling subordinates what to do: ''Barbara and

Bill will watch the children eating in the cafeteria while John and Jane monitor them on the playground and Mary and Mark organize games for them in the field so that six other faculty members can eat lunch.'' Coordinated activities include staffing and other ways of deploying resources, making decisions about how goods are going to be made and sold and about how services are going to be delivered and sold.

None of those activities are necessary to leadership as a relationship, primarily because leadership is not about producing and selling goods and/or services. Some of these activities may not even be helpful to particular leaders and followers who intend real changes. The leadership relationship allows for a great many activities that would not be classified as coordinated activities in the ordinary sense of the term: revolution, reform, demonstrations, rallies, breaking unjust laws, charismatic behaviors, intuitive decisions, behaving according to new governing assumptions, ad hoc committees, disrupting coordinated activities, unplanned actions, and so on. These kinds of activities may be clues that leadership is happening and that management is not.

Of course, a leadership relationship may involve coordinated activities, but the crucial point is that these coordinated activities are not essential to leadership. They are, however, essential to management. It is impossible to conceive of people in a management relationship producing and selling goods and/or services without coordinated activities.

7

Leadership and Ethics in the 1990s

INTRODUCTION

The difficulty with the word *ethics* is that it can be applied in two areas of human relationships.

The first area is that of process. The question regarding process is: Does one act ethically in one's relations with other human beings while attempting to influence them? Thus, if we want to deal with the ethics of leadership, part of our concern must be with the ways leaders and followers interact as they attempt to influence one another and other people not in the leadership relationship.

The second area is that of content. The question regarding content is: Are the changes (decisions, policies, positions) that one supports morally acceptable? Thus, if we want to deal with the ethics of leadership, part of our concern must be with the ethical content of the proposed changes that leaders and followers intend for an organization and/or society.

If this distinction makes sense, people could expect to see leaders and followers using ethical process to pursue unethical changes, and also see leaders and followers using unethical processes to support ethical changes. The ideal situation, of course, is for leaders and followers to use ethical processes in working for ethical changes. Figure 7.1 shows the four combinations that are possible in conceptualizing the ethics of leadership.

Figure 7.1
The Ethics of Leadership

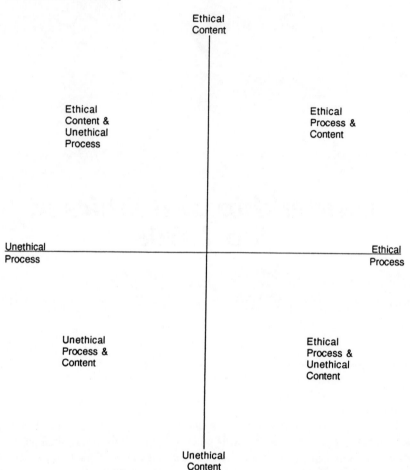

Leadership, being an influence relationship among leaders and followers who intend real changes that reflect their mutual purposes, is concerned with both process and content. The reason for this double concern is clear from the definition. Since leaders and followers interact to influence one another about the changes they intend, that interaction—those attempts to influence one another—are crucial to the relationship and to its health, mutuality, growth, development, and success. The way leaders and followers use influence, power, and authority to process decisions about the relationship and about the changes they intend is important to the relationship, to the people who make up the relationship. To take a worst-case scenario, some followers may decide that they do not want to continue in the leadership relationship because one or more of the leaders have not used a collaborative process to make those important decisions. Or some leaders may decide that they want to quit the leadership relationship because many of the followers have been too passive.

Conversely, since leaders and followers intend real changes that reflect their mutual purposes, the content of those changes is crucial to the relationship that is leadership. What changes are proposed, what specifics are in the proposal, and how the changes impact the people and groups in the organization and/or society are important issues to the relationship, to the people who make up the relationship. Some followers, for instance, may decide that they want to drop out of the leadership relationship because they disagree with the specific changes in a proposal although they may agree with its general thrust. Or some leaders may wish to discontinue their involvement in the leadership relationship because they believe the proposed changes are not consistent with their vision of the organization. In both cases, the followers and leaders want to break off the relationship because they believe the proposed changes do not reflect their mutual interests.

If the above analysis is accurate, leaders and followers must pay close attention to both the process and the content of the leadership relationship. The reality is, however, that both leaders and followers in the United States pay much more attention to the content of the proposed changes than they do to the process of the relationship when questions of ethics arise. There may be some change toward more concern for process in the political arena throughout the United States. (One interpretation of the Speaker Jim Wright affair, for example, is that a concern for ethical processes in the leadership of the House of Representatives brought his downfall.) Be that as it may, there does not seem to be much movement to deal with ethical process issues in leadership relationships in businesses and professional organizations. One certainly does not see much change in the overemphasis on content issues in the ethics literature used in graduate programs in professional schools.

This state of affairs may be understandable in view of the management and professional interests to which that ethics literature appeals. That literature does not attend to the relationship I have defined here as leadership. Again, the confusion in the literature of equating leadership with management appears.

THE ETHICS OF THE LEADERSHIP PROCESS

If leadership is an influence relationship, then the process whereby leaders and followers interact becomes crucial to the ethics of leadership. The process defines both the nature of leadership and its ethical integrity.

Ethics and the Definition of Leadership

Using influence as a definitional standard, leaders and followers must be attentive to the influence process that forges the relationship. They must guard their relationship from attempts by both leaders and followers to use coercive and authoritarian methods to control the relationship, to promote their own purposes, or to win approval of their specific proposals. The tendency, of course, is for leaders to manipulate the relationship by coercive and/or authoritarian means, but followers can also be guilty of these behaviors.

The reason why these types of behaviors cause definitional problems is twofold: They go against standard, commonsense notions of influence that characterize leadership relationships, and they contradict elemental notions of the mutuality that the changes must reflect. In common terms, then, coercive and authoritarian demands are neither influential nor mutual. When coercive and authoritarian processes are characteristic of a relationship, we can no longer call it leadership.

It is important to be clear on this point because we can set too high a standard for a relationship to be called leadership. We also have to take into account the human condition, since we humans are far from perfect in the way we develop relationships. Thus, it is important, I believe, to state that one or two authoritarian commands or coercive actions do not a relationship make. Most human relationships are going to be marred by lapses, by straying from the path, by unwanted behaviors. Such situations are inevitable in leadership relationships, and a discussion of the ethics of leadership behavior must take them into account.

In dealing with the nature of leadership, what we need to assess and analyze is the pattern of behaviors that make up the relationship, the pattern of interactions that characterize the process of leadership. Here, the standard of influence can be used by leaders and followers to decide what kind of relationship they are in. A relationship in which the pattern of behaviors is classified as predominantly coercive and authoritarian is not leadership.

If, on the other hand, the pattern of behaviors is classified as predominantly influential, if the pattern of interactions is multidirectional, then influence can be used as an ethical standard to make judgments about any individual or group behaviors that might be questionable or a cause of concern. In this situation, defining the relationship is not the concern; rather, the concern is the ethics of particular actions of individual leaders and/or followers who are engaged in leadership.

Ethical Perspectives of the Leadership Process

Influence is not an easy concept to define in practical and meaningful ways. Part of the problem is that no matter what the general definition might be, and even given some assent to the definition, what each of us sees as influential is always going to be based, in part, on our perceptual and personal screens. John uses his perceptual screen to evaluate particular behaviors as attempts to influence, but Peter may see the same behaviors as coercive even though he is using the same definition of influence, because of his perceptual screen. Some part of our perceptual screens may be gender-induced, so that Jane may see certain behaviors are influential and James may see the same behaviors as coercive, even though both agree upon a definition of influence.

When certain actions are directed at me personally, I may see them as coercive;

but when those same actions are directed at another person in the organization or society, I may see them as influential. We human beings often tend to take different perspectives concerning behaviors that affect us personally as opposed to behaviors that affect other persons.

I do not think there is any way of getting around the perceptual and personal problems of applying ethical standards to particular behaviors in a relationship. Perceptual and personal screens are not going to go away, so people have to learn to live with them both conceptually and practically. No matter how much conceptual clarity scholars can give to the notion of influence, the way people use the concept of influence to evaluate individual behaviors will always be susceptible to assumptions that make up our perceptual and personal screens. That again is the human condition, which inevitably makes behavioral science messy.

Having said that, I think that the concept of influence must be clarified if we are going to make any progress concerning the ethics of the leadership process. A beginning definition might be: Influence is an interactive process in which people attempt to convince other people to believe and/or act in certain ways. In an effort to flesh out that definition and help clarify what actions would fall within the concept of influence, I offer the following points.

First, certain actions that use physical force can be ruled out completely. Such actions are quintessentially coercive and can never be assessed as falling within the concept of influence.

Second, specific actions that overtly command obedience in the name of some recognized and legitimate authority also can be eliminated completely. Such actions may be entirely proper, legal, acceptable, and even necessary within organizations, but they must be judged as falling within the concept of authority (management), not the concept of influence. Influence allows individuals in a relationship the ability to choose a course of action without leaving the relationship. Actions that command obedience do not.

Third, actions that include a threat of certain consequences if one does not agree or behave in prescribed ways are more or less coercive, depending on the seriousness of the consequences to the person(s) being threatened and, perhaps, on other criteria. Threats may be in the form of either rewards or punishments. Some of these actions (especially those which threaten serious punishments) are more properly termed *power wielding*, since these actions are done in order to gain the actor's objectives, not the mutual purposes of the people in the relationship.

Generally, people tend to view these behaviors as coercive, especially if the actions are directed toward them. The primary reason for this evaluation is that these behaviors tend to inhibit choice. But the reality is that consequences— whether overtly stated, implied, or rationally analyzed—are part of the way we human beings make decisions, solve problems, and choose alternatives. Not much of importance in our lives is without consequences, and a fact of life is that these consequences greatly *influence* our choices and our actions. Threatening consequences, therefore, cannot be eliminated from a realistic concept of influence.

The above discussion suggests why scholars and practitioners have been unable to clearly understand power and influence as relationships and to distinguish between them. Power resources can be used to influence and, conversely, can be used to coerce. When power resources are used to influence, are the concepts of power and influence, defined as interactive relationships (see Bell, 1975), clearly distinguishable? Perhaps not.

The ethics of threatening consequences in a leadership relationship must be based on considerations other than the use of threats. Threatening consequences can be of considerable service to many people in a leadership relationship because the threats may more clearly point up problems and difficulties of various proposals for change—or, alternatively, may point up their benefits and promises. The bottom line of deciding the ethics of threatening consequences goes to the heart of the meaning of influence: Do the people in the relationship (leaders and followers) have freedom of choice or is it, for all practical purposes, taken away? If the people have the ability to choose, the threatening behaviors are within the concept of influence. If they do not have the practical possibility of making a choice, the threatening behaviors are coercive and are not within the concept of influence.

Fourth, actions that intend to psychologically intimidate others are more or less coercive, depending on the extent of the intimidation and, perhaps, on other criteria. The emphasis here is on the word *psychological*. Physical abuse, authoritative commands, and power-wielding threats are more overt and obvious forms of intimidation, and are excluded from consideration here because they have already been dealt with in the first three points. The actions being discussed here tend to be more covert, more subtle, more clever, and more indirect. They may be played out over a longer period of time than other forms of power, authority, and influence.

Intimidation is a good example of where perceptual and personal differences enter the concept of influence. Some people are hard to intimidate, others are quite easy to intimidate, and the majority of us fall somewhere in the middle. Actions directed at a group of people will intimidate some people in the group and not others. John could be intimidated by a particular behavior, and that same behavior could have no intimidating effect on Jane.

Another confounding factor in judging the ethics of intimidation is the issue of intention and motive. Some actions show clear intentions and motivations, and are easy to assess from an ethical perspective. However, some people in a relationship may intimidate others by the force of their personalities or their habits of assertiveness. Colors, clothes, and posture, as well as the size and gender of a person, have all been shown to be sources of unintended intimidation of people. What is the ethics of unintentionally intimidating others? I think that behaviors which produce unintended intimidation cannot be ruled out of ethically based leadership relationships.

While the ethics of intimidation in a leadership relationship may be decided partially on the basis of intention or motive of the actor, I believe the key determinant is the extent of intimidation, the impact the intimidation has on the relationship that is leadership. Do these intimidating actions seriously lessen or weaken the mutuality of the relationship? Do they, for all practical purposes, eliminate the multidirectionality of the interaction and influence? Do they make choice practically impossible? Do they encourage passivity on the part of the followers in particular?

Again, I think that we have to be careful not to set too strict a criterion within which leaders and followers must operate. Leadership is, after all, a process oriented to changing organizations and societies. Change is not easily done, nor does it come naturally. The research on change unanimously confirms that the normal reaction of people is to resist change. People who want to involve themselves in leadership relationships should have realistic expectations of how organizations and societies change and how the people who are members of these organizations and societies change. Use of power resources to threaten consequences (the third point above) and use of psychological intimidation to encourage movement from fixed positions or from rigid, self-interested considerations may be essential to influencing some human beings to change their organizations and societies. Lacking those tactics, the only other methods to change organizations may be physical force, authoritative commands, and power wielding. Intimidation may look good when compared with those alternatives. In summary, I think we have to leave a little room for intimidation in the ethics of the leadership process.

Fifth, actions that are aimed at persuading others to one's point of view, toward one's vision of the organization or society, toward one's proposal for change are generally thought of as within the concept of influence. People view persuasive behavior as noncoercive because persuasion allows the element of choice to operate in the interaction among the people in a leadership relationship. In fact, most people involved in some change process expect that others will attempt to persuade them and that they will attempt to persuade others.

Dictionaries define *persuade* as "to cause (someone) to do something by means of argument, reasoning, or entreaty" and "to win over (someone) to a course of action by reasoning or inducement" and "to make (someone) believe something" (*The American Heritage Dictionary*). Note the connotative differences in those definitions.

Neustadt (1980) has an extended discussion of persuasion. He frames his discussion around the U.S. presidency, but I have taken the liberty of generalizing his framework by using brackets. Neustadt states that the essence of persuasion is "to convince [people] that what [you] want of them is what they ought to do for their own sake and on their own authority. Persuasive power, thus defined, amounts to more than charm or reasoned argument" (p. 27). Status and authority are important to persuasion because they give some people clear advantages. But other people have similar or other advantages. In the end, Neustadt concluded, "Persuasion is a two-way street." (p. 28). "The power to persuade is the power to bargain" (p. 28). "Power is persuasion and persuasion becomes bargaining'' (p. 30). ''Influence derives from bargaining advantages; power is a give-and-take'' (p. 30).

The essence of a [person's] persuasive task with [others who have authority] and everybody else, is to induce them to believe that what he [she] wants of them is what their own appraisal of their own responsibilities requires them to do in their interests, not his [hers]. Because men [women] may differ in their views on public policy, because differences in outlook stem from differences in duty—duty to one's office, one's constituents, oneself—that task is bound to be more like collective bargaining than like a reasoned argument among philosopher kings. Overtly or implicitly, hard bargaining has characterized all illustrations offered up to now. This is the reason why: persuasion deals in the coin of self-interest with men [women] who have some freedom to reject what they find counterfeit. (p. 35)

My own view of persuasion adheres rather closely to Neustadt's. Along with rational discourse, persuasion involves the use of reputation, prestige, personality, purpose, status, content of the message, interpersonal and group skills, give-and-take behaviors, authority or lack of it, symbolic interaction, perception, motivation, gender, race, religion, and choices, among countless other things. I call these things power resources. Influence does not come out of thin air. It comes from leaders and followers using power resources to persuade.

Having defined persuasion as more than reasoned argument to convince others to believe or do something, the ethics of using persuasion to influence takes on new meaning for those interested in the ethics of the leadership process. If persuasion is more than reasoned argument, the ethical question becomes: How much of one's power resources can one put into the persuasive process before the power of persuasion becomes power wielding? Particulars aside, the answer must revolve around the same bottom line that has been given twice—the freedom to choose alternatives different from what the persuader has in mind. This freedom is not just theoretical, nor does it involve the freedom to leave the relationship. It means the practical possibility that I may choose not to be persuaded, that I may decide to believe and act in ways of my own—choosing despite attempts by others to convince me to believe and act in ways they have chosen. It means the practical possibility of so choosing and still belonging to and being actively involved in the leadership relationship. If such practical possibilities do not exist, the persuasive behavior is unethical in the leadership process because it goes beyond the bounds of influence within which leaders and followers must interact.

Summary: The Ethics of the Leadership Process

Pastin (1986), in a very thought-provoking book on the ethics of management, makes the following point: ''An ideal [ethical] organization adds to the autonomy and value of the individuals who are the organization. It does not require that individuals sacrifice some of their integrity to belong to the organization''

(p. xiv). I want to paraphrase that statement in terms of leadership, and I would claim that the statement reflects not an ideal notion of leadership but, in a very strict sense, an accurate concept of how leadership *really* works. Leadership, correctly understood, operates this way: "Leadership adds to the autonomy and value of the individuals who are in the relationship. Leadership does not require that individuals sacrifice some of their integrity to be in the relationship."

This is the reason why: Leadership is an influence relationship wherein leaders and followers propose real changes that reflect their mutual purposes. Since leaders and followers use influence to agree upon proposals for change that reflect their mutual purposes, they use their autonomy and value in the leadership relationship and do not have to sacrifice their integrity to belong to that relationship. The very essence of multidirectional influence and mutuality requires that individual autonomy, value, and integrity be maintained. The ethics of the leadership process requires that the leaders and followers use influence in their interactions to achieve this mutuality. All other behaviors are unethical in a leadership relationship.

In a discussion of social contract ethics in a later chapter, Pastin (1986) developed a two-pronged test for deciding the ethics of a contract that could well be translated to the concept of leadership and used as the bottom-line criteria for evaluating the ethics of the leadership process.

"Social contract ethics offers a standard: A contract is sound if the parties to the contract would enter the contract *freely* and *fairly*" (p. 136). Pastin does not define *freely* except to equate it with *voluntarily* in later chapters of the book. He does, however, define *fairly* quite descriptively. "A contract is fair if the parties would freely agree to the contract even if their roles might be switched upon enactment of the contract. . . . If you grasp the single turnabout-is-fair-play idea of this paragraph, you know the secret" (p. 137).

It is an interesting and perceptive secret. Translated to the leadership process, the ethical standard of any leadership relationship would be stated this way: "The leadership process is ethical if the people in the relationship (the leaders and followers) *freely* agree that the intended changes *fairly* reflect their mutual purposes."

In order for the people in the relationship to freely agree that the changes fairly reflect their mutual purposes, the leaders and followers would have to have used persuasive and similar behaviors that allow for interactive (multidirectional) influence. Such a process would more or less guarantee that they would freely agree to the proposed changes even if their places might be changed upon enactment of the changes. Leadership by free and fair agreement thus becomes the ethical standard for the leadership process.

The sine qua non of free and fair agreements is persuasion, defined as using rational discourse and other power resources to convince the people in the relationship to believe or do something. The antithesis of free and fair agreements is physical force, authoritarian commands, and other forms of coercion to gain compliance. Falling somewhere between persuasion and compliance are efforts to manipulate behavior by threats of consequences and psychological intimidation. The ethics of manipulation involve the same standard: free and fair agreements. How much room do the threats and intimidations leave for the people in the relationship to freely agree that the proposed changes fairly reflect the mutual purposes of the followers and leaders? If there is little or no room for free and fair agreement, the threats and intimidations are unethical. If there is considerable room for free and fair agreement, the threats and intimidations are ethical. In the first instance, those behaviors would be evaluated as power wielding and not influence. In the second situation, the behaviors would be evaluated as influential, and therefore ethical.

Messy? Absolutely! So is the human condition. So is change. And so is the relationship we call leadership.

THE ETHICS OF LEADERSHIP CONTENT

Leaders and followers intend real changes. Those changes are filled with content: organized facts gathered in patterned ways, conceptual frameworks that help to make sense of the data, rational analyses of various proposals based on some personal and/or professional criteria, and ethical judgments of the value of alternative proposals based on some moral criteria. Leaders and followers have numerous options in supporting various change proposals, and not all the options are necessarily good from an ethical perspective. Changes are not value free; they have ethical ramifications for leaders and followers. That is the subject I wish to explore in this section.

The content of leadership has to do with the issues that leaders and followers tackle, and more specifically with the changes that leaders and followers propose concerning those issues. For instance, the issue might be abortion. Some leaders and followers support a policy favoring the baby's right to life. Other leaders and followers support a policy favoring the woman's right to make decisions about her own body. The ethical content of leadership has to do with the moral judgments that leaders and followers make when they support one or the other of those policies. Which one of those proposed changes is ethically acceptable? Which one of those proposed changes is ethically unacceptable?

In another example, the issue might be AIDS. Some leaders and followers propose a policy that encourages people to use condoms when having sex. Other leaders and followers propose a policy that encourages people not to have sex outside of marriage. What is the ethics of supporting either of those proposed changes? Or, concerning the treatment of AIDS, some leaders and followers support a policy that opens up various experimental medical treatments to people who have AIDS, while other leaders and followers want to control experimental medical treatments until they have been proven safe and effective. What is the ethics of supporting either of those proposed changes?

These are the questions that leaders and followers have to ask about the ethical content of leadership. The reader will note that these are very different questions from those posed about the process of leadership. To repeat an earlier statement, I suggested that it is possible for leaders and followers to engage in the leadership process ethically but to propose unethical changes. Alternatively, it is possible for leaders and followers to propose ethical changes by using an unethical process of leadership. The point is that the two areas of ethical concern are not the same. Making sure that the leadership process is ethical does not mean that the content of leadership will be ethical. Not all ethical leadership processes result in leadership content (changes) that are ethical. There is no cause-and-effect relationship between the process and the content of leadership.

Some Ethical Ambiguities of the Content of Leadership

The issues with which modern leaders and followers have to deal and the proposed changes that leaders and followers support often have no clear-cut ethical advantage. Indeed, in some cases it may be very difficult to discern what option has an ethical advantage. Modern problems are sometimes so complex that all options have some ethical advantages and some ethical disadvantages, leaving the leaders and followers with an ethical ambiguity at best.

Rationally, we have the same difficulty with modern problems of organizations and societies. Many of these problems do not admit of any one best solution or any permanent solution. So our leaders and followers constantly struggle to find partial solutions to problems that continuously recycle themselves through the policy-making process of an organization or society.

Little wonder, then, that the people who are unable to find the best rational solution to a problem are unable to agree on the ethical solution to that problem. Indeed, the two difficulties are related because some of the best solutions to modern problems are considered unethical and are, as a result, rejected by leaders and followers. In such instances, they are left with selecting second-best solutions, and the recycling of problems continues.

People of high morals take opposite sides in proposing changes to deal with modern, controversial issues. Leaders and followers of considerable moral integrity are constantly debating the higher moral ground of proposed changes to solve such problems as population control, unfair competition, nuclear energy, discrimination, polluted air and streams in urban areas, euthanasia, affirmative action, highway construction through residential neighborhoods, acid rain, capital punishment, smoking in public places, abortion, placement of garbage dumps, standardized tests in education, the destruction of rain forests, quality control, bribery in foreign countries where it is an accepted practice, nuclear deterrence, privacy vs. information networks, drugs, excessive charges for products and services, private lives of public officials, terrorist impact on citizens, and resource conservation. The list of such problems that admit of proposed changes which have ambiguous ethical ramifications is almost endless. So what can be said about the ethics of the content of leadership?

Transformational Leadership

One answer that is popular these days came from James MacGregor Burns, who developed the concept of transformational leadership in his 1978 book on the subject. Transformational leadership, according to Burns, "occurs when one or more persons *engage* with others in such a way that leaders and followers raise one another to higher levels of motivation and morality" (p. 20).

As explained in previous chapters, Burns conceived of another kind of leadership that he called transactional leadership. His definition of transactional leadership does not contain any moral element. Thus, leaders and followers engaging in transactional leadership could support what they and others might evaluate as immoral changes to solve organizational and societal problems. Burns did not claim that all leadership has to be morally uplifting; only transformational leadership had to have that quality. Many readers—followers—of Burns's leadership framework seem to forget or choose to ignore his theory of transactional leadership.

Be that as it may, I have come to the conclusion that Burns's notion of transformational leadership does not help leaders and followers deal realistically with the conceptual ambiguities of the ethical content of leadership. I have three problems with his understanding of the ethics of leadership.

First, Burns focuses on individual motivation and morality. That locus of control may be a good place to start, but it is wholly inadequate to deal with the ethics of changes that leaders and followers may propose to solve complex modern problems. Our individual motivations and morality as leaders and followers may be oriented to justice, but the ethical issue is not our motivations and morality. The ethical question is: Will the changes that the leaders and followers propose eliminate discriminatory practices in this organization so that justice can be served? The two issues are not the same, and the ethical content of leadership has to do with the second issue. Unfortunately, Burns dealt with the first issue in constructing his theory of transformational leadership.

Second, Burns emphasized that "leaders and followers raise one another to higher levels of motivation and morality." There is nothing in his notion of transformational leadership that speaks to organizations and societies being raised to higher levels of motivation and morality. Personal redemption may be the function of organized religion (although many would claim that is too narrow a definition of purpose for the church in society), but personal redemption is certainly not the ethical purpose of leadership. That purpose has to do with the ethical impact of proposed changes on organizations and societies. The ethical content of leadership is concerned about leaders and followers proposing specific changes that they believe will raise organizations and societies to higher levels of motivation and morality (using the word *levels* in a colloquial, not a scientific, sense).

Third, Burns, and even more his followers who have adopted transformational leadership as *the* model of leadership, assumes that leaders and followers know what the higher moral ground (to use Jesse Jackson's phrase) is regarding the many controversial issues in the United States and the world. The reality of ethical pluralism is that there is no consensus as to the higher moral ground. Two sets of leaders and followers often propose two different changes that would push an organization in diametrically opposed directions, and yet both groups argue vehemently that their proposed changes will bring the organization to a higher level of motivation and morality, to the higher moral ground. Using Burns's model, both groups would be evaluated as engaging in transformational leadership. But that is conceptually inconsistent, since they cannot both raise the level of morality and at the same time push the organization in opposite directions. The ethical content of leadership must account for the fact that leaders and followers often do not know, and different sets of leaders and followers cannot agree on, what the higher moral ground is concerning any number of changes that they may propose to solve the complex problems which real human beings face in this modern world.

The Definition of Leadership and Its Ethical Content

Many scholars, practitioners, and watchers of leadership are so disgusted with the unethical conduct of many people in positions of power and authority that they want to make ethical conduct a moral imperative for leaders and leadership. In sum, these people include a moral dimension in their definition of leadership. This position is, as I indicated earlier, an outgrowth of the popularity of Burns's transformational leadership model. Bennis, another popular writer on leadership, has joined this movement. "Managers," he and Nanus asserted in 1985, "are people who do things right [process] and leaders are people who do the right thing [content]" (p. 21). Bennis reiterated the same conclusion in one of his 1989 books and added: "I often observe people in top positions doing the wrong thing well. . . . They do not pay enough attention to doing the right thing, while they pay too much attention to doing things right (1989b, p. 18).

There is no clear definition of leadership in either book, but it is clear that Bennis has adopted Burns's notion of transformational leadership. ("This is 'transformative leadership,' the province of those leaders we've been discussing throughout this book"; Bennis & Nanus, 1985, p. 217.)

Extrapolating from Bennis and Nanus's definition of leaders and the characteristics of leadership ("Leadership is morally purposeful and elevating"; Bennis & Nanus, 1985, p. 218), but using the structure of my definition of leadership, a moral definition of leadership would go like this: "Leadership is an influence relationship among leaders and followers who intend [Bennis and Nanus said "do"] the right changes [things] in organizations and societies." Or "Leadership is an influence relationship among leaders and followers who intend [do] real changes [things] that morally elevate organizations and the people in them." Both definitions are basically the same because they make the moral dimension as essential element of the nature of leadership.

The reader will notice that the moral element relates to the content of leadership—the changes/things that leaders and followers intend/do. It does not relate to the process of leadership. Bennis is clear about this: "I often observe people in top positions doing the wrong thing well" (1989b, p. 18). Bennis indicated that when people use ethical processes to do the wrong thing, they are not doing leadership.

So it goes. Such is the popular opinion of many people today about the nature of leadership. The trouble with that opinion is that it does not account for the reality that is leadership. The moral definition of leadership is a wish list, not an explanation of what is, or what will be. We may wish that our leaders and followers exercise leadership so that we and our organizations and societies are morally uplifted, but that wishful definition of leadership does not describe what has happened throughout history, what happened in the 1980s, nor what will happen in the 1990s and the twenty-first century.

Why? Because we can point to numerous real examples of leadership in the past and present that have not raised us, our organizations, or our societies to higher levels of morality. A good example of such a leadership relationship is that of President Ronald Reagan, his co-leaders, and his millions of followers. I do not know of a single commentator who has claimed that the leadership of Reagan and his followers raised the people of the United States, the federal government as an organization, or the United States of America as a society to a higher level of morality. But practically everyone, including Burns (1984, p. 45) but not Bennis (1989b, p. 39), has concluded that Reagan and his followers exerted leadership. Reagan and his followers, they argue, changed many of us, the national government, and the United States as a society in real, significant ways. These changes were not imposed on us against our will (in other words, they were the result of an influence process) and were not haphazard but intentional. They reflected the mutual purposes of Reagan and his followers (the millions of voters who, among other ways of showing support, reelected him to office in 1984). All the essential elements of leadership are there, and the overwhelming majority of commentators and scholars attest to that. Some people—commentators, scholars, and common folk—may not like what Reagan and his followers did, but they recognize that it was leadership. Bennis and others who include a moral dimension in their definition of leadership insist that Reagan and his followers did not do leadership.

My view, as should be clear by now, is that these scholars have confused the nature of leadership with the practice of morally good leadership. While I am all in favor of morally good leadership and have for years deplored what Reagan and his followers did to the United States and its citizens, I can distinguish between what leadership is and the kind of leadership I would like to see practiced. In trying very hard to attain some conceptual clarity as to the nature of leadership, it is very important that we not confuse what leadership is with what leadership should be. The two are not the same and never will be, even in the twenty-first century.

Figure 7.2
Leadership and the Ethics of Change

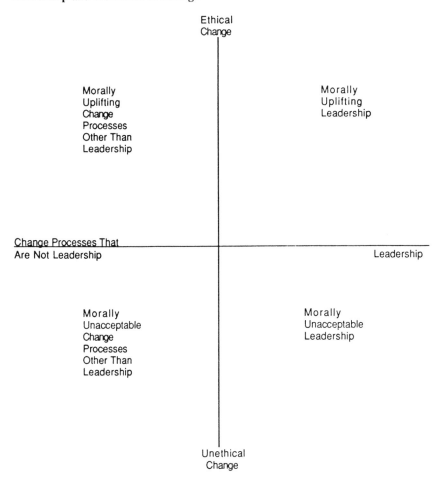

Thus, using moral or ethical criteria, one can determine the ethics of a proposed change; and, using definitional criteria, one can determine whether a change process is leadership. The two concepts are on two different continua that intersect as a cross. This understanding of leadership and the ethics of change is diagrammed in Figure 7.2. This model makes it clear that some change processes can be both leadership and ethical, and others can be neither. Or the change process can be one but not the other. The continua in the model also suggest that there are degrees of certainty with which any of us can make these judgments, but that in reality these degrees are often fairly ambiguous and the judgments are quite tenuous.

Ethical Perspectives on the Content of Leadership

Now that a distinction has been made between the nature of leadership and leadership that is ethical, what can be said about the ethics of the content of leadership?

The first thing I want to emphasize is that the ethics of what is intended by leaders and followers in proposing changes may not be the same as the ethics of those changes once they have been implemented. This troubling distinction is not often developed in books on professional ethics, but it does turn up time and again in real life. Thus, ethical judgments are made (or should be made) several times during any change process. Ethical issues can be debated at the time changes are proposed and at the time the results of the changes are discernible. Thereafter, ethical evaluations can be made intermittently during the life of any program to change an organization or society.

This distinction causes some difficulties in judging the content of leadership according to ethical standards because there are obvious differences in evaluating proposed changes and evaluating implemented changes. In the first instance people can only judge intentions whereas in the second instance they can judge results.

By far, most commentators and scholars use results to make ethical judgments about leadership. The problem with this approach is that it is too late for the people involved in the change process except as a way of revising a program that has been implemented.

The core of leadership goes on before changes are implemented. Leadership is the process wherein leaders and followers decide what changes they intend to implement in an organization. The crucial time for people to make ethical judgments about the content of leadership is the time at which decisions concerning proposed changes are being made. If people avoid or delay the questions of ethics at that time, they may have to wait for months or years to make ethical judgments about the results of such decisions. It seems to me that such a time lag in making ethical evaluations is not in our best interests as members of organizations and societies.

How, then, to proceed? Professional ethicists suggest that people make ethical judgments by applying one or more systems of ethical thought to the issues. In what follows, I try to do that and then see how well it works.

Utilitarian Ethics

One system of ethical thought is utilitarian ethics. Judgments are made by a cost-benefit analysis of the probable effects of the proposed change on the people in the organization and society. Pastin stated the utilitarian principle this way: '' A person, organization, or society should do that which promotes the greatest balance of good over harm for everyone'' (1986, p. 79).

Utilitarian ethics emphasizes the consequences of the proposed changes. ''The most fundamental idea underlying the theory is that in order to determine whether

an action is right, we should look at *what will happen as a result of doing it*"
(Rachels, 1986, p. 93). As any evaluation expert would tell us, we increase our
accuracy of judgment significantly if we make the cost-benefit analysis after we
know what the consequences are rather than when we predict what they will be.
Therein lies the first major problem of putting this ethical system to work in
making judgments about the ethics of proposed changes.

The second problem is in trying to count by either quantitative or qualitative
methods the goods and harms for a specific number of people. The larger the
number of good and harmful consequences, and the larger the number of people,
the greater the difficulty in achieving some basic accuracy.

The third problem is that counting everyone's goods and harms is practically
impossible, so one is left with making preliminary decisions as to who the
stakeholders are, what groups they are aligned with, and how important the
groups are in the organization or society. As a result, these preliminary decisions
produce an estimate of, not an actual counting of, the goods and harms, which
estimate determines the eventual ethical judgment about the balance of good
over harm.

The fourth problem of applying utilitarian ethics to the content of leadership
can be stated in two questions. Is the greatest balance of good over harm for
everyone equal to the common good? Is it in the public interest always to do
what is the greatest balance of good over harm for everyone? My own view is
that the answer to both questions is "not always." Cost-benefit estimations of
the ethical consequences that proposed changes will have on organizations and
societies do not necessarily add up to a judgment based on the common good
or on the public interest. What these evaluations give people is precisely what
they count or estimate—the most goods and the fewest harms for the largest
number of people. The ethical system does not factor in holistic notions of good.
Utilitarianism does not allow us to evaluate the good or the interest of the public.

Rule Ethics

Another system of ethical thought is rule ethics. Judgments are made by
evaluating the proposed change against ethical standards to which the leaders
and followers agree. Moral standards abound in all cultures. Some of them are
propagated by religions. Examples would be the Ten Commandments and the
Golden Rule. Other standards are developed using rational processes of deduc-
tion. Two examples would be the natural laws developed by Thomas Aquinas
and the categorical imperatives developed by Immanuel Kant. Other standards
are part of an ideological belief system such as democracy or communism, and
these are often imbedded in the organizations and societies that have adopted
the ideology. Standards are sometimes expressed as rights that all members of
an organization or society have. Alternatively, standards can be stated as values.
Burns, for instance, used the concept of end-values as the standard against which
people should judge real, intended change to determine if it is morally uplifting.

There are several problems in using ethical standards to make decisions about the ethics of proposed changes. One is the problem of obtaining agreement on which moral standards to use in making ethical evaluations. Leaders and followers may not agree on the same standards, and the larger the number of people in the leadership relationship, the greater the probability that there will be some disagreement over what standards to use.

Second, leaders and followers can interpret any specific moral standard or set of moral standards differently. Freedom, justice, and equity, for instance, are open to quite different interpretations by people of reputedly high moral standards.

Third, people in a leadership relationship may not reach the same conclusion when moral standards are applied to a proposed change. The specifics of any complex change proposal are particularly open to various, sometimes contradictory, conclusions using the same moral standards. This problem results in part from the practice of stating moral standards at a rather high degree of abstraction and generalization.

Fourth, many moral rules are stated and propagated as standards of personal morality. Do these personal rules of ethics help leaders and followers to know the higher moral ground of such issues as those listed in the last section of this chapter? I am not sure. While some personal ethical standards may fit organizations and societies, the ethical standards needed by organizations and societies may be more communal and may involve totally different principles than personal ethical standards.

Social Contract Ethics

A third system of ethics is social contract ethics. "Morality consists of a set of rules, governing how people are to treat one another that rational people will agree to accept, for their mutual benefit, on the condition that others follow those rules as well" (Rachels, 1986, p. 129). Pastin simplified this view of ethics to "The social contract is an implicit agreement about the basic principles or ethics of a group" (1986, pp. 199–200). The web of such agreements forms the basic set of ground rules of the organization or society.

Using social contract ethics, leaders and followers could make judgments of the ethics of proposed changes by determining if the changes are consistent with the contracts already agreed upon by the people in the leadership relationship and in the organization and society.

Again, there are several problems in using social contract ethics to evaluate the ethics of the content of leadership. First, there is the fundamental problem of whether the contracts are actually morally uplifting. We know from experience that many relationships (organizations, leadership, management) develop social contracts that are not very high on any moral scale of development. Social contract ethics basically states that whatever has been decided is good as long as the decision process was fair and voluntary. I have already indicated that there is no cause-and-effect relationship between the process and the content of leadership. Thus social contract ethics is fundamentally flawed.

Secondly, what if the leaders and followers want to change one of the ground rules, the constitution, or a basic contract that has operated in an organization or society for a long period of time? They obviously cannot use social contract ethics (the web of agreements) to make judgments about the ethics of such a proposed change because the answer would automatically be "no."

Ethical Relativism

A fourth system of ethics might be termed moral relativism, which, to me at least, is not very clear as a systemic approach to ethics. It seems that moral relativism comes in several forms. One form is hedonism, which would judge the ethics of whatever is at issue on the basis of the pleasure or happiness each individual person experienced. The reason this view of ethics is relativistic is because there is no general agreement on what is pleasurable or what is happiness. Both are inherently subjective insofar as they are based on experiential data as constructed by individual persons. Using hedonism, a proposed change would be evaluated on the basis of the pleasure or happiness it would bring to the leaders and followers, and to the other people in the organization or society. If the majority declared it pleasurable or gained happiness from the change, it would be ethical.

Another relativistic view of ethics is emotivism, which holds that moral statements are not statements of facts but statements used to influence others by expressing one's attitudes. Emotivism is relativistic because it bases ethical judgments on individual attitudes that may or may not be based on sound moral reasoning. Emotivism allows people to use any criteria to make ethical judgments. In applying emotivism to the ethics of leadership content, a proposed change is ethical when the leaders and followers have convinced one another that it is. Ethical evaluation is reduced to whose attitude is more influential.

A third relativistic notion of ethics can be called ethical egoism, which boils down to simple self-interest. Each person decides whether a proposed change is ethical based on an evaluation of how the change would impact on that person's well-being. Whatever factors the person wants to include in the ethical equation are up to her/him. The leaders and followers then determine if the proposed change is ethical by counting the yeas and nays of the people in the relationship. The majority wins.

A final relativistic ethical perspective was one proposed by Pastin (1986). He called it the ethics of design or of purpose.

The purpose of managerial and employee actions in organizations is no more or less than to act with purpose. (p. 193)

The new organization will have many internal and external stakeholder groups; they cannot share one purpose, but they can share a commitment to purposefulness. . . . The new organization will put a premium on principled action. Since the principles by which we should operate in organizations are not settled, principles should be close to the surface of organizational life. . . . In short, the new organization will maximize the sense of purposefulness for each stakeholder. (p. 194)

An ethics of design will focus not on a common good, but on purpose differentiated by stakeholder groups. . . . What is needed is the recognition that purpose, not goals, gives direction, and that purpose resides in the stakeholders—not in the government, in dated organizations and institutions, or in the cosmos. (p. 196)

While Pastin's explication of the ethics of design or purpose is not very clear, what is presented suggests a relativistic framework wherein ethical judgments are made by using the purposes developed by the people in an organization or society. What makes this ethical view relativistic is its lack of any common criteria that the stakeholders use to develop purpose. Applying the ethics of design or purpose to the content of leadership, leaders and followers would judge whether a proposed change is ethical by evaluating whether it fulfills the stakeholder's purpose for him/herself and/or the organization or society. Since there is no agreement on the purpose among the leaders and followers or among the other stakeholders in an organization or society, only an agreement to be purposeful, the people are left to make individual judgments based on their individual purposes. If the yeas are more numerous than the nays, the proposed change would be ethical.

The first problem of relativistic ethics is its basic design for deciding what is right or wrong by majority rule. A good process (majority rule) does not automatically ensure good proposed changes, ethical programs, or moral results. Procedural justice does not ensure substantive justice.

The second problem is the lack of reasonable criteria used in applying relativistic ethics to the content of leadership. The criteria may vary from the sensible to the nonsensical, from the principled to the unprincipled. Many commentators have concluded that relativistic ethics cannot be taken seriously until the criteria used to make ethical judgments are narrowed significantly to what reasonable people can accept.

The third problem is that relativistic ethics ignores any notion of the common good. It assumes that the common good will be well served when individual goods, defined idiosyncratically by each person, are well served.

In essence, the relativists believe that the public interest is taken care of when the self-interests of a majority of those involved are accommodated. While that bottom line has a comfortable ring to it, many people now believe that what is most comfortable is not the most effective way of making ethical decisions about important organizational and societal issues.

CONCLUSION: AN ETHICAL FRAMEWORK OF LEADERSHIP CONTENT

The first conclusion is rather easy to make. None of the ethical systems is particularly valuable in helping leaders and followers make decisions about the ethics of the changes they intend for an organization or society.

Utilitarian ethics suffers from doing a results analysis before the results are in, from its counting inaccuracies, and from its inability to focus on the common good.

Rule ethics is not very helpful because many leaders and followers will not agree on the moral standards, do not interpret the standards uniformly, and often reach different conclusions when a moral standard is applied to a specific change proposal.

Social contract ethics is better used to make decisions about the ethics of the leadership process than about the leadership content because the ethical criteria have more to do with the fairness and voluntariness of the process used to make the contract than with its content. It is certainly no help when the basic contract of an organization or society is in ethical dispute.

Relativistic ethics is of little use because all of its various models have a majority rule basis for making decisions about ethics, the criteria used to make decisions are questionable at best and unacceptable to many, and the models do not have a plausible notion of the common good.

Thus, the conclusion is this: The systems of ethical thought people have been using create as many problems as they provide solutions in the attempt to make ethical sense of the content of leadership.

If that conclusion is accurate, then the question, again, is: How do we proceed? How do leaders and followers make ethical judgments about the changes they intend for organizations and societies? There are two answers to that question which follow from the discussion above. These answers are, perhaps, more helpful than the ethical frameworks given above, and they lead to two conclusions that are more positive than the conclusion just given.

Personal responsibility for making ethical judgments is essential to any ethical framework of leadership content. This is the first answer: Leaders and followers have the responsibility and the duty to make ethical judgments concerning the changes they intend for organizations and societies. While this answer may seem unduly subjective and relativistic in light of the discussion above, this criticism can be overcome by stressing two points: (1) personal responsibility is only one part of a two-part answer, and (2) the ethical framework that informs the personal responsibility must include more than self-interest. (More on that later.)

A basic fact of life is that human beings have a free will, and with that comes the ability to make choices or decisions. In choosing to support a particular change proposal, leaders and followers exercise that fundamental human characteristic. To downplay the responsibility of each of us to make such personal, ethical decisions is to minimize the fundamental moral purpose of human existence, and I want no part of that. My view is that an ethical framework of leadership must make individual leaders and followers accountable to their ethical responsibilities as human beings. Without that component, the ethical framework is not workable. Rather, it is dehumanizing.

Placing the ethics of the content of leadership on the individual shoulders of the leaders and followers adheres to the time-honored practice of placing the ethics of personal actions on the shoulders of the person doing the acting. People must accept moral responsibility for their actions. Choosing to support a proposed change is that kind of personal action because the person decides to give or withhold her/his support of the proposal. That choice is the person's—the leader's or the follower's—and an ethical framework of leadership content must require people to be ethically responsible for such choices.

Leadership, however, is not a personal or individual "thing." It is a relationship, a process whereby people influence one another concerning real changes they intend for organizations or societies. Thus, the act of choosing to support a proposed change and the responsibility to make an ethical evaluation of that proposed change cannot be a once-and-for-all-time, individualistic decision because such a concept of personal responsibility does not admit of an understanding of leadership as an ongoing process of influence. Thus, the personal responsibility for making ethical judgments cannot be conceived as an isolated action because that obliterates any notion of a person being influenced by others in making an ethical evaluation of a proposed change. The person's ethical choice to support a change proposal must be integrated with the person's attempt to influence others concerning that proposal and with the attempts of other leaders and followers to influence that person and other persons in the leadership relationship. This is the process of developing a mutual purpose that is so crucial to an accurate notion of leadership.

In developing a mutual purpose, leaders and followers are going to have to let go of self-interest criteria for making ethical judgments and move to a consensus on common criteria for evaluating the ethics of the changes they intend for an organization or society. A mutual purpose is more than independent goals mutually held, self-interested objectives that are accommodated. Mutual purposes are common purposes, and common purposes require some fundamental common criteria that individuals in an influence relationship can use to develop a change proposal that reflects common purpose. Thus, the personal responsibility for making an ethical evaluation that must be part of an ethical framework of leadership content cannot be based solely on individualistic ethical criteria. That will not work because it will not develop change proposals that reflect the mutual purpose of the leaders and followers.

The second answer flows in part from the discussion of the personal responsibility of leaders and followers for making ethical judgments concerning the content of leadership. A succinct answer is this: An ethical framework of leadership content requires that leaders and followers use a moral standard of the common good to make ethical judgments about the real changes they intend for organizations and societies. Some elaboration of this statement follows.

The content of leadership—change proposals that leaders and followers intend—transcends the individual moral responsibility of the leaders and followers as persons because a proposal is agreed upon by a number of people through an interactive process of influence. In a very real sense, the proposal becomes, through that process, the property (for want of a better word) of the people involved in the leadership relationship. It no longer is any individual's proposal— especially the leader's—because the proposal reflects the mutual purposes of the leaders and followers. As a result, the proposal cannot reflect the ethics of any one person—for instance, of the leader's ethics—because it reflects the ethics of the people involved in the leadership relationship. Thus, the proposal is the moral responsibility of the leaders and followers as a community.

While leaders and followers each individually making moral judgments about change proposals is a necessary and important part of leadership viewed from an ethical perspective, it is *insufficient* to deal realistically with the ethics of the content of leadership. The collective group of leaders and followers has to be able to make an ethical evaluation of the change proposal that has, through the process of leadership, become the collective's proposal. I believe that this kind of ethical judgment can be made only by using some understanding—however poorly formed—of the common good.

Bellah et al. (1985) wrote at length of this problem, although they did not discuss it in terms of leadership. I would like to quote several statements from *Habits of the Heart* to give the reader a flavor of their discussion.

There is no rationale here for developing public institutions that would tolerate the diversity of a large, heterogeneous society and nurture common standards of justice and civility among its members. (p. 185)

It was difficult for them [the people the authors interviewed] to conceive of a common good or a public interest that recognizes economic, social, and cultural differences between people but sees them all as parts of a single society on which they all depend. (pp. 191–192).

The extent to which many Americans can understand the workings of our economic and social organizations is limited by the capacity of their chief moral language to make sense of human interaction. The limit set by individualism is clear: events that escape the control of individual choice . . . cannot coherently be encompassed in a moral calculation. But that means that much, if not most, of the workings of the interdependent political economy . . . cannot be understood in terms that make coherent moral sense. (p. 204)

Americans seem to lack the resources to think about the relationship between groups that are culturally, socially, or economically quite different. (p. 206)

Even the most articulate of those to whom we talked found it difficult to conceive of a social vision that would embody their deepest moral commitments. (p. 252)

That, indeed, seems to be the heart of the problem. Our moral systems of thought, our moral language, do not encompass a concept of a social vision, a common good, a public interest.

Neither Montesquieu in France nor the founding fathers in the United States who used his ideas had this problem. "Montesquieu defined a republic as a self-regulating political society whose mainstream is the identification of one's own good with the common good, calling this identity civic virtue. For Montesquieu, the virtuous citizen was one who understood that personal welfare is dependent on the general welfare and could be expected to act accordingly" (Bellah et al., 1985, p. 254). In the twentieth century, the people in the United States and other Western democracies have turned the notion of civic virtue around to mean the accommodation of self-interests, the pursuit of private advancement with little or no concern for the public interest. As a result, our first moral language is that of individualism, either utilitarian or expressive/therapeutic (Bellah et al. 1985, has extended discussions of these traditions and the language we use today to express them). With only the language of individualism to use and with only an interest accommodation model to inform that language when it comes to making decisions about changes in our organizations and societies, the people in the United States are without both the language and the moral systems of thought necessary to make morally coherent judgments about the content of leadership— proposals that indicate the real changes leaders and followers intend for our organizations and societies.

What is needed is some ability to deal with the ethical issues that these change proposals inherently bring to the public agenda. We need to be able to think about the ethics of leadership content as a community, we need to develop a second language that will enable us to talk about the common good of the community, we need to infuse the leadership relationship with some dedication to the social ecology of organizations and of societies (Bellah et al., 1985, pp. 283–286) as the bottom line in which all of us—leaders and followers alike— have a huge stake and to which all of us should be committed.

What is needed is a reconstruction of our understanding as leaders and followers of the concept of civic virtue, the elemental notion that all of our goods as individuals and groups are bound up in the common good, or, to put it another way, that all of our self- and group interests are bound up in the public interest. This is the essential message of Bellah et al. as well as of MacIntyre (1984) and Sullivan (1986). It is also the essential message of this book on leadership in the twenty-first century.

Applying the notion of civic virtue to the problem at hand—the ethics of the content of leadership—I think it becomes clear that making ethical judgments about proposed changes involves leaders and followers in more than the ethics of personal responsibility. An ethical framework of leadership cuts to the core of what the common good is because in proposing changes in organization and societies, leaders and followers are dealing not only with their individual interests mutually accommodated but also with the public interest mutually developed; not only with their own goods mutually attained but also with the common good mutually integrated into their individual goods; not only with their own private purposes mutually pursued but also with the community purpose mutually transformed.

Civic virtue demands that leaders and followers put ethics to work in a larger framework than being personally responsible. The common good is not achieved when we use an ethical framework that only helps us achieve our individual goods.

- The balance of good over harm for everyone affected by change proposal is not the common good.

- The moral standards of right or wrong that we use to govern our private lives are not adequate to ensure that a change proposal will effect the common good in our public lives.

- The social contracts we agree to freely and fairly do not promote the common good in our organizations and societies because there are no content criteria fundamental to a social contract.

- The use of relativistic, individualistic criteria to evaluate change proposals does not address the notion of the common good and therefore is useless.

Clearly, the systems of ethical thought people have used in the past and that are still in use are inadequate to the task of making moral judgments about the content of leadership. Leaders and followers need to develop a new language of civic virtue to discuss and make moral evaluations of the changes they intend for organizations and societies. This new language of ethics must center on an integrated concept of the common good, of our social ecology as a community. Only then will leaders and followers begin to make some moral sense out of the changes they propose to transform our organizations and societies. Out of this new language will evolve a new ethical framework of leadership content, a system of ethical thought applied to the content of leadership, that actually works.

8

Leadership in the Future

"Leadership," Chester Barnard wrote in 1948, "has been the subject of an extraordinary amount of dogmatically stated nonsense" (p. 80). If he could say that in 1948, when the leadership literature, if piled together, would amount to only a small hill, what would he say in 1990, when the leadership literature approaches the size of a small mountain?

In one way, I agree with Barnard's assessment. A large number of works on leadership cannot be taken seriously when the authors of those works either do not define what leadership is or provide a definition that does not distinguish leadership from numerous other relationships or social processes which some human beings use to coordinate, direct, control, and govern other human beings. That assessment includes roughly 450 of the almost 600 books, chapters, and journal articles reviewed in this study (see Table 3.1). This literature, in essence, sees leadership as being all things to all people, and that view is literally nonsensical, as Barnard said. When leadership is anything anyone wants to say it is, the concept of leadership is meaningless, hence nonsense.

A different assessment is, perhaps, necessary for approximately 150 of the works reviewed for this study. In these books, chapters, and journal articles, which are about one-fourth of the total number of works, the authors struggled with a definition of leadership, and they were more or less successful in trying to understand the phenomena they called leadership. They tried to put boundaries around the phenomena of leadership, but they were only partially successful. Many of these scholars established that leadership relationships are substantially different from other human relationships, but they were hard pressed to articulate that difference clearly. Many of these scholars understood leadership as an influence process that human beings use to give direction to their organizational and societal lives, but only a few of them were able to consistently explain how and why the leadership process is distinct from other processes that human beings use to order their existence.

In the end, many commentators, including myself, have roundly criticized these scholars for not coming to grips with the nature of leadership in order to develop a school of leadership that clearly and consistently articulates an understanding of what leadership is. Instead, these authors have tended to confuse their readers with contradictory conceptual frameworks, their theories and models have not added up to any meaningful conclusion about the nature of leadership, and they have been accused of emphasizing the peripheral elements of leadership: traits, styles, preferred behaviors, contingencies and situations, and effectiveness. In other words, though practitioners read the leadership definitions of these scholars and study their models of leadership, they find it almost impossible to integrate and synthesize a clear, consistent picture of what leadership is and how leaders and followers actually engage in leadership. They find only contradictory and confusing understandings of the nature of leadership and almost no explanation of how leaders and followers really do leadership.

At a deeper level of analysis, however, I have suggested that what does not make sense when a first-cut analysis is done may make sense when a second or third cut penetrates the background assumptions embedded in the definitions and looks behind the words in the theories and models. When that kind of analysis is done, a consistent picture of the nature of leadership appears and begins to make sense. In short, the picture paints what should have been obvious all along: Leadership is good management. In a more detailed, bigger picture, the painted surface reveals this: Leadership is great men and women with certain preferred traits influencing followers to do what the leaders wish in order to achieve group/organizational goals that reflect excellence defined as some kind of higher-level effectiveness.

This understanding of leadership, I have argued, is pervasive in the leadership literature, both the serious works and those which could be evaluated as nonsense. And it permeates the works in all of the major academic disciplines that address the subject of leadership. This understanding is what I have called the industrial leadership paradigm. It is industrial because it accepts almost all of the major characteristics of the industrial paradigm: (1) a structural-functionalist view of organizations, (2) a view of management as the preeminent profession, (3) a personalistic focus on the leader, (4) a dominant objective of goal achievement, (5) a self-interested and individualistic outlook, (6) a male model of life, (7) a utilitarian and materialistic ethical perspective, and (8) a rational, technocratic, linear, quantitative, and scientific language and methodology.

The problem with the industrial leadership paradigm is that it increasingly ill serves the needs of a world rapidly being transformed by a massive paradigm shift in societal values. There is more and more evidence to conclude that the industrial paradigm is losing its hold on the culture of Western societies (and perhaps all societies in the world—but that is another issue) and that some kind of postindustrial paradigm will dominate these societies in the twenty-first century. In this view of paradigmatic change, the 1980s and 1990s are seen as a transition period wherein the dominant values and cultural norms shift from an industrial to a postindustrial frame. While no one knows with certainty when the postindustrial paradigm will achieve dominance, many analysts assume it will be sometime in the early twenty-first century. No one knows with certainty, either, what values will form the core of the postindustrial paradigm; but if the shift is going to have any significance of note, the values will have to be quite different from, and even opposed to, the core values of the industrial paradigm. In trying to develop a way out of the problems that the industrial era has produced in the world, many commentators have pointed to the importance of such values as collaboration, common good, global concern, diversity and pluralism in structures and participation, client orientation, civic virtues, freedom of expression in all organizations, critical dialogue, qualitative language and methodologies, substantive justice, and consensus-oriented policy-making process.

If these values and other like them are going to achieve dominance in the future, they must be embedded in a new understanding of what leadership is, in a postindustrial school of leadership. Such a school of leadership is not possible without a paradigm shift in leadership studies as an academic discipline, in the definition of leadership, in the theories and models that flow from a new definition of leadership, and in the practice of leadership in our organizations and societies. While Burns made a serious attempt in 1978 to initiate such a paradigm shift in the nature and practice of leadership and to begin to construct a new school of leadership, the overwhelming evidence presented in Chapter 4 indicates that, contrary to early, more optimistic assessments, not much has changed in leadership studies. The industrial paradigm of leadership continues to dominate the study and practice of leadership as we begin the 1990s. This important work remains ahead of us.

I think it is time to attack the problem head-on. Building on what Burns accomplished but differing in significant ways from his conceptual framework, this book presents a definition of leadership that does not accept the values of the industrial paradigm. Rather, the predicted values of the postindustrial paradigm are build into the definition of leadership, and in developing such a definition, I have deliberately set out to construct a postindustrial school of leadership. Such a school is crucial to the development of leadership theory and practice and to the transition from an industrial to a postindustrial society. By its very nature, leadership understood as intending change should be one of the primary social processes that people use to make paradigmatic changes. On the contrary and by its very nature, leadership understood as good management would be one of the primary social processes people use to maintain the old order, the industrial paradigm. Thus, only a new paradigm of leadership will help the people in the Western world transform their societies according to postindustrial frames.

I do not want to be misunderstood. I am not suggesting that a new postindustrial paradigm of leadership will save the world or Western societies, or will solve the problems left over from the industrial era—pollution, population explosion, poverty and hunger, warming of the atmosphere, atomic destruction, garbage, self-interested politics, greed, individualism, racial injustice, expressive therapeutic life-styles, economic inequities, and so on. The larger, societal paradigm shift to a postindustrial era will be an effort to resolve some of those issues by coming to grips with many of the problems that the industrial era was unwilling and unable to solve. A new paradigm of leadership is not the solution to those problems. Rather, a postindustrial school of leadership will help people change the dominant paradigm governing their society, thereby empowering them to transform their society and, one hopes, solve some of these outstanding problems. There are no guarantees that any of this paradigmatic change will be successful. We are not sure that the postindustrial era will be any better than the industrial era. All we know with certainty is that the industrial paradigm has not had a very good record in solving certain intractable problems that stem from the industrial era. Thus many people say, "Let's give a new paradigm a chance." The new paradigm of leadership might help make that chance work.

THE STUDY AND PRACTICE OF LEADERSHIP IN THE FUTURE

Leadership studies as an academic discipline needs to come out of the woodwork of management science in all of its guises (business, education, health, public, nonprofit) and out of such disciplines as social psychology, political science, and sociology wherein academics have developed an interest in leadership as a subspecialty. Leadership scholars need to develop an academic presence as an interdisciplinary area of studies serving both undergraduate and graduate students in specialized programs that deal with the study and practice of leadership in organizations and in societies.

Looking at leadership through the lens of a single discipline has not worked well in the past, and it will not work any better in the future. Indeed, a case could be made that organizations and societies in the future, with their collaborative, community, and global orientations, may not be hospitable to a concept of leadership that is grounded in only one academic discipline.

Universities are institutions that have been molded and shaped by the industrial paradigm. They have not been particularly hospitable to professors and students engaging in interdisciplinary programs of study; thus the recommendation given above may be difficult to operationalize. Universities themselves may have to go through their own paradigm shift in order to promote and develop such programs and make them work successfully.

In the meantime there are some prototypes that can serve as models. There are multidisciplinary leadership programs (some may actually be interdisciplinary) at perhaps fifty colleges and universities serving undergraduate and graduate students who major and minor in leadership studies or take graduate degrees in leadership. I expect that these programs will increase in size and number in the 1990s. Most of these programs, I suspect, are wedded to the industrial paradigm of leadership as good management, but many of them will be transformed and move to a postindustrial concept of leadership in the near future. Some of these programs have established centers on leadership to reach out into the community. Several business persons have recently endowed centers, and it will be interesting to see what impact these centers will have on the study and practice of leadership.

Leadership scholars in the future are going to have to think new thoughts about leadership, using postindustrial assumptions about human beings, organizations, societies, and the planet Earth. With that kind of thinking, scholars must settle on a definition of leadership, conduct research based on that definition, and construct new theories and models of leadership that will address the wants and needs of the people in a postindustrial society. With that kind of thinking, leadership scholars must experiment with different research designs and methodologies. They must invent new research strategies that enable them to explain what leadership is and how it operates at all levels of organizations and societies.

With this new kind of thinking, leadership scholars must develop a new school of leadership that is grounded in what is real, what actually happens when leaders and followers do engage in leadership. With this new kind of thinking, leadership scholars must critically analyze one another's theories and models and engage in dialogic conversations about those conceptual frameworks. Leadership studies would be vastly improved with a large dose of critical thought and methodology.

As evidence of this kind of new thinking, I can point to several dissertations by leadership doctoral candidates at the University of San Diego. Shay Sayre (1986) studied a nonmale model of leadership that transformed a business organization. Kevin Freiberg (1987) did a study of transformational leadership in an airline corporation. Alex Kodiath (1987) researched the commonalities and differences of male and female spiritual leaders. Rita King (1988) researched how mentor teachers changed schools and a school district by working from the bottom up and using a collaborative notion of leadership. Stuart Grauer (1989) developed an interactive model of leadership in studying educators' attempts to internationalize schools. Richard Henrickson (1989) developed a cultural model of leadership from his studies of anthropology. James Kelly, Jr. (1989), did a historical study of leadership in the transformation of a mature organization. Bertha Pendleton (1989) investigated the impact of leadership among various members of a Schools of the Future Commission in a large, urban school district. Kathleen Allen (1990) interviewed alternative (nonstandard) types of reputed leaders to see if they voiced different models of leadership. Dallas Boggs (1990) studied several literary classics in each of four eras in an effort to understand how leadership was understood in those eras. Robert Fink (1990) completed a study of a national professional association using an interactive model of transformational leadership. James Ford (1990) researched nonordained pastors and religious education coordinators in the Roman Catholic Church and analyzed their concepts of leadership according to a postindustrial model of leadership. Rita Marinoble (1990) studied the connection between spirituality and leadership. And there are more exciting research projects in the works for 1991 and 1992.

While not all these research projects were entirely successful, they were all serious attempts to study leadership from a postindustrial perspective and had a clearly articulated definition of leadership at work in the analysis. Some of the studies were exploratory in design and methodology; most of them were exploratory in the leadership they described and in the conclusions they developed. These authors were not afraid of studying leadership from the perspective of alternative frameworks because they did not see the traditional framework as providing answers to the fundamental questions they wanted to ask about leadership. When hundreds of people all over the country complete research studies such as these, we will begin to get some answers about the nature of leadership and how leaders and followers do leadership in organizations and societies.

But scholars cannot do it alone. In fact, what it means to be a scholar may change radically in the postindustrial paradigm. Scholars may include training and development experts who translate theories into action through professional development and practitioners who put new theories of leadership to work and then reflect critically on those experiences. Leadership studies as an academic discipline needs both of these types of scholars as well as academics based in universities and think tanks.

How do we translate a new paradigm of leadership to leaders and followers who are actually engaged in leadership? Centers on leadership are one obvious way, but such centers have not been particularly good at doing that in the past. Most, if not all, of these centers are solidly entrenched in the industrial paradigm of leadership. Consultants, training and development specialists, professional development packages, and electronic media software are other methods that have been used to inculcate newer aspects of the old paradigm with some success. But these vehicles would themselves have to be transformed before they could begin to translate a new paradigm of leadership so that others could use it. Indeed, vast numbers of people throughout our society, including many professional people in our organizations, would have to rethink their commitment to professional development and take it more seriously.

While consultants, trainers, packagers, and software designers who are dedicated to the application of postindustrial leadership models will be of enormous help in achieving some praxis of leadership theory and practice, it is becoming more apparent that leaders and followers in the future will need new and different relationships with these translations experts. The usual short-term consulting contracts, inservice workshops, convention speeches, one-day seminars, simulations, and organizational development tricks of the trade will not do the job.

These specialists may, first of all, have to see themselves as scholars who are doing grounded research on the nature and practice of leadership in organizations, and they should view their scholarship as being as important as that done by academics in universities and think tanks. They may have to see their relationships with clients as leadership relationships wherein they and the clients influence one another concerning intended real changes that reflect their mutual purposes. They may have to develop long-term contracts that allow for the possibility of transformation rather than incremental change. They may have to insist on week-long professional development sessions and follow-up peer coaching or collaborative mentoring strategies. They may have to create computer simulations that teach consensus policy-making processes and interactive decision-making strategies among diverse populations. If not by computer simulations, they will somehow have to learn, and then teach others, how to build consensus from diverse points of view without compromising end-values. They may have to model the kinds of influence behaviors that the postindustrial leadership paradigm calls for and engage in the kind of critical, honest, dialectical analysis that the new leadership models require of leaders and followers. They may have to create a new moral language that will help leaders and followers to practice civic virtues rather than self-interest politics, that will help them serve the common good rather than individualistic goods, that will help them move to substantive justice instead of being satisfied with procedural justice.

Practitioners are also going to have to think new thoughts if leadership studies is going to be taken seriously in the future. My guess is that practitioners are going to have to become leadership scholars as well. I don't mean the kind of scholars who conduct formal research on leadership and publish the results in books and journal articles, although that is possible in some instances. There are practitioners who do that now. Rather, these practitioners are going to have to be the kind of scholars who do critical thinking as they do leadership.

The kind of scholars I have in mind are those thinking women and men who understand that leadership is more complex than the mythology of leadership would have us believe. They are those thinking men and women who will surely be dissatisfied with one-minute leadership, quick and simple leadership models that can be mastered in a three-hour seminar, slick presentations on leadership at conventions, and the kind of nonsense that pervades the leadership literature from about 1930 up to and including 1990. These scholars know that such minimalist efforts will not give them what they need to know about the new paradigm of leadership to meet the wants and needs of the people, organizations, and societies of the twenty-first century.

These scholars are reflective practitioners (Schon, 1984), thinking women and men who reflect on their reflections-in-actions (the more or less automatic actions that result from countless previous experiences upon which they have reflected).

They do research about leadership in context, leadership in this organization, this community, this society. They see themselves as doing action research because they are at the center of where the action is, because they are involved in the paradigm shift, because they are agents of transformational change. They understand that there are quite literally no other people who have the perspective on leadership that they have because they are the ones who have been doing postindustrial leadership.

These practitioners think of themselves as educators, scholars who have the expertise to help other women and men understand what leadership is all about and inform their practice of leadership in their organizations and societies. In this sense, these thinking men and women share their leadership expertise in order to generate other leaders and followers who have a deep understanding of postindustrial leadership and the practical experience to put that understanding to work.

In the end, leadership studies as an academic discipline would be significantly improved if practitioners, translation specialists, and academic scholars would collaborate in research projects on postindustrial leadership. In fact, such collaborative efforts may be the only way to find out and document how leadership actually occurs in organizations and societies. With that kind of documentation, leadership scholars would have a much better chance of developing grounded conceptual frameworks that make sense and inform the practice of leadership in the future.

CONCLUDING COMMENTS

When did the last societal paradigm shift transpire? The industrial revolution happened over two centuries ago. While there have been paradigmatic shifts since the 1930s in sciences and technology that have ushered in the atomic age, the space age, and the computer age, none of these shifts has been massive enough or deeply antithetical enough to the values of the industrial era to cause a societal paradigm shift. Indeed, many commentators have argued that atomic energy, space engineering, and computer technology fit comfortably into the industrial paradigm and, in truth, have made that paradigm stronger and more intractable. These shifts have given our Western culture the self-image that it has been updated or transformed, and thus they have given the industrial culture new life. If anything, these shifts have made the transition to a postindustrial paradigm more difficult because scientific and technological innovations have shored up the industrial paradigm and made it more acceptable to people who otherwise would have grown intolerant of the industrial era and its problems.

The people in this generation may be the first in history who can reflect upon a societal paradigm shift, who can watch themselves go through the transition from an industrial era to a postindustrial era. All kinds of potential futures are possible. If the events in Eastern Europe have taught us nothing else, they should teach us that many of the things we thought were impossible using the old paradigm are very possible using a new paradigm.

Transforming leadership is one such possibility or impossibility, depending on which paradigm is used. The 1990s are upon us, and it is time to forsake the old paradigm and begin a new life for leadership study and practice by consciously thinking and acting in ways that are consistent with a postindustrial framework. If academic scholars, translation specialists, and practitioners can all do that, and do it collaboratively, leadership studies has no place to go but up. Leadership studies, itself, will be transformed.

References

Abboua, A. G. (1953). *Selection for industrial leadership*. London: Oxford University Press.

Ackerman, L. (1985). Leadership and management. *Leadership and Organizational Development Journal*, 6(2), 17–19.

Adair, J. (1984). *The skills of leadership*. New York: Nichols.

Adams, J. & Yoder, J. D. (1985). *Effective leadership for women and men*. Norwood, NJ: Ablex.

Adams, J. A. (Ed.). (1986). *Transforming leadership*. Alexandria, VA: Miles River Press.

Adams, J. D., & Spencer, S. A. (1986). The strategic leadership perspective. In J. A. Adams (Ed.), *Transforming leadership* (pp. 5–16). Alexandria, VA: Miles River Press.

Allen, K. E. (1990). *Leadership in a different voice: Different rhythms and emerging harmonies*. Doctoral dissertation, University of San Diego.

Allison, G. T. (1984). Public and private administrative leadership: Are they fundamentally alike in all unimportant respects? In T. J. Sergiovanni & J. E. Corbally (Eds.), *Leadership and organizational culture* (pp. 214–239). Urbana: University of Illinois Press.

Allport, F. H. (1924). *Social psychology*. Boston: Houghton Mifflin.

Andrade, K. M., & Ontiveros, S. R. (Eds.). (1986). *Organizational behavior: Contemporary viewpoints*. Santa Barbara, CA: ABC-Clio.

Argyris, C. (1953). *Executive leadership*. New York: Harper & Brothers.

Argyris, C. (1976). *Increasing leadership effectiveness*. New York: Wiley.

Argyris, C. (1979). How normal science methodology makes leadership research less additive and less applicable. In J. G. Hunt and L. L. Larson (Eds.), *Crosscurrents in leadership* (pp. 47–63). Carbondale: Southern Illinois University Press.

Argyris, C., & Cyert, R. M. (1980). *Leadership in the 80's*. Cambridge, MA: Harvard University, Institute for Educational Management.

Avolio, B. J., & Bass, B. M. (1988). Transformational leadership, charisma, and beyond. In J. G. Hunt, B. R. Baliga, H. P. Dachler, & C. A. Schriesheim (Eds.), *Emerging leadership vistas* (pp. 29–49). Lexington, MA: Lexington Books.

Badaracco, J. L., Jr., & Ellsworth, R. R. (1989). *Leadership and the quest for integrity*. Boston: Harvard Business School Press.

Bailey, F. G. (1988). *Humbuggery and manipulation: The art of leadership*. Ithaca, NY: Cornell University Press.

Baldridge, J. V., Curtis, D. V. Ecker, G., & Riley, G. L. (1978). *Policy making and effective leadership*. San Francisco: Jossey-Bass.

Baliga, B. R., & Hunt, J. G. (1988). An organizational life cycle approach to leadership. In J. G. Hunt, B. R. Baliga, H. P. Dachler, & C. A. Schriesheim (Eds.), *Emerging leadership vistas* (pp. 129–149). Lexington, MA: Lexington Books.

Ball, S. J. (1987). *The micro-politics of the school*. London: Methuen.

Barnard, C. I. (1938). *The functions of the executive*. Cambridge, MA: Harvard University Press.

Barnard, C. I. (1948). *Organizations and management*. Cambridge, MA: Harvard University Press.

Barr, L., & Barr, N. (1989). *The leadership equation*. Austin, TX: Eakins Press.

Bass, B. M. (1960). *Leadership, psychology and organizational behavior*. New York: Harper.

Bass, B. M. (1981). *Stogdill's handbook of leadership* (rev. ed.). New York: The Free Press.

Bass, B. M. (1985). *Leadership and performance beyond expectations*. New York: The Free Press.

Bates, R. (1989). Leadership and the rationalization of society. In J. Smyth (Ed.), *Critical perspectives on educational leadership* (pp. 131–156). London: Falmer.

Bateson, G. (1972). *Steps to an ecology of mind*. New York: Chandler.

Batten, J. D. (1989). *Tough minded leadership*. New York: AMACOM.

Bavelas, A. (1960). Leadership: Man and function. *Administrative Science Quarterly, 4*, 491–498.

Beal, G. M., Bohlen, J. M., & Randabaugh, J. N. (1962). *Leadership*. Ames: Iowa State University Press.

Behrman, J. N. (1988). *Essays on ethics in business and the professions*. Englewood Cliffs, NJ: Prentice-Hall.

Bell, D. (1973). *The coming of the post-industrial society*. New York: Basic Books.

Bell, D. J. (1975). *Power, influence, and authority*. New York: Oxford University Press.

Bell, W., Hill, R. J., & Wright, C. R. (1961). *Public leadership*. San Francisco: Chandler.

Bellah, R. N., Madsen, R., Sullivan, W. M., Swidler, A., & Tipton, S. M. (1985). *Habits of the heart*. New York: Harper & Row.

Bellows, R. (1959). *Creative leadership*. Englewood Cliffs, NJ: Prentice-Hall.

Bennis, W. G. (1959). Leadership theory and administrative behavior: The problem with authority. *Administrative Science Quarterly, 4*, 259–301.

Bennis, W. G. (1976). *The unconscious conspiracy*. New York: AMACOM.

Bennis, W. G. (1977, March–April). Where have all the leaders gone? *Technological Review*, 3–12.

Bennis, W. G. (1983). The artform of leadership. In S. Srivastra & Associates (Eds.), *The executive mind*. San Francisco: Jossey-Bass.

Bennis, W. G. (1984). Transformative power and leadership. In T. J. Sergiovanni & J. E. Corbally (Eds.), *Leadership and organizational culture* (pp. 64–71). Urbana: University of Illinois Press.

Bennis, W. G. (1989a). *On becoming a leader*. Reading, MA: Addison-Wesley.

Bennis, W. G. (1989b). *Why leaders can't lead*. San Francisco: Jossey-Bass.

Bennis, W., & Nanus, B. (1985). *Leaders: The strategies for taking charge*. New York: Harper & Row.

Berger, P., & Luckman, T. (1966). *The social construction of reality*. New York: Anchor Books.

Bernard, L. L. (1927). Leadership and propaganda. In J. Davis & H. E. Barnes (Eds.), *An introduction to sociology*. New York: Heath.

Betz, D. (1981). *Cultivating leadership: An approach*. Washington, DC: University Press of America.

Blackmar, F. W. (1911). Leadership in reform. *American Journal of Sociology, 16*, 626–644.

Blades, J. W. (1986). *Rules for leadership*. Washington, DC: National Defense University Press.

Blake, R. R., & Mouton, J. S. (1964). *The managerial grid*. Houston, TX: Gulf.

Blake, R. R., & Mouton, J. S. (1978). *The new managerial grid*. Houston, TX: Gulf.

Blake, R. R., & Mouton, J. S. (1986a). *Executive achievement*. New York: McGraw-Hill.

Blake, R. R., & Mouton, J. S. (1986b). Theory and research for developing a science of leadership. In T. Heller, J. Van Til, & L. A. Zurcher (Eds.), *Leaders and followers: Challenges for the future* (pp. 157–175). Greenwich, CT: JAI Press.

Blanchard, K., Zigarmi, P., & Zigarmi, D. (1985). *Leadership and the one minute manager*. New York: Morrow.

Block, P. (1987). *The empowered manager*. San Francisco: Jossey-Bass.

Blondel, J. (1987). *Political leadership*. Beverly Hills, CA: Sage.

Blumberg, A., & Greenfield, W. (1986). *The effective principal: Perspectives on school leadership* (2nd ed.). Boston: Allyn & Bacon.

Boal, K. B., & Broyson, J. M. (1988). Charismatic leadership: A phenomenological and structural approach. In J. G. Hunt, B. R. Baliga, H. P. Dachler, & C. A. Schriesheim (Eds.), *Emerging leadership vistas* (pp. 11–28). Lexington, MA: Lexington Books.

Bogardus, E. S. (1934). *Leaders and leadership*. New York: Appleton-Century.

Boggs, D. B. (1990). *Literary perceptions of leadership* Doctoral dissertation, University of San Diego.

Bogue, E. G. (1985). *The enemies of leadership*. Bloomington, IN: Phi Delta Kappan.

Boje, D. M. & Ultich, D. (1985). The qualitative side of leadership. In R. Tannenbaum, N. Margulies, & F. Massarik (Eds.), *Human systems development*. San Francisco: Jossey-Bass.

Boles, H. W., & Davenport, J. A. (1975). *Introduction to educational leadership*. New York: Harper & Row.

Bothwell, L, (1983). *The art of leadership*. Englewood Cliffs, NJ: Prentice-Hall.

Bowen, W. (1974, June). Almost everything you ever wanted to know about leadership. *Fortune, 80*, 241–242.

Bradford, D. L., & Cohen, A. R. (1984). *Managing for excellence*. New York: Wiley.

Brent, C. H. (1980). *Leadership: The William Belden Noble lectures*. New York: Longman.

Bridges, E. M. (1977). The nature of leadership. In L. L. Cunningham, W. G. Hack, & R. O. Nystrand (Eds.), *Educational administration: The developing decades* (pp. 202–230). Berkeley, CA: McCutchan.

Brittel, L. R. (1984). *Leadership: The key to management success*. New York: Franklin Watts.

Britton, P. R., & Stallings, J. W. (1986). *Leadership is empowering people*. Washington, DC: University Press of America.

Broedling, L. A. (1981). The psychology of leadership. In J. H. Ruck & L. J. Korb (Eds.), *Military leadership* (pp. 71–94). Beverly Hills, CA: Sage.

Brown, D. C. (1979). *Leadership vitality*. Washington, DC: American Council on Education.

Brown, J. D. (1973). *The human nature of organizations*. New York: AMACOM.

Browne, C. G., & Cohn, T. S. (Eds.). (1958). *The study of leadership*. Danville, IL: Interstate.

Bryman, A. (1986). *Leadership and organizations*. London: Routledge & Kegan Paul.

Bryson, J. M., & Kelly, G. (1981). Leadership, politics and the function of complex organizations and interorganizational networks. In G. W. England, A. R. Negandlir, & B. Wilpert (Eds.), *The functioning of complex organizations* (pp. 203–236). Cambridge MA: Oelgeschlager, Gunn & Hain.

Buckley, K. W., & Steffy, J. (1986). The invisible side of leadership. In J. A. Adams (Ed.), *Transforming leadership* (pp. 233–243). Alexandria, VA: Miles River Press.

Bundel, C. M. (1930). Is leadership losing its importance? *Infantry Journal, 36*, 339–349.

Burack, E. H. (1979). Leadership findings and applications: The viewpoint of four from the real world—David Campbell, Joseph L. Moses, Paul J. Patinka, and Blanchard B. Smith. In J. G. Hunt & L. L. Larson (Eds.), *Crosscurrents in leadership* (pp. 25–46). Carbondale: Southern Illinois University Press.

Burdin, J. L. (Ed.). (1989). *School leadership*. Newbury Park, CA: Sage.

Burdy, R. J. (1972). *Fundamentals of leadership: A guide for the supervisor*. Reading, MA: Addison-Wesley.

Burke, W. W. (1986). Leadership as empowering others. In S. Srivastra & Associates (Eds.), *Executive power* (pp. 51–77). San Francisco: Jossey-Bass.

Burns, J. M. (1978). *Leadership*. New York: Harper & Row.

Burns, J. M. (1984). *The power to lead*. New York: Simon & Schuster.

Burr, W. (1929). *Community leadership*. New York: Prentice-Hall.

Busch, H. M. (1934). *Leadership in group work*. New York: Association Press.

Bussom, R. S., Larson, L. L., & Vicars, W. M. (1982). Unstructured, nonparticipant observation and study of leaders' interpersonal contact. In J. G. Hunt, U. Sekaran, & C. A. Schriesheim (Eds.), *Leadership: Beyond establishment views* (pp. 31–49). Carbondale: Southern Illinois University Press.

Calas, M. B., & Smircich, L. (1988). Reading leadership as a form of cultural analysis.

In J. G. Hunt, B. R. Baliga, H. P. Dachler, & C. A. Schriesheim (Eds.), *Emerging leadership vistas* (pp. 201–226). Lexington, MA: Lexington Books.

Calder, B. J. (1977). An attribution theory of leadership. In B. Shaw & G. Salanick (Eds.), *New Directions in organizational behavior*. Chicago: St. Clair Press.

Campbell, D. T. (1956). *Leadership and its effects upon the group*. Columbus: Ohio State University, Bureau of Business Research.

Campbell, J., with Moyers, W. (1988). *The power of myth*. Garden City, NY: Doubleday.

Campbell, J. P. (1977). The cutting edge of leadership: An overview. In J. G. Hunt & L. L. Larson (Eds.), *Leadership: The cutting edge* (pp. 221–234). Carbondale: Southern Illinois University Press.

Caplan, A. L., & Callahan, D. (Eds.). (1981). *Ethics in hard times*. New York: Plenum.

Carroll, S. J. (1984). Feminist scholarship on political leadership. In B. Kellerman (Ed.), *Leadership: Multidisciplinary perspectives* (pp. 139–156). Englewood Cliffs, NJ: Prentice–Hall.

Carter, L. G. (1953/1958). Leadership and small group behavior. In M. Sherif & M. O. Wilson (Eds.), *Group relations at the crossroads*. New York: Harper. (Reprinted in Browne & Cohn, 1958, pp. 22–25.)

Cartwright, D. (1965). Influence, leadership, control. In J. G. March (Ed.), *Handbook of organizations*. Chicago: Rand McNally.

Cartwright, D., & Zander, A. (1953). Leadership and performance of group functions: Introduction. In D. Cartwright & A. Zander (Eds.), *Group dynamics: Research and theory*. Evanston, IL: Row, Peterson.

Cassel, R. N. (1975). Psychological dimensions of leadership. In R. N. Cassel & R. L. Heichberger (Eds.) *Leadership development: theory and practice*. North Quincy, MA: Christopher.

Cassel, R. N., & Heichberger, R. L. (Eds.) (1975). *Leadership development: Theory and practice*. North Quincy, MA: Christopher.

Cattell, R. B. (1951). New concepts for measuring leadership in terms of group syntality. *Human Relations, 4*, 161–184.

Cavanagh, G. F. (1984). *American business values*. Englewood Cliffs, NJ: Prentice-Hall.

Center for Creative Leadership. (n.d.). *Looking Glass, Inc., A management simulation of a day in the life of top management*. Greensboro, NC: Author.

Champlin, J. (1987). Leadership: A change agent's view. In L. T. Sheive & M. B. Schoenbelt (Eds.), *Leadership: Examining the elusive* (pp. 49–63). Alexandria, VA: Association for Supervision and Curriculum Development.

Chemers, M. M. (1984). The social, organizational and cultural context of effective leadership. In B. Kellerman (Ed.), *Leadership: Multidisciplinary perspectives* (pp. 91–112). Englewood Cliffs, NJ: Prentice-Hall.

Child, J., & Hosking, D. M. (1979). Commentary on what should be studied. In J. G. Hunt & L. L. Larson (Eds.), *Crosscurrents in leadership* (pp. 148–156). Carbondale: Southern Illinois University Press.

Chomsky, N. (1972). *Language and mind* (enl. ed.). New York: Harcourt, Brace, Jovanovich.

Christopher, E. M., & Smith, L. E. (1987). *Leadership training through gaming*. New York: Nichols.

Cleeton, G. U., & Mason, C. W. (1934). *Executive ability: Its discovery and development*. Yellow Springs, OH: Antioch Press.

Clemens, J. K., & Mayer, D. F. (1987). *The classic touch: Lessons in leadership from Homer to Hemingway.* Homewood, IL: Dow Jones-Irwin.

Cleveland, H. (1985). *The knowledge executive.* New York: Dutton.

Clifford, D. K., Jr., & Cavanagh, R. E. (1985). *The winning performance.* New York: Bantam Books.

Cohen, A. R., & Bradford, D. L. (1990). *Influence without authority.* New York: Wiley.

Cohen, M. D., & March, J. G. (1974/1986). *Leadership and ambiguity.* Boston: Harvard Business School Press. (Original published in 1974.)

Cohen, W. A. (1990). *The art of the leader.* Englewood Cliffs, NJ: Prentice-Hall.

Collins, E.G.C. (Ed.). (1983). *Executive success: Making it in management.* New York: Wiley.

Colwill, N. L. (1982). *The new partnership: Women and men in organizations.* Palo Alto, CA: Mayfield.

Conger, J. A. (1989a). *The charismatic leader.* San Francisco: Jossey-Bass.

Conger, J. A. (1989b). Leadership: The art of empowerment. *Executive, 3*(1), 17–24).

Conger, J. A., & Kanungo, R. N. (Eds.). (1988). *Charasmatic leadership: The elusive factor in organizational effectiveness.* San Francisco: Jossey-Bass.

Copeland, N. (1942). *Psychology and the soldier.* Harrisburg, PA: Military Service Publications.

Corwin, R. G. (1978). Power. In E. Sagarin (Ed.), *Sociology: The basic concepts.* New York: Holt, Rinehart & Winston.

Covey, S. R. (1989). *The seven habits of highly effective people.* New York: Simon & Schuster.

Cox, C. J., & Cooper, G. L. (1988). *High flyers.* Oxford: Basil Blackwell.

Cribbin, J. J. (1981). *Leadership: Your competitive edge.* New York: AMACOM.

Cronin, T. E. (1980). *The state of the presidency* (2nd ed.). Boston: Little, Brown.

Crosby, P. B. (1990). *Leading: The art of becoming an executive.* New York: McGraw-Hill.

Crowley, W. H. (1928, July–September). Three distinctions in the study of leaders. *Journal of Abnormal and Social Psychology, 23*, 144–157.

Cuban, L. (1988). *The managerial imperative and the practice of leadership in schools.* Albany: State University of New York Press.

Dachler, H. P. (1984). On refocusing leadership from a social systems perspective of management. In J. G. Hunt, D. M. Hosking, C. A. Schriesheim, & R. Stewart (Eds.), *Leaders and managers* (pp. 100–108). New York: Pergamon.

Dachler, H. P. (1988). Constraints on the emergence of new vistas in leadership and management research: An epistemological overview. In J. G. Hunt, B. R. Baliga, H. P. Dachler, & C. A. Schriesheim (Eds.), *Emerging leadership vistas* (pp. 261–285). Lexington, MA: Lexington Books.

Dahl, R. A. (1961). *Who governs?* New Haven, CT: Yale University Press.

Daniels, M. M. (1983). *Realistic leadership.* Englewood Cliffs, NJ: Prentice-Hall.

Dansereau, F., Graen, G., & Haga, W. A. (1975). A vertical dyad linkage approach to leadership within formal organization: A longitudinal investigation of the role making process. *Organizational Behavior and Human Performance, 13*, 46–78.

Davis, K. (1962). *Human relations at work.* New York: McGraw-Hill.

Davis, K. E. (1986). The status of black leadership: Implications for black followers in the 1980s. In T. Heller, J. Van Til, & L. A. Zurcher (Eds.), *Leaders and followers: Challenges for the future* (pp. 193–208). Greenwich, CT: JAI Press.

Davis, R. C. (1942). *The fundamentals of top management*. New York: Harper & Row.

Davis, S. M. (1987). *Future perfect*. Reading, MA: Addison-Wesley.

Deal, T. E., & Kennedy, A. A. (1982). *Corporate cultures: The rites and rituals of corporate life*. Reading, MA: Addison-Wesley.

DeBruyn, R. L. (1976). *Causing others to want your leadership*. Manhattan, KS: DeBruyn & Associates.

DePree, M. (1989). *Leadership is an art*. New York: Doubleday.

Dietz, M. G. (1987, Fall). Context is all: Feminism and theories of citizenship. *Daedalus*, pp. 1–24.

Dilenschneider, R. L. (1990). *Power and influence*. Englewood Cliffs, NJ: Prentice-Hall.

Doll, R. C. (1972). *Leadership to improve schools*. Worthington, OH: Jones.

Donaldson, G., & Lorsch, J. W. (1983). *Decision making at the top*. New York: Basic Books.

Dowd, J. (1936). *Control in human societies*. New York: Appleton-Century.

Downton, J. M. (1973) *Rebel leadership*. New York: The Free Press.

Dubin, R. (1962). *Leadership in union-management relations as an intergroup system*. New York: Wiley.

Dubin, R. (1979). Metaphors of leadership: An overview. In J. G. Hunt & L. L. Larson (Eds.), *Crosscurrents in leadership* (pp. 225–238). Carbondale: Southern Illinois University Press.

Dubin, R., Homans, C. C., Mann, F. C., & Miller, D. C. (1965). *Leadership and productivity*. San Francisco: Chandler.

Duke, D. L. (1987). *School leadership and instructional improvement*. New York: Random House.

Duke, D. L. (1989). The aesthetics of leadership. In J. L. Burdin (Ed.), *School leadership* (pp. 345–365). Newbury Park, CA: Sage.

Dunn, K., & Dunn, R. (1983). *Situational leadership for principals*. Englewood Cliffs, NJ: Prentice-Hall.

Edelman, M. (1964). *The symbolic uses of politics*. Urbana: University of Illinois Press.

Edelman, M. (1971). *Politics are symbolic actions*. Chicago: Markham.

Edinger, L. J. (1967). Editor's introduction. In L. J. Edinger (Ed.), *Political leadership in industrialized societies* (pp. 1–25). New York: Wiley.

Edwards, G. C., III. (1989). *At the margins: Presidential leadership of Congress*. New Haven, CT: Yale University Press.

Eichler, M. (1972). Leadership in social movements. *Sociological Inquiry, 47*(2), pp. 99–107.

Ellis, A. (1975). A rational approach to leadership. In R. N. Cassel & R. L. Heichberger (Eds.), *Leadership development: Theory and practice* (pp. 23–53). North Quincy, MA: Christopher.

England, G. W., Negandlir, A. R., & Wilpert, B. (1981). *The functioning of complex organizations*. Cambridge, MA: Oelgeschlager, Gunn & Hain.

Engstrom, T. W. (1976). *The making of a Christian leader*. Grand Rapids, MI: Zondervan.

Enochs, J. C. (1981, November). Up from management. *Phi Delta Kappan*, pp. 175–178.

Erickson, D. A. (1965). Some misgivings concerning a study of leadership. *Educational Administration Quarterly, 1*(3), 52–59.

Etzioni, A. (1965). Dual leadership in complex organizations. *American Sociological Review, 30*, pp. 688–698.

Fallon, W. F. (Ed.). (1981). *Leadership on the job* (3rd ed.). New York: AMACOM.

Faris, J. H. (1981). Leadership and enlisted attitudes. In J. H. Ruck & L. J. Korb (Eds.), *Military leadership* (pp. 139–164). Beverly Hills, CA: Sage.

Fay, B. (1977). How people change themselves: The relationship between critical theory and its audience. In T. Ball (Ed.), *Political theory and praxis: New perspectives* (pp. 200–233). Minneapolis: University of Minnesota Press.

Ferguson, M. (1980). *The Aquarian conspiracy*. Los Angeles: Tarcher.

Fiedler, F. E. (1967). *A theory of leadership effectiveness*. New York: McGraw-Hill.

Fiedler, F. E., & Garcia, J. E. (1987). *New approaches to effective leadership*. New York: Wiley.

Filley, A. C. (1978). *The compleat manager*. Middleton, WI: Green Briar Press.

Finch, F. E. (1977). Collaborative leadership in work settings. *The Journal of Applied Behavioral Science, 12*(3), 292–302.

Fink, R. A. (1988, April). Leadership, culture and change on the college campus. *Campus Activities Programming*, pp. 64–69.

Fink, R. A. (1990). *Vision: An essential component of transformational leadership*. Doctoral dissertation, University of San Diego.

Fisher, L. F. (1948). *A philosophy of social leadership according to Thomistic principles*. Doctoral dissertation, Catholic University of America, Washington, DC.

Fleishman, J. L., Liebman, L., & Moore, M. H. (1981). *Public duties: The moral obligations of government officials*. Cambridge, MA: Harvard University Press.

Ford, J. F. (1990). *Education for Christian leadership*. Doctoral dissertation, University of San Diego.

Foster, W. F. (1986a). *Paradigms and promises*. Buffalo, NY: Prometheus Books.

Foster, W. F. (1986b). *The reconstruction of leadership*. Victoria, Australia: Deakin University Press.

Foster, W. F. (1989). Toward a critical practice of leadership. In J. Smyth (Ed.), *Critical perspectives on educational leadership* (pp. 39–62). London: Falmer.

Freiberg, K. L. (1987). *The heart and spirit of transformational leadership: A qualitative case study of Herb Kelleher's passion for Southwest Airlines*. Doctoral dissertation, University of San Diego.

Fritz, R. (1986). The leader as creator. In J. A. Adams (Ed.), *Transforming leadership* (pp. 159–182). Alexandria, VA: Miles River Press.

Frost, P. J., Moore, L. F., Louis, M. R., Lundberg, C. C., & Martin, J. (1985). *Organizational culture*. Beverly Hills, CA: Sage.

Gabler, J. E. (1987). Leadership: A woman's view. In L. T. Sheive & M. B. Schoenbelt (Eds.), *Leadership: Examining the elusive* (pp. 64–77). Alexandria, VA: Association for Supervision and Curriculum Development.

Gardner, J. W. (1961). *Excellence*. New York: Harper & Row.

Gardner, J. W. (1965/1984). The antileadership vaccine. In W. E. Rosenbach & R. E. Taylor (Eds.), *Contemporary issues in leadership* (pp. 318–325). Boulder, CO: Westview Press. (Original published in 1965.)

Gardner, J. W. (1986). *The nature of leadership*. Washington, DC: Independent Sector.

Gardner, J. W. (1990). *On leadership*. New York: The Free Press.

Garfield, C. (1986). *Peak performance*. New York: Morrow.

Gast, I. F. (1984). Leader discretion as a key component of a manager's role. In J. G. Hunt, M. Hosking, C. A. Schriesheim, & R. Stewart (Eds.), *Leaders and managers* (pp. 350–359). New York: Pergamon Press.

Gerth, H., & Mills, C. W. (1953). *Character and social structure*. New York: Harcourt, Brace.

Gibb, C. A. (1954) Leadership. In G. Lindzey (Ed.), *Handbook of social psychology* (Vol. 2, pp. 877–920). Reading, MA: Addison-Wesley.

Gibb, C. A. (1968). Leadership: Psychological aspects. In D. L. Sills (Ed.), *International encyclopedia of the social sciences* (Vol. 9, pp. 91–101). New York: Macmillan.

Gibb, C. A. (1969). Leadership. In G. Lindzey & E. Aronson (Eds.), *Handbook of social psychology* (2nd ed., Vol. 2, pp. 205–282). Reading, MA: Addison-Wesley.

Gibb, J. R. (1967/1983). Dynamics of educational leadership. In W. R. Lassey & M. Sashkin (Eds.), *Leadership and social change* (3rd ed., pp. 188–202). San Diego: University Associates. (Original published in 1967.)

Gilligan, C. (1982). *In a different voice*. Cambridge, MA: Harvard University Press.

Gilmore, T. N. (1986). Leadership and boundary management. *The Journal of Applied Behavioral Science, 18*(3), 343–356.

Gilmore, T. N. (1988). *Making a leadership change*. San Francisco: Jossey-Bass.

Gilmour, P. (1986). *The emerging pastor*. Kansas City, MO: Sheed & Ward.

Glasman, N. S. (1986). *Evaluation-based leadership*. Albany: State University of New York Press.

Goble, F. (1972). *Excellence in leadership*. New York: American Management Association.

Gordon, T. (1955). *Group-centered leadership*. Boston: Houghton Mifflin.

Gordon, T. (1977). *Leader effectiveness training*. New York: Bantam Books.

Gouldner, A.W. (1950). *Studies in leadership*. New York: Russell and Russell.

Gouldner, A. W. (1970). *The coming crisis of Western sociology*. New York: Basic Books.

Graen, G., & Cashman, J. F. (1975). A role making model of leadership in formal organizations: A developmental approach. In J. G. Hunt & L. L. Larson (Eds.), *Leadership frontiers* (pp. 143–165). Kent, OH: Kent State University Press.

Graham, J. W. (1982, August). *Leadership: A critical analysis*. Paper presented at the 42nd Annual Meeting of the Academy of Management, New York City.

Graham, J. W. (1988). Transformational leadership: Fostering follower autonomy, not automatic followership. In J. G. Hunt, B. R. Baliga, H. P. Dachler, & C. A. Schriescheim (Eds.), *Emerging leadership vistas* (pp. 73–79). Lexington, MA: Lexington Books.

Grauer, S. R. (1989). *Think globally, act locally: A Dephi study of educational leadership through the development of international resources in the local community*. Doctoral dissertation, University of San Diego.

Green, T. F. (1987). The conscience of leadership. In L. T. Sheive & M. B. Schoenbelt (Eds.), *Leadership: Examining the elusive* (pp. 105–115). Alexandria, VA: Association for Supervision and Curriculum Development.

Greenfield, T. B. (1984). Leaders and schools: Wilfullness and nonnatural order in organizations. In T. F. Sergiovanni & J. E. Corbally (Eds.), *Leadership and organizational culture* (pp. 142–169). Urbana: University of Illinois Press.

Greenleaf, R. K. (1977). *Servant leadership*. New York: Paulist Press.

Griffiths, D. E. (1986). Lead me or leave me. In S. Packard (Ed.), *The leading edge* (pp. 45–64). Washington, DC: American Association of Colleges for Teacher Education.

Grob, L. (1984). Leadership: The Socratic model. In B. Kellerman (Ed.), *Leadership:*

Multidisciplinary perspectives (pp. 263–280). Englewood Cliffs, NJ: Prentice-Hall.

Guetzkow, H. S. (Ed.). (1951). *Groups, leadership and men*. Pittsburgh: Carnegie Press.

Guild, P. B. (1987). How leaders' minds work. In L. T. Sheive & M. B. Schoenbelt (Eds.), *Leadership: Examining the elusive* (pp. 81–92). Alexandria, VA: Association for Supervision and Curriculum Development.

Hagberg, J. O. (1984). *Real power*. Minneapolis, MN: Winston Press.

Haiman, F. S. (1951). *Group leadership and democratic action*. Boston: Houghton Mifflin.

Halpin, A. W. (1966). *Theory and research in administration*. New York: Macmillan.

Halpin, A. W., & Winter, B. J. (1952). *The leadership behavior of the airplane commander*. Columbus: Ohio State University, Bureau of Personnel Research.

Halsey, G. D. (1938). *How to be a leader*. New York: Harper.

Hargrave, E. C. (1967). Popular leadership in Anglo-American democracies. In L. J. Edinger (Ed.), *Political leadership in industrialized societies* (pp. 182–219). New York: Wiley.

Harman, W. W. (1979). *An incomplete guide to the future*. New York: Norton.

Harman, W. W. (1986). Transformed leadership: Two contrasting concepts. In J. D. Adams (Ed.), *Transforming leadership* (pp. 105–160). Alexandria, VA: Miles River Press.

Harrison, F. C. (1989). *Spirit of leadership: Inspiring quotations for leaders*. Germantown, TN: Leadership Education and Development.

Harrison, R. (1984). Leadership and strategies for a new age. In J. D. Adams (Ed.), *Transforming organizations* (pp. 97–112). Alexandria, VA: Miles River Press.

Hart, L. B. (1980). *Moving up! Women and leadership*. New York: AMACOM.

Heider, J. (1985). *The Tao of leadership*. Atlanta: Humanics Limited.

Heifetz, R. A., & Sinder, R. M. (1988). Political leadership: Managing the public's problem solving. In R. B. Reich (Ed.), *The power of public ideas* (pp. 179–203). Cambridge, MA: Ballinger.

Heifetz, R. A., Sinder, R. M., Jones, A., Hodge, L. M., & Rowley, K. A. (1989). Teaching and assessing leadership courses at the John F. Kennedy School of Government. *Journal of Policy Analysis and Management, 8*, 536–562.

Heller, T. (1982). *Women and men as leaders*. New York: Praeger.

Heller, T., & Van Til, J. (1986). Leadership and followership: Some summary propositions. In T. Heller, J. Van Til, & L. A. Zurcher (Eds.), *Leaders and followers: Challenges for the future* (pp. 251–263). Greenwich, CT: JAI Press.

Heller, T., Van Til, J., & Zurcher, L. A. (Eds.). (1986). *Leaders and followers: Challenges for the future*. Greenwich, CT: JAI Press.

Hemphill, J. K. (1949a). The leader and his group. *Journal of Educational Research, 28*, 225–229, 245–246.

Hemphill, J. K. (1949b). *Situational factors in leadership*. Columbus: Ohio State University, Bureau of Educational Research.

Hemphill, J. K. (1952). *Theory of leadership*. Unpublished staff report. Ohio State University, Bureau of Personnel Research.

Hemphill, J. K. (1958). Administration as problem solving. In A. W. Halpin (Ed.), *Administrative theory in education* (pp. 89–118). New York: Macmillan.

Hemphill, J. K., & Coons, A. E. (1957). Development of the Leader Behavior Description Questionnaire. In R. M. Stogdill & A. E. Coons (Eds.), *Leader behavior:*

Its description and measurement. Columbus: Ohio State University, Bureau of Business Research.

Henrickson, R. L. (1989). *Leadership and culture*. Doctoral dissertation, University of San Diego.

Hersey, P., & Blanchard, K. (1988). *Management of organizational behavior: Utilizing human resources* (5th ed.). Englewood Cliffs, NJ: Prentice-Hall.

Hersey, P., & Stinson, J. (1980). *Perspectives in leader effectiveness*. Oberlin: Ohio University, Center for Leadership Studies.

Heyns, R. W. (Ed.). (1977). *Leadership for higher education*. Washington, DC: American Council on Education.

Hickman, C. R., & Silva, M. A. (1984). *Creating excellence: Managing corporate culture, strategy, and change in the new age*. New York: NAL Books.

Higham, J. (Ed.). (1978). *Ethnic leadership in America*. Baltimore: John Hopkins University Press.

Hitt, W. D. (1989). *The leader-manager: Guidelines for action*. Columbus, OH: Battelle Press.

Hocking, W. E. (1924). Leaders and led. *Yale Review, 13*, 625–641.

Hodgkinson, C. (1983). *The philosophy of leadership*. New York: St. Martin's Press.

Hollander, E. P. (1964). *Leaders, groups, and influence*. New York: Oxford University Press.

Hollander, E. P. (1978a). *Leadership dynamics*. New York: The Free Press.

Hollander, E. P. (1978b). What is the crisis of leadership? *Humanitas, 14*(3), 285–296.

Hollander, E. P. (1985). Leadership and power. In G. Lindzey & E. Aronson (Eds.), *Handbook of social psychology* (3rd ed., Vol. 2, pp. 485–537). New York: Random House.

Hollander, E. P., & Juban, J. W. (1969). Contemporary trends in the analysis of leadership processes. *Psychological Bulletin, 71*, 387–397.

Hollenback, D. (1989). The common good revisited. *Theological Studies, 50*(1), 70–94.

Holloman, C. R. (1984). Leadership and headship: There is a difference. In W. E. Rosenbach & R. L. Taylor (Eds.), *Contemporary issues in leadership* (pp. 109–116). Boulder, CO: Westview Press.

Homans, G. C. (1950). *The human group*. New York: Harcourt, Brace & World.

Hook, S. (1943). *The hero in history*. New York: John Day.

Horbon, T. R. (1986). *What works for me*. New York: Random House.

Hosking, D. M. & Hung, J. G. (1982). "Leadership research and the European connection: An epilogue." In J. G. Hunt, U. Sekaran, & C. E. Shriesheim (Eds.) *Leadership: Beyond establishment views* (pp. 278–289). Carbondale, IL: Southern Illinois University Press.

Hosking, D. M., & Morley, I. E. (1988). The skills of leadership. In J. G. Hunt, B. R. Baliga, H. P Dachler, & C. A. Schriesheim (Eds.), *Emerging leadership vistas* (pp. 89–106). Lexington, MA: Lexington Books.

Hosking, D. M., Hunt, J. G., Schriesheim, C. A., & Stewart, R. (1984). Conclusions: On paradigm shifts in studying leadership. In J. G. Hunt, D. M. Hosking, C. A. Schriesheim, & R. Stewart (Eds.), *Leaders and managers* (pp. 417–424). New York: Pergamon Press.

House, R. J. (1977). A 1976 theory of charismatic leadership. In J. G. Hunt & L. L. Larson (Eds.), *Leadership: The cutting edge* (pp. 189–207). Carbondale: Southern Illinois University Press.

House, R. J., & Baetz, M. L. (1979). Leadership: Some empirical generalizations and new research directions. In B. M. Staw (Ed.), *Research in organizational behavior* (Vol. 1, pp. 341–423). Greenwich, CT: JAI Press.

House, R. J., & Mitchell, T. R. (1974). Path-goal theory of leadership. *Journal of Contemporary Business, 3*, 81–97.

Huggins, N. I. (1978). Afro-Americans. In J. Higham (Ed.), *Ethnic leadership in America* (pp. 91–118). Baltimore: Johns Hopkins University Press.

Hunsaker, J., & Hunsaker, P. (1986). *Managerial women*. Cincinnati, OH: South-Western.

Hunt, J. G. (1984a). *Leadership and managerial behavior*. Chicago: Science Research Associates.

Hunt, J. G. (1984b). Managerial behavior from a "radical" perspective. In J. G. Hunt, D. M. Hosking, C. A. Schriesheim, & R. Stewart (Eds.), *Leaders and managers* (pp. 275–277). New York: Pergamon Press.

Hunt, J. G. (1984c). Organizational leadership: The contingency paradigm and its challenges. In B. Kellerman (Ed.), *Leadership: Multidisciplinary perspectives* (pp. 113–138). Englewood Cliffs, NJ: Prentice-Hall.

Hunt, J. G., & Blair, J. D. (Eds.). (1985) *Leadership on the future battlefield*. McLean, VA: Pergamon-Brassey.

Hunt, J. G., & Larson, L. L. (Eds.). (1975). *Leadership frontiers*. Kent, OH: Kent State University Press.

Hunt, J. G., & Larson, L. L. (Eds.). (1977). *Leadership: The cutting edge*. Carbondale: Southern Illinois University Press.

Hunt, J. G., & Larson, L. L. (Eds.). (1979). *Crosscurrents in leadership*. Carbondale: Southern Illinois University Press.

Hunt, J. G., & Osborn, R. N. (1980). A multiple-influence approach to leadership for managers. In P. Hersey & J. Stinson (Eds.), *Perspectives in leader effectiveness* (pp. 47–62). Oberlin: Ohio University, Center for Leadership Studies.

Hunt, J. G., Baliga, B. R., Dachler, H. P. & Schriesheim, C. A. (Eds.). (1988). *Emerging leadership vistas*. Lexington, MA: Lexington Books.

Hunt, J. G., Hosking, M., Schriesheim, C. A., & Stewart, R. (Eds.). (1984). *Leaders and managers*. New York: Pergamon Press.

Hunt, J. G., Sekaran, U., & Schriesheim, C. A. (Eds.). (1982). *Leadership: Beyond establishment views*. Carbondale: Southern Illinois University Press.

Hunt, S. M. (1984). The role of leadership in the construction of reality. In B. Kellerman (Ed.), *Leadership: Multidisciplinary perspectives* (pp. 157–178). Englewood Cliffs, NJ: Prentice-Hall.

Hunter, F. (1953). *Community power structure*. Chapel Hill: University of North Carolina Press.

Hunter, F. (1959). *Top leadership, U.S.A.* Chapel Hill: University of North Carolina Press.

Iacocca, L. (1984). *Iacocca: An autobiography*. New York: Bantam.

Immegart, G. L. (1988). Leadership and leader behavior. In N. J. Boyan (Ed.), *Handbook of research on educational administration* (pp. 259–277). New York: Longman.

Jacobs, T. O. (1970). *Leadership and exchange in formal organizations*. Alexandria, VA: Human Resources Research Organization.

Jacobson, S. L., & Conway J. A. (Eds.). (1990). *Educational leadership in an age of reform*. New York: Longman.

Jago, A. G. (1982). Leadership: Perspectives in theory and research. *Management Science, 28*, 315–336.

Janda, K. F. (1960). Towards the explication of the concept of leadership in terms of the concept of power. *Human Relations, 13*, 345–363.

Janis, I. L. (1989). *Crucial decisions: Leadership in policymaking and crisis management.* New York: The Free Press.

Jennings, E. E. (1960). *An anatomy of leadership: Princes, heroes and supermen.* New York: Harper & Brothers.

Jennings, H. H. (1944). Leadership: A dynamic redefinition. *Journal of Educational Sociology, 17*, 431–433.

Jennings, H. H. (1958). Sociometry of leadership. In C. G. Browne & T. S. Cohn (Eds.), *The study of leadership* (pp. 41–45). Danville, IL: Interstate.

Jentz, B. C., & Wofford, J. W. (1979). *Leadership and learning.* New York: McGraw-Hill.

Johannesson, B., & Suanberg, K. (1982). *Scandinavian management: The boss as leader.* Bromley, Kent, UK: Chartwell-Bratt.

Joiner, C. W., Jr. (1987). *Leadership for change.* Cambridge, MA: Ballinger.

Juran, J. M. (1989). *Juran on leadership for quality.* New York: The Free Press.

Kahn, R. L., & Katz, D. (1953). Leadership practices in relation to productivity and morale. In D. Cartwright & A. Zander (Eds.), *Group dynamics: Research and theory* (pp. 612–628). Evanston, IL: Row-Peterson.

Kanter, R. M. (1977). *Men and women of the corporation.* New York: Basic Books.

Kanter, R. M. (1983). *The change masters.* New York: Simon & Schuster.

Kanter, R. M. (1989, November–December). The new managerial work. *Harvard Business Review*, pp. 85–92.

Katz, D., & Kahn, R. L. (1966/1978). *The social psychology of organizations* (2nd ed.). New York: Wiley, (Original published in 1966.)

Kegan, R., & Lahey, L. L. (1984). Adult leadership and adult development. In B. Kellerman (Ed.), *Leadership: Multidisciplinary perspectives* (pp. 199–230). Englewood Cliffs, NJ: Prentice-Hall.

Keller, S. (1963). *Beyond the ruling class.* New York: Random House.

Kellerman, B. (1984a). Leadership as a political act. In B. Kellerman (Ed.), *Leadership: Multidisciplinary perspectives* (pp. 63–89). Englewood Cliffs, NJ: Prentice-Hall.

Kellerman, B. (Ed.). (1984b). *Leadership: Multidisciplinary perspectives.* Englewood Cliffs, NJ: Prentice-Hall.

Kellerman, B. (Ed.). (1986). *Political leadership: A source book.* Pittsburgh: University of Pittsburgh Press.

Kelly, C. M. (1988). *The destructive achiever.* Reading, MA: Addison-Wesley.

Kelly, J. F., Jr. (1989). *The transformation of a corporate culture in a mature organization.* Doctoral dissertation, University of San Diego.

Kelly, R. E. (1988, November–December). In praise of followers. *Harvard Business Review*, pp. 142–148.

Kennedy, D. M., & Parish, M. E. (Eds.). (1986). *Power and responsibility in American leadership.* San Diego: Harcourt Brace Jovanovich.

Ket deVries, M.F.R. (1989). *Prisoners of leadership.* New York: Wiley.

Khare, R. S., & Little, D. (1984). *Leadership: Interdisciplinary reflections.* Lanham, MD: University Press of America.

Kiechel, Walter, III. (1988, November 21). The case against leaders. *Fortune*, pp. 217–219.

Kieper, C. (1986). Leadership in metanoic organizations. In J. A. Adams (Ed.), *Transforming Leadership* (pp. 185–197). Alexandria, VA: Miles River Press.

Killian, R. A. (1979). *Managers must lead* (rev. ed.). New York: AMACOM.

King, R. M. (1988). *A study of shared instructional leadership by mentor teachers in Southern California*. Doctoral dissertation, University of San Diego.

Kiser, S. L. (1954). *The American concept of leadership*. New York: Pageant Press.

Klopp, O. E. (1964). *Symbolic leaders*. Chicago: Aldine.

Kmetz, J. L. (1981). Leadership and organizational structure: A critique and an argument for synthesis. In G. W. England, A. R. Negandlir, & B. Wilpert (Eds.), *The functioning of complex organizations* (pp. 145–171). Cambridge, MA: Oelgeschlager, Gunn & Hain.

Knickerbocker, I. (1948/1958). Leadership: A conception and some implications. *Journal of Social Issues*, *4*, 23–40. (Reprinted in Browne & Cohn, 1958, pp. 3–11).

Knowles, M., & Knowles, H. (1955). *How to develop better leaders*. New York: Association Press.

Kochan, T. A., Schmidt, S. S., & DeCotis, T. A. (1975). Superior–subordinate relations: Leadership and headship. *Human Relations*, *28*, 279–294.

Kodiath, A. (1987). *A study of the commonalities and differences of male and female spiritual leaders*. Doctoral dissertation, University of San Diego.

Koestenbaum, P. (1987). *The heart of business: Ethics, power, and philosophy*. San Francisco: Saybrook.

Kohlberg, L. (1981). *The philosophy of moral development*. New York: Harper & Row.

Korton, D. C. (1968). Situational determinants of leadership structure. In D. Cartwright & A. Zander (Eds.), *Group dynamics: Research and theory* (3rd ed., pp. 351–361). New York: Harper & Row.

Kotter, J. P. (1988). *The leadership factor*. New York: The Free Press.

Kouzes, J. M., & Posner, B. Z. (1987). *The leadership challenge*. San Francisco: Jossey-Bass.

Kracke, W. H. (1978). *Force and persuasion: Leadership in an Amazonian society*. Chicago: University of Chicago Press.

Kuhn, A., & Beam, R. D. (1982). *The logic of organizations*. San Francisco: Jossey-Bass.

Kuhn, T. S. (1970). *The structure of scientific revolutions* (2nd ed.). Chicago: University of Chicago Press.

Kuhnert, K. W., & Lewis, P. (1987). Transactional and transformational leadership: A constructive/developmental analysis. *Academy of Management Review*, *12*, 648–657.

Kuzmits, F. E. (1979). *Leadership in a dynamic society*. Indianapolis, IN: Bobbs-Merrill.

Laird, D. A., & Laird, E. C. (1956). *The new psychology of leadership*. New York: McGraw-Hill.

Lane, J. J., & Walberg, H. J. (Eds.) (1987). *Effective school leadership*. Berkeley, CA: McCutchan.

Lassey, W. R., & Sashkin, M. (Eds.). (1983). *Leadership and social change* (3rd ed.). San Diego: University Associates.

Lasswell, H. D. (1948). *Power and personality*. New York: Norton.

Lasswell, H. D. (1967). Political systems, styles, and personalities. In L. J. Edinger

(Ed.), *Political leadership in industrialized societies* (pp. 316–347). New York: Wiley.

Lawler, E. E., III. (1984). Leadership in participation. In J. G. Hunt, M. Hosking, C. A. Schriesheim, & R. Stewart (Eds.), *Leaders and managers* (pp. 316–332). New York: Pergamon Press.

Lawson, J. D., Griffin, L. S., & Donant, F. D. (1976). *Leadership is everybody's business*. San Luis Obispo, CA: Impact.

Lazarus, R. (1964). *Leaders, groups and influence*. New York: Oxford University Press.

Leadership expert: Ronald Heifetz. (1988, October). *INC.*, pp. 37–48.

Leavitt, H. J. (1986). *Corporate pathfinders*. Homewood, IL: Dow Jones-Irwin.

Lee, L. (1989, July). Can leadership be taught? *Training*, pp. 19–26.

Leigh, R. D. (1936). *Group leadership*. New York: Norton.

Levinson, H. (1968). *The exceptional executive*. Cambridge, MA: Harvard University Press.

Levinson, H. (1981). *Executive*. Cambridge, MA: Harvard University Press.

Levinson, H., & Rosenthal, S. (1984). *CEO: Corporate leadership in action*. New York: Basic Books.

Levy, A., & Merry, U. (1986). *Organizational transformation: Approaches, strategies, theories*. New York: Praeger.

Lewin, K., Lippitt, R., & White, R. K. (1939). Patterns of aggressive behavior in experimentally created social climates. *Journal of Social Psychology*, *10*, 271–301.

Likert, R. (1961) *New patterns of management*. New York: McGraw-Hill.

Lindblom, D. E. (1968). *The policy-making process*. Englewood Cliffs, NJ: Prentice-Hall.

Lindgren, H. C. (1954). *Effective leadership in human relations*. New York: Hermitage House.

Lindy, J. (1986). *Lead, follow, or get out of the way*. San Diego: Avant Books.

Lippitt, G. L. (1969). *Organizational renewal*. New York: Appleton-Century-Crofts.

Lippitt, R. (1986). The changing leader-follower relationships of the 1980s. *The Journal of Applied Behavioral Science*, *18*(3), 395–403.

Lips, H. M. (1981). *Women, men and the psychology of power*. Englewood Cliffs, NJ: Prentice-Hall.

Lloyd, A. H. (1922). *Leadership and progress*. Boston: Stratford.

Loden, M. (1985). *Feminine leadership or how to succeed in business without being one of the boys*. New York: Times Books.

Lombardo, M. M. (1978). *Looking at leadership: Some neglected issues*. Greensboro, NC: Center for Creative Leadership.

Lombardo, M. M., & McCall, M. W., Jr. (1982). Leaders on line: Observations from a simulation of managerial work. In J. G. Hunt, U. Sekaran, & C. A. Schriesheim, *Leadership: Beyond establishment views* (pp. 50–67). Carbondale: Southern Illinois University Press.

Long, N. E. (1963). The political act as an act of will. *Sociology*, *69*(1), 126–138.

Long, S. L. (Ed.). (1951). *The handbook of political behavior* (Vols. 1 & 3). New York: Plenum Press.

Lord, R. G. (1979). Leadership valence: A transactional measure of the leadership emergence process. In J. G. Hunt & L. L. Larson (Eds.), *Crosscurrents in leadership* (pp. 156–160) Carbondale: Southern Illinois University Press.

Losoney, L. (1985). *The motivating leader*. Englewood Cliffs, NJ: Prentice-Hall.

Lowry, R. P. (1962). *Who's running the town?* New York: Harper & Row.

Loye, D. (1977). *The leadership passion*. San Francisco: Jossey-Bass.

Lundborg, L. B. (1981). *The art of being an executive*. New York: The Free Press.

Luthans, F. (1979). Leadership: A proposal for social learning theory base and observational and functional analysis techniques to measure leader behavior. In J. G. Hunt & L. L. Larson (Eds.), *Crosscurrents in leadership* (pp. 201–208). Carbondale: Southern Illinois University Press.

Maccoby, M. (1981). *The leader: A new face for American management*. New York: Simon & Schuster.

Maccoby, M. (1988). *Why work?* New York: Simon & Schuster.

MacIntyre, A. (1984). *After virtue*. Notre Dame, IN: University of Notre Dame Press.

Maguire, D. C. (1980). *A new American justice*. Garden City, NY: Doubleday.

Main, J. (1987, September 28). Wanted: Leaders who can make a difference. *Fortune*, pp. 92–102.

Mant, A. (1983). *Leaders we deserve*. Oxford: Robertson.

Manz, C. C., & Sims, H. (1989). *Super-leadership*. New York: Prentice-Hall.

March, J. G., & Olsen, J. P. (1979). *Ambiguity and choice in organizations* (2nd ed.). Bergen, Norway: Universitetsforlaget.

Marinoble, R. M. (1990). *Faith and leadership: The spiritual journeys of transformational leaders*. Doctoral dissertation, University of San Diego.

Mauriel, J. J. (1989). Strategic leadership for schools. San Francisco: Jossey-Bass.

Mazlish, B. (1984). History, psychology and leadership. In B. Kellerman (Ed.), *Leadership: Multidisciplinary perspectives* (pp. 1–23). Englewood Cliffs, NJ: Prentice-Hall.

McCall, M. W., Jr. (1978). *Leadership as a design problem*. Greensboro, NC: Center for Creative Leadership.

McCall, M. W., Jr. (1979/1984). Conjecturing about creative leaders. In W. E. Rosenbach & R. L. Taylor (Eds.), *Contemporary issues in leadership* (pp. 271–280). Boulder, CO: Westview Press. (Original published in 1979).

McCall, M. W., Jr. (1981). *Leadership and the professional*. Greensboro, NC: Center for Creative Leadership.

McCall, M. W., Jr., & Lombardo, M. M. (Eds.). (1978). *Leadership: Where else can we go?* Durham, NC: Duke University Press.

McCorry, J. J. (1978). *Marcus Foster and the Oakland Public Schools: Leadership in an urban bureaucracy*. Berkeley: University of California Press.

McElroy, J. C., & Hunger, J. D. (1988). Leadership theory as causal attributions of performance. In J. G. Hunt, B. R. Baliga, H. P. Dachler, & C. A. Schriesheim (Eds.), *Emerging leadership vistas* (pp. 169–182). Lexington, MA: Lexington Books.

McFarland, A. S. (1969). *Power and leadership in pluralistic systems*. Palo Alto, CA: Stanford University Press.

McGregor, D. (1960). *The human side of enterprise*. New York: McGraw-Hill.

McGregor, D. (1966). *Leadership and motivation*. Cambridge, MA: M.I.T. Press.

Meindl, J., Ehrlich, S., & Dukerich, J. (1985). The romance of leadership. *Administrative Science Quarterly, 30*, 78–102.

Melia, J., & Lyttle, P. (1986). *Why Jenny can't lead*. Saquache, CO: Operational Politics.

Merton, R. K. (1969). The social nature of leadership. *American Journal of Nursing*, 69, 2614–2618.

Millett, J. D. (1980). *Management, governors, and leadership*. New York: AMACOM.

Miner, J. B. (1975). The uncertain future of the leadership concept: An overview. In J. G. Hunt & L. L. Larson (Eds.). *Leadership frontiers* (pp. 197–208). Kent, OH: Kent State University Press.

Miner, J. B. (1986). The uncertain future of the leadership concept: Revisions and clarifications. In T. Heller, J. Van Til, & L. A. Zurcher (Eds.), *Leaders and followers: Challenges for the future* (pp. 39–56). Greenwich, CT: JAI Press.

Mintzberg, H. (1982). If you're not serving Bill and Barbara, then you're not serving leadership. In J. G. Hunt, U. Sekaran, & C. A. Schriesheim (Eds.), *Leadership: Beyond establishment views* (pp. 239–250). Carbondale: Southern Illinois University Press.

Misumi, J. (1985). *The behavioral science of leadership*. Ann Arbor: University of Michigan Press.

Mitchell, T. R. (1979). Organizational behavior. *Annual Review of Psychology*, 30, 243–281.

Moloney, M. M. (1979). *Leadership in nursing*. Saint Louis: Mosby.

Montgomery, B. L. (1961). *The path to leadership*. New York: G. P. Putnam's Sons.

Montor, K., McNicholas, T. M., Jr. Ciotti, A. J., Hutchenson, T. H., III, & Wehmueller, J. E. (Eds.). (1987). *Naval leadership: Voices of experience*. Annapolis, MD: Naval Institute Press.

Moore, B. V. (1927). The May conference on leadership. *Personnel Journal*, 6, 124–128.

Morley, I. E. (1984). On imagery in the cycling of decision making. In J. G. Hunt, D. M. Hosking, C. A. Schriesheim, & R. Stewart (Eds.), *Leaders and managers* (pp. 267–274). New York: Pergamon Press.

Morris, G. B. (1985). A futuristic cognitive view of leadership. *Educational Administration Quarterly*, 21(1), 7–27.

Morris, R. T., & Seeman, M. (1950/1958). The problem of leadership. In C. G. Browne, & T. S. Cohn (Eds.), *The study of leadership* (pp. 12–21). Danville, IL: Interstate. (Original published in 1950).

Morrison, A. M., White, R. P., & VanVelso, E. (1987). *Breaking the glass ceiling: Can women reach the top of America's largest corporations?* Reading, MA: Addison-Wesley.

Moyer, W. (1987). *The hero's journal*. [videotape]. New York: Public Broadcasting Service.

Mueller, R. K. (1984). Leading edge leadership. In W. E. Rosenbach & R. L Taylor (Eds.), *Contemporary issues in leadership* (pp. 326–344). Boulder, CO: Westview Press.

Mumford, E. (1906–1907). The origins of leadership. *American Journal of Sociology*, 12, 216–224, 367–397, 500–531.

Munson, E. L. (1921). *The management of men*. New York: Holt.

Munson, E. L. (1942). *Leadership for American Army leaders*. Washington, DC: Infantry Journal.

Murphy, J. (1988). The unheroic side of leadership: Notes from the swamp. *Phi Delta Kappan*, 69(9), 654–659.

Naisbitt, J., & Aburdene, P. (1990). *Megatrends 2000*. New York: Morrow.

Nanus, B. (1989). *The leader's edge*. Chicago: Contemporary Books.

Naylor, J. C., Pritchard, R. D., & Ilgen, D. R. (1980). *A theory of behavior in organizations*. New York: Academic Press.

Neustadt, R. (1960/1980). *Presidential power* (2nd ed.). New York: Wiley. (Original published in 1960.)

Nicoll, D. (1986). Leadership and followership: Fresh views on an old subject. In J. A. Adams (Ed.), *Transforming leadership* (pp. 29–38). Alexandria, VA: Miles River Press.

Nix, H. L. (1969). Concepts of community and community leadership. *Sociology and Social Research, 53*(4), 500–510.

Oates, J. F. (1970). *The contradictions of leadership*. New York: Appleton-Century-Crofts.

Orren, G. R. (1988). Beyond self-interest. In R. B. Reich (Ed.), *The power of public ideas* (pp. 13–29). Cambridge, MA: Ballinger.

Osborn, R. N. & Hunt, J. G. (1975). An adaptive-reactive theory of leadership. In J. G. Hunt & L. L. Larson (Eds.), *Leadership frontiers* (pp. 27–44). Kent, OH: Kent State University Press.

Osborn, R. N., Morris, F. A., & Connor, P. E. (1984). Emerging technologies: The challenge to leadership theory. In J. G. Hunt, D. M. Hosking, C. A. Schriesheim, & R. Stewart (Eds.), *Leaders and managers* (pp. 360–374). New York: Pergamon Press.

O.S.S. Staff. (1948). *The assessment of men*. New York: Rinehart.

O'Toole, J. (1985). *Vanguard management: Redesigning the corporate future*. Garden City, NY: Doubleday.

Owen, H. (1986). Leadership by indirection. In J. A. Adams (Ed.), *Transforming leadership* (pp. 111–122). Alexandria, VA: Miles River Press.

Owens, R. G. (1987). The leadership of educational clans. In L. T. Sheive & M. B. Schoenbelt (Eds.), *Leadership: Examining the elusive* (pp. 16–29). Alexandria, VA: Association for Supervision and Curriculum Development.

Paige, G. D. (1977). *The scientific study of political leadership*. New York: The Free Press.

Pastin, M. (1986). *The hard problems of management: Gaining the ethics edge*. San Francisco: Jossey-Bass.

Pendleton, B. O. (1989). *The Schools of the Future Commission of San Diego City Schools: An ethnographic study*. Doctoral dissertation, University of San Diego.

Pennington, L. A., Hough, R. B., & Case, H. W. (1943). *The psychology of military leadership*. New York: Prentice-Hall.

Perrow, C. (1979). *Complex organizations: A critical essay* (2nd ed.). Glenview, IL: Scott, Foresman.

Peters, T. J. (1987). *Thriving on chaos*. New York: Knopf.

Peters, T. J., & Austin, N. (1985). *A passion for excellence: The leadership difference*. New York: Random House.

Peters, T. J., & Waterman, R. H. (1982). *In search of excellence*. New York: Harper & Row.

Petrullo, L., & Bass, B. M. (Eds.). (1961). *Leadership and interpersonal behavior*. New York: Holt, Rinehart & Winston.

Peyer, H. (1962). Excellence and leadership: Has Western Europe any lessons for us?

In S. R. Granbard & G. Holton (Eds.), *Executives and leadership in a democracy* (pp. 1–24). New York: Columbia University Press.

Pfeffer, J. (1977). The ambiguity of leadership. *Academy of Management Review*, 2(1), 104–112.

Pfeffer, J. (1981). Management as symbolic action: The creation and maintenance of organizational paradigms. In L. K. Cunning & B. M. Shaw (Eds.), *Research in organizational behavior* (Vol. 3, pp. 1–52). Greenwich, CT: JAI Press.

Pigors, P. (1935). *Leadership or domination*. Boston: Houghton Mifflin.

Pitner, N. (1986). Substitutes for principal leader behavior: An exploratory study. *Educational Administration Quarterly*, 22(2), 23–42.

Plachy, R. (1978). *When I lead, why don't they follow?* (2nd ed.). Chicago: Teach 'em.

Pondy. L. R. (1978). Leadership is a language game. In M. W. McCall, Jr., & M. M. Lombardo (Eds.), *Leadership: Where else can we go?* (pp. 87–99). Durham, NC: Duke University Press.

Popper, S. H. (1989). The instrumental value of the humanities in administrative preparation. In J. L. Burdin (Ed.), *School leadership* (pp. 366–389). Newburg Park, CA: Sage.

Portnoy, R. A. (1986). *Leadership: What every leader should know about people*. Englewood Cliffs, NJ: Prentice-Hall.

Potts, M., & Behr, P. (1987). *The leading edge*. New York: McGraw-Hill.

Prentice, W.C.H. (1961, September). Understanding leadership. *Harvard Business Review*, pp. 143–148 + .

Presthus, R. (1964). *Men at the top*. New York: Oxford University Press.

Prince, H. T., and Associates (Eds.). (1985). *Leadership in organizations* (3rd ed.). West Point, NY: United States Military Academy.

Quinn, R. E. (1988). *Beyond rational management*. San Francisco: Jossey-Bass.

Rachels, J. (1986). *The elements of moral philosophy*. New York: Random House.

Rainio, K. (1955). *Leadership quality: A theoretical inquiry and an experimental study on forement*. Helsinki, Finland: No publisher indicated.

Rallis, S. F., & Highsmith, M. C. (1986, December). The myth of "great principal": Questions of school management and instructional leadership. *Phi Delta Kappan*, pp. 300–304.

Rauch, C. F., & Behling, O. (1984). Functionalism: Basis for an alternative approach to the study of leadership. In J. G. Hunt, D. M. Hosking, C. A. Schriesheim, & R. Stewart (Eds.), *Leaders and managers* (pp. 45–62). New York: Pergamon Press.

Redl, F. (1942). Group emotion and leadership. *Psychiatry*, 5, 575–584.

Reed, P. B., Jr. (1943). *Personal leadership for combat officers*. New York: Whitlesey House.

Reich, R. B. (Ed.). (1988). *The power of public ideas*. Cambridge, MA: Ballinger.

Rejai, M., & Phillips, K. (1983). *World revolutionary leaders*. New Brunswick, NJ: Rutgers University Press.

Rejai, M., & Phillips, K. (1988). *Loyalists and revolutionaries: Political leaders compared*. New York: Praeger.

Reuter, E. B. (1941). *Handbook of sociology*. New York: Dryden Press.

Rice, A. K. (1965). *Learning for leadership*. London: Tavistock.

Ridge, W. J. (1989). *Follow me*. New York: AMACOM.

Ritscher, J. A. (1986). Spiritual leadership. In J. A. Adams (Ed.), *Transforming leadership* (pp. 61–80). Alexandria, VA: Miles River Press.

Roberts, W. (1989). *The leadership secrets of Attila the Hun*. New York: Warner.

Rosen, D. M. (1984). Leadership systems in world cultures. In B. Kellerman (Ed.), *Leadership: Multidisciplinary perspectives* (pp. 39–62). Englewood Cliffs, NJ: Prentice-Hall.

Rosen, N. A. (1969). *Leadership change and work group dynamics*. Ithaca, NY: Cornell University Press.

Rosenbach, W. E., & Taylor, R. L. (Eds.). (1984). *Contemporary issues in leadership*. Boulder, CO: Westview Press.

Roskill, S. W. (1964). *The art of leadership*. London: Collins.

Ross, M. G., & Hendry, C. E. (1957). *New understandings of leadership*. New York: Association Press.

Rost, J. C. (1985, October). *Distinguishing leadership and management: A new consensus*. Paper presented at the Organizational Development Network National Conference, San Francisco.

Rost, J. C., (1986). *A leadership theory of policy making*. Unpublished manuscript, University of San Diego, School of Education.

Rost, J. C. (1988). *The politics of instructional leadership*. Unpublished manuscript, University of San Diego, School of Education.

Rost, J. C., & Cosgrove, T. J. (1987, Summer). The politics of student leadership. *Campus Activities Programming*, pp. 36–40.

Rothstein, S. W. (1986). *Leadership dynamics*. Lanham, MD: University Press of America.

Ruck, J. H., & Korb, L. J. (Eds.). (1981). *Military leadership*. Beverly Hills, CA: Sage.

Ruch, R. S., & Goodman, R. (1983). *Image at the top*. New York: The Free Press.

Rustow, D. A. (Ed.). (1970). *Philosophers and kings: Studies in leadership*. New York: Braziller.

Sadler, P. (1988). *Managerial leadership in the post-industrial society*. Aldershot Hants, UK: Gower.

Safire, W., & Safir, L. (1990). *Leadership*. New York: Simon & Schuster.

Sanford, F. A. (1951). Leadership identification and acceptance. In H. S. Guetzkow (Ed.), *Groups, leadership and men* (pp. 158–176). Pittsburgh: Carnegie Press.

Sarkesian, S. C. (1981). A personal perspective. In R. S. Ruch & L. J. Korb, (Eds.), *Military leadership* (pp. 243–247). Beverly Hills, CA: Sage.

Sashkin, M. (1986). True vision in leadership. *Training and Development Journal, 40*(5), 58–61.

Sashkin, M., & Fulmer, R. M. (1988). Toward an organizational leadership theory. In J. G. Hunt, B. R. Baliga, H. P. Dachler, & C. A. Schriesheim (Eds.), *Emerging leadership vistas* (pp. 51–65). Lexington, MA: Lexington Books.

Sashkin, M., & Garland, H. (1979). Laboratory and field research on leadership: Integrating divergent streams. In J. G. Hunt & L. L. Larson (Eds.), *Crosscurrents in leadership* (pp. 64–87). Carbondale: Southern Illinois University Press.

Saville, A. (1971). Conflict: New emphasis in leadership. *Clearing House, 46*, 52–55.

Sayles, L. R. (1979). *Leadership: What effective managers really do . . . and how they do it*. New York: McGraw-Hill.

Sayles, L. R. (1989). *Leadership: Managing in real organizations*. New York: McGraw-Hill.

Sayre, S. (1986). *Leadership communication and organizational culture: A field study.* Doctoral dissertation, University of San Diego.

Schatz, K., & Schatz, L. (1986). *Managing by influence.* Englewood Cliffs, NJ: Prentice-Hall.

Schein, E. H. (1985). *Organizational culture and leadership.* San Francisco: Jossey-Bass.

Schenk, C. (1928). Leadership. *Infantry Journal, 33,* 111–122.

Schlesinger, J. A. (1967). Political careers and political leadership. In L. J. Edinger (Ed.), *Political leadership in industrialized societies* (pp. 266–293). New York: Wiley.

Schmidt, R. (1933). Leadership. In E.R.A. Seligman (Ed.), *Encyclopaedia of the social sciences* (Vol. 9, pp. 282–286). New York: Macmillan.

Schon, D. A. (1984). Leadership as reflection in action. In T. J. Sergiovanni & J. E. Corbally (Eds.), *Leadership and organizational culture* (pp. 36–63). Urbana: University of Illinois Press.

Shriesheim, C. A., Hunt, J. G., & Sekaran, U. (1982). Conclusion: The leadership management controversy revisited. In J. G. Hunt, U. Sekaran, & C. A. Shriesheim (eds.) *Leadership: Beyond establishment views* (pp. 290–298) Carbondale, IL: Southern Illinois University Press.

Schriesheim, C. A., Tolliver, J. M., & Behling, O. C. (1984). Leadership theory: Some complications for managers. In W. E. Rosenbach & R. L. Taylor (Eds.), *Contemporary issues in leadership* (pp. 124–134). Boulder, CO: Westview Press.

Schutz, W. (1977). *Leaders of schools.* La Jolla, CA: University Associates.

Schwandt, T. A. (1989, November). Recapturing moral discourse in evaluation. *Educational Research,* pp. 12–16.

Scott, E. L. (1956). *Leadership and perceptions of organizations.* Columbus: Ohio State University, Bureau of Business Leadership.

Seeman, M. (1960). *Social status and leadership.* Columbus: Ohio State University, Bureau of Educational Research.

Segal, D. R. (1981). Leadership and management: Organizational theory. In R. H. Ruch & L. J. Korb, (Eds.), *Military leadership* (pp. 41–69). Beverly Hills, CA: Sage.

Seligman, L. G. (1967). Political parties and the recruitment of political leadership. In L. J. Edinger (Ed.), *Political leadership in industrialized societies* (pp. 294–315). New York: Wiley.

Seligman, L. G. (1968). Leadership: Political aspects. In D. L. Sills (Ed.), *International encyclopedia of the social sciences* (Vol. 9, pp. 107–113). New York: Macmillan.

Selvin, H. C. (1960). *The effects of leadership.* New York: The Free Press.

Selznick, P. (1957). *Leadership in administration: A sociological interpretation.* Evanston, IL: Row, Peterson.

Sergiovanni, T. J. (1984). Leadership as cultural expression. In T. J. Sergiovanni & J. E. Corbally (Eds.), *Leadership and organizational culture* (pp. 105–114). Urbana: University of Illinois Press.

Sergiovanni, T. J. (1987a). *The principalship: A reflective practice perspective.* Boston: Allyn & Bacon.

Sergiovanni, T. J. (1987b). The theoretical bases for cultural leadership. In L. T. Sheive & M. B. Schoenbelt (Eds.), *Leadership: Examining the elusive* (pp. 116–129). Alexandria, VA: Association for Supervision and Curriculum Development.

Sergiovanni, T. J. (1989). The leadership needed for quality schooling. In T. J. Sergiovanni & J. H. Moore (Eds.), *Schooling for tomorrow* (pp. 213–226). Boston: Allyn & Bacon.

Sergiovanni, T. J. (1990). *Value-added leadership*. San Diego: Harcourt Brace Jovanovich.

Sergiovanni, T. J., & Corbally, J. E. (Eds.). (1984). *Leadership and organizational culture*. Urbana: University of Illinois Press.

Shartle, C. L. (1956). *Executive performance and leadership*. Englewood Cliffs, NJ: Prentice-Hall.

Sheive, L. T., & Schoenbelt, M. B. (Eds.). (1987). *Leadership: Examining the elusive*. Alexandria, VA: Association for Supervision and Curriculum Development..

Sherif, M. (Ed.). (1962). *Intergroup relations and leadership*. New York: Wiley.

Shivers, J. S. (1980). *Recreational leadership*. Princeton, NJ: Princeton Book Co.

Simon, H. (1947). *Administrative behavior*. New York: Macmillan.

Simonton, D. K. (1987). *Why presidents succeed: A political psychology of leadership*. New Haven, CT: Yale University Press.

Singer, M. S. (1985). Transformational vs. transactional leadership: A study of New Zealand company managers. *Psychological Reports, 57*, 143–146.

Smircich, L., & Morgan, G. (1982). Leadership: The management of meaning. *Journal of Applied Behavior Science, 18*(3), 257–273.

Smith, H. G., & Kruger, L. M. (1933). *A brief summary of literature on leadership*. Bloomington: Indiana University, School of Education, Bureau of Cooperative Research.

Smith, M. (1935). Leadership: The management of social differentials. *Journal of Abnormal and Social Psychology, 30*, 348–358.

Smith, P. B., & Peterson, M. F. (1988). *Leadership, organizations and culture*. Beverly Hills, CA: Sage.

Smith, S. C., Mazzarella, J. A., & Piele, P. K. (1981). *School leadership: Handbook for survival*. Eugene, OR: Clearinghouse on Educational Management.

Smyth, J. (1989a). A "pedagogical" and "educative" view of leadership. In J. Smyth (Ed.), *Critical perspectives on educational leadership* (pp. 179–204). London: Falmer.

Smyth, J. (Ed.) (1989b). *Critical perspectives on educational leadership*. London: Falmer.

Sola, P. A. (Ed.) (1984). *Ethics, education and administrative decisions: A book of readings*. New York: Peter Lang.

Spoor, W. H. (1986, February 13). *The leadership riddle*. Speech given at the inauguration of the William H. Spoor Dialogues on Leadership Lectures at Dartmouth College, Hanover, NH.

Srivastua, S., & Associates. (Eds.). (1983). *The executive mind*. San Francisco: Jossey-Bass.

Srivastua, S., & Associates. (Eds.). (1986). *Executive power*. San Francisco: Jossey-Bass.

Srivastra, S., & Associates. (Eds.). (1988). *Executive integrity*. San Francisco: Jossey-Bass.

Stage, S. (1986). From domestic science to social housekeeping: The career of Ellen Richards. In D. M. Kennedy & M. E. Parrish (Eds.), *Power and responsibility in American leadership* (pp. 211–228). San Diego: Harcourt Brace Jovanovich.

Staw, B. M. (1984). Leadership and persistence. In T. J. Sergiovanni & J. E. Corbally

(Eds.), *Leadership and organizational culture* (pp. 72–84). Urbana: University of Illinois Press.

Staw, B. M., & Ross, J. (1980). Commitment in an experimenting society: An experiment on the attribution of leadership from administrative scenarios. *Journal of Applied Psychology*, *65*, 249–260.

Stewart, R. (1984). Integrative comments: A look at research methodologies for exploring managerial behavior. In J. G. Hunt, D. M. Hosking, C. A. Schriesheim, & R. Stewart (Eds.). *Leaders and managers* (pp. 220–222). New York: Pergamon Press.

Stogdill, R. M. (1948). Personal factors associated with leadership: A survey of the literature. *Journal of Psychology*, *25*, 35–71. (Reprinted in Bass, 1981, pp. 43–72).

Stogdill, R. M. (1950/1958). Leadership, membership and organizations. *Psychological Bulletin*, *47*, 1–14. (Reprinted in Browne & Cohn, 1958,, pp. 31–40).

Stogdill, R. M. (1974). *Handbook of leadership*. New York: The Free Press.

Stogdill, R. M. & Coons, A. E. (Eds.). (1957). *Leader behavior: Its description and measurement*. Columbus: Ohio State University, Bureau of Business Research.

Stott, J. W. (1985). What makes leadership Christian? *Christianity Today*, *29*(11), 24–27.

Stout, R., & Brener, C. (1969). Leadership. In R. L. Ebel (Ed.), *Encyclopedia of educational research* (4th ed., pp. 699–706). New York: Macmillan.

Strike, K. A., Haller, E. J., & Soltis, J. F. (1988). *The ethics of school administration*. New York: Teachers College Press.

Stozier, C. B., & Offer, D. (1985). *The leader: Psychohistorical essays*. New York: Plenum Press.

Sullivan, W. M. (1986). *Reconstructing public philosophy*. Berkeley: University of California Press.

Sweetser, T., & Holden, C. W. (1987). *Leadership in a successful parish*. San Francisco: Harper & Row.

Tannenbaum, A. S. (1968). Leadership: Sociological aspects. In D. L. Sills (Ed.), *International encyclopedia of the social sciences* (Vol. 9, pp. 101–107). New York: Macmillan.

Tannenbaum, R., & Schmidt, W. H. (1958). How to choose a leadership pattern. *Harvard Business Review*, *36*, 95–101. (Retrospective with additional comments published in May–June, 1973, *55*, 95–102).

Tannenbaum, R., Margulies, N., & Massarik, F. (1985). *Human systems development*. San Francisco: Jossey-Bass.

Tannenbaum, R., Wechsler, I. R., & Massarick, F. (1961). *Leadership and organizations: A behavioral science approach*. New York: McGraw-Hill.

Tarcher, M. (1966). *Leadership and the power of ideas*. New York: Harper & Row.

Tead, O. (1935). *The art of leadership*. New York: McGraw-Hill.

Thebald, R. (1987). *The rapids of change*. Indianapolis, IN: Knowledge Systems.

Tichy, N., & Devanna, M. A. (1986). *The transformational leader*. New York: Wiley.

Timm, P. R., & Peterson, B. D. (1982). *People at work*. St. Paul, MN: West.

Titus, C. H. (1950). *The processes of leadership*. Dubuque, IA: Brown.

Toffler, B. L. (1986). *Tough choices: Managers talk ethics*. New York: Wiley.

Tosi, H. J., Jr. (1982). Toward a paradigm shift in the study of leadership. In J. G.

Hunt, U. Sekaran, & C. A. Schriesheim (Eds.), *Leadership: Beyond establishment views* (pp. 222–233). Carbondale: Southern Illinois University Press.

Tralle, H. E. (1925). *The psychology of leadership*. New York: Century.

Tramel, M. E., & Reynolds, H. (1981). *Executive leadership*. Englewood Cliffs, NJ: Prentice-Hall.

Tucker, R. C. (1970). The theory of charismatic leadership. In D. A. Rustow (Ed.), *Philosophers and kings*. New York: Braziller.

Tucker, R. C. (1981). *Politics as leadership*. Columbia: University of Missouri Press.

United States Army (1961). *Military leadership*. Washington, DC: Headquarters, Department of the Army.

United States Marine Corps. (1973). *Adventures in leadership*. Quantico, VA: USMC Development and Educational Command.

United States Military Academy. (1925). *Leadership*. West Point, NY: Department of Tactics.

United States Naval Institution. (1949). *Naval leadership*. Annapolis, MD: Author.

Uris, A. (1953). *Techniques of leadership*. New York: McGraw-Hill.

Vaill, P. B. (1984). The purposing of high-performing systems. In T. J. Sergiovanni & J. E. Corbally (Eds.), *Leadership and organizational culture* (pp. 85–104). Urbana: University of Illinois Press.

Vaill, P. B. (1989). *Managing as a performing art*. San Francisco: Jossey-Bass.

Vardaman, G. T. (1973). *Dynamics of managerial leadership*. Philadelphia: Auerbach.

Verba, S. (1961). *Small groups and political behavior: A study leadership*. Princeton, NJ: Princeton University Press.

Vidich, A. J., & Bensman, J. (1958). *Small town in mass society*. Princeton, NJ: Princeton University Press.

Vroom, V. H. (1976). Leadership. In M. Dunnette (Ed.), *Handbook of Industrial and organizational psychology* (pp. 1527–1551). Chicago: Rand McNally.

Vroom, V. H., & Jago, A. G. (1988). *The new leadership: Managing participation in organizations*. Englewood Cliffs, NJ: Prentice-Hall.

Vroom, V. H., & Yetton, P. W. (1973). *Leadership and decision making*. Pittsburgh: University of Pittsburgh Press.

Walker, D. E. (1979). *The effective administrator*. San Francisco: Jossey-Bass.

Wall, J. (1986). *Bosses*. Lexington, MA: Lexington Books.

Waterman, R. H. Jr. (1987). *The renewal factor*. New York: Bantam.

Watkins, P. (1989). Leadership, power and symbols in educational administration. In J. Smyth (Ed.), *Critical perspectives on educational leadership* (pp. 9–37). London: Falmer.

Wayson, W. W. (1979). Misconceptions about leadership. In F. Griffith (Ed.), *Administrative theory in education* (pp. 181–190). Midland, MI: Pendell.

Weber, M. (1921/1947). *The theory of social and economic organizations*. Translated by A. M. Henderson and T. Parsons (Eds.). New York: The Free Press. (Originally published in 1921).

Weiss, W. (1986). *The management of change*. New York: Praeger.

Well, K. A. (1956). *Guide to good leadership*. Chicago: Science Research Associates.

White, R. K., & Lippitt, R. (1960). *Autocracy and democracy: An experimental inquiry*. New York: Harper.

Whitehead, J. D., & Whitehead, M. A. (1986). *The emerging laity: Returning leadership to the faith community*. Garden City, NY: Doubleday.

Whitehead, T. N. (1936). *Leadership in a free society*. Cambridge, MA: Harvard University Press.

Who's excellent now? (1984, November 5). *Business Week*, pp. 65–86.

Whyte, W. F. (1943). *Street corner society*. Chicago: University of Chicago Press.

Wildavsky, A. (1964). *Leadership in a small town*. Totowa, NJ: Bedminster Press.

Williamson, J. N. (Ed.). (1984). *The leader/manager*. New York: Wiley.

Willner, A. R. (1984). *The spellbinders: Charismatic political leaders*. New Haven, CT: Yale University Press.

Wilpert, B. (1982). Commentary on part 1: Various paths beyond establishment views. In J. G. Hunt, U. Sekaran, & C. A. Schriesheim (Eds.), *Leadership: Beyond establishment views* (pp. 68–74). Carbondale: Southern Illinois University.

Wilson, L. C. (1978). *School leadership today*. Boston: Allyn & Bacon.

Wilson, W. (1890/1952). *Leaders of Men*. Edited by T. H. Vail Motter. Princeton, NJ: Princeton University Press. (Original published in 1890.)

Wissler, D. F., & Oritz, F. I. (1988). The Superintendent's leadership in school reform. London: Falmer.

Wolf, F. E. (1937). *Leadership in the new age*. Boston: New Age Publications.

Wolfe, M. E., & Mulholland, F. J. (1957). *Selected readings in leadership*. Annapolis, MD: United States Naval Institution.

Wynne, E. A. (1989). Managing effective schools: The moral element. In M. Holmes, K. A. Leithwood, & D. F. Musella (Eds.), *Educational policy for effective schools* (pp. 128–142). New York: Teachers College Press.

Yukl, G. A. (1989). *Leadership in organizations* (2nd ed.). Englewood Cliffs, NJ: Prentice-Hall.

Yukl, G. A., & Nemeroff, W. F. (1979). Identification and measurement of specific categories of leadership behavior: A progress report. In J. G. Hunt & L. L. Larson (Eds.), *Crosscurrents in leadership* (pp. 164–200). Carbondale: Southern Illinois University Press.

Zaleznik, A. (1966). *Human dilemmas of leadership*. New York: Harper & Row.

Zaleznik, A. (1977). Managers and leaders: Are they different? *Harvard Business Review*, *15*(3), 67–84.

Zaleznik, A. (1989). *The managerial mystique: Restoring leadership in business*. New York: Harper & Row.

Zaleznik, A., & Ket de Vries, M.F.R. (1975). *Power and the corporate mind*. Boston: Houghton Mifflin.

Index

Adams, Jerome, 76
Adams, John D., 85–86, 88
Allen, Kathleen, 183
Allison, Graham, 136–37
American Heritage Dictionary, 42
Argyris, C., 6, 91, 134
authority, 106, 130, 145–46, 157
Avolio, Bruce, 132

Badaracco, Joseph, Jr., 82
Baetz, Mary, 32, 57, 63
Bailey, F. G., 72–73
Baliga, B. Rajaram, 79
Barnard, Chester, 179
Bass, Bernard, 4, 28, 32, 33, 37–38, 42, 45, 55, 71, 84, 85, 87, 118, 131
Bates, Richard, 84
Bavelas, Alex, 56
Beal, G. M., 48
Beam, Robert, 78
Behling, Orlando, 76
Bellah, Robert, 120–23, 175–77

Bellows, Robert, 51
Bennis, Warren, 5, 19, 28, 52, 75, 82, 133, 141, 165
Betz, Donald, 81
biblical tradition, 121–23
Blair, J. D., 79
Blake, Robert, 33
Blanchard, Kenneth, 28, 33, 75, 82
Blondel, Jean, 38, 72
Blumberg, Arthur, 80
Boal, Kimberly, 17
Bogardus, Emory, 47
Boggs, Dallas, 183
Bohen, J. M., 53
Boles, Harold, 33, 58
Bowen, W., 81
Brittell, L. R., 80
Browne, Clarence, 24, 45, 52, 53
Bryman, Alan, 80, 134–35
Bryson, John, 17, 84
Buckley, Karen, 83

Bundel, C. M., 48
Burack, Elmer, 137–38
Burns, James MacGregor, 5, 9, 10, 11, 35, 57, 61, 64–65, 71, 75, 82–83, 87, 88, 91, 101–2, 113–17, 118–22, 130–32, 164–65, 181

Calas, Marta, 21
Calder, Bobby, 57, 62–63
Campbell, Donald, 52
Campbell, Joseph, 7–8
Carroll, Susan, 89
Carter, Launor, 52
Cartwright, Dorwin, 32, 51
Case, H. W., 49
Cassel, Russell, 58
Cattel, Raymond, 52
Center for Creative Leadership, 33, 133–36
Century Dictionary, 40, 41
Cleeton, Clen, 48
coercion, 105–7, 146, 157–60
Cohen, William, 82
Cohn, Thomas, 24, 45, 52, 53
Conger, Jay, 82–85
Connor, Patrick, 80
Coons, A. F., 33, 51
Copeland, Norman, 48–49
Corwin, Richard, 59
Cribbin, James, 82, 84
Cronin, Thomas, 84
Cuban, Larry, 76

Dachler, H. Peter, 21, 78
Davenport, James, 33, 58
Davis, R. C., 49
DeBruyn, Robert, 58
definitions, criteria for, 103–4. *See also* leadership, definitions
DePree, Max, 82
Devanna, Mary Anne, 87
dictatorial relationships, 106
Dictionary of Modern Usage, 43
Doll, Ronald, 59
Dubin, Robert, 35, 132–33

Eastern Europe, events of 1989, 87–88, 102, 142–43, 186

Edelman, Murray, 31–32
Edinger, Lewis, 54
Ellsworth, Richard, 82
end values, 123
English Synonymes, 39
Engstrom, Ted, 59
Enochs, James, 132
ethical relativism, 171–72, 173
ethics and leadership, 153–82; civic virtue, 175–77; common good, 173–77; personal responsibility, 173–74; self-interest, 174
expressive individualism, 120–21

Faris, J. H., 84
Fay, B., 84
Fiedler, Fred, 29, 33, 78, 137
Filley, Alan, 59
Fink, Robert, 184
followers, 107–9, 122
Ford, James, 184
Foster, William, 28, 83–84, 111, 118, 122, 139
Freiberg, Kevin, 87, 183
Fritz, Robert, 85
Funk and Wagnalls' Dictionary, 42

Garcia, Joseph, 28, 33, 78
Gardner, John, 72
Gibb, Cecil, 32, 42, 50–51, 53, 55, 57
Gordon, Thomas, 52–53, 58
Graham, Jill, 80, 131–32
Grauer, Stuart, 183
Greenberg, William, 80
Greenfield, Thomas, 83
Greenleaf, Robert, 35
Griffiths, Daniel, 87
Grob, Leonard, 89

Hagberg, Janet, 86
Haiman, Franklyn, 52
Halpin, Andrew, 51
Harman, Willis, 85
Hart, Lois, 76
Heifitz, Ronald, 75, 76, 83
Hemphill, John, 49–50, 51
Hersey, Paul, 33, 75

Hollander, Edwin, 32, 33, 54, 57, 61, 75–76
Hosking, Dian-Marie, 6, 19, 25, 35, 83, 91, 138–40
Hough, R. B., Jr., 49
House, Robert, 32, 57, 63, 85
Hunger, J. David, 17, 28
Hunsaker, Johanna, 78
Hunsaker, Phillip, 78
Hunt, John, 28, 31, 57, 59, 78–79, 83, 85, 137–39
Hunt, Sonja, 28

Ilgen, Daniel, 80–81
Immegart, Glenn, 31, 32, 45, 89–90
industrial paradigm, 27–28, 29, 91–95, 97–101, 129–30
influence: definition, 156; and ethics, 155–60; intimidation, 158–59; perceptual problems and, 156–59; persuasion, 159–60; threatening consequences, 157–58

Jacobs, T. O., 19–20, 57, 60–61, 130–31, 134
Jago, Arthur, 76
Janda, Kenneth, 56
Jennings, Eugene, 56
Jennings, Helen H., 49
Johnson, Samuel, 38–39

Kahn, Daniel, 62, 131
Kanter, Rosabeth, 71
Kanungo, Rabindra, 85
Katz, Robert, 62, 131
Kegan, Robert, 78
Kellerman, Barbara, 28, 72
Kelley, James, Jr., 183
Kelly, George, 84
Ket de Vries, M.F.R., 85
King, Rita, 183
Knickerbocker, Irving, 49
Kodiath, Alex, 183
Kotter, John, 28, 81
Kouzes, James, 28, 33, 81, 82, 141
Kracke, Waud, 57, 64
Kuhn, Alfred, 78
Kuhn, Thomas, 92

Lahey, Lisa, 78
Larson, Lars, 57
Lasswell, Harold, 54–55
leadership, charismatic, 85
leadership, confusion with leader, 43–44, 58, 134
leadership, definitions, 6–9; cultural permissiveness, 13, 17, 102; dictionary, 39–44; English origins of the word, 37–38, 42–43; scholarly, 44–47, 99; 1900–1929, 47; 1930s, 47–48; 1940s, 48–50; 1950s, 50–53; 1960s, 53–57; 1970s, 57–65; 1980s, 69–90. *See also individual definitions under scholar's name*
leadership, feminist views, 35, 44–45, 89. *See also feminist definitions under scholar's name*
leadership, industrial school, 91–95, 99, 130, 134, 180–81
leadership, nature of, 97–128; cultural permissiveness in defining leadership, 13–17, 137; essential elements of definition, 103–5; influence relationship, 105–7; intend real changes, 113–18; leaders and followers, 107–11; mutual purposes, 118–23; outline of definitional elements, 102–3
leadership, political aspects, 25, 52, 54–55
leadership, postindustrial school, 9–11, 97–128, 140, 181–82
leadership, rituals, 33–35
leadership as being number one, 97–98
leadership as collective leaders in office, 98
leadership as directing other people, 98
leadership effectiveness, 52–53, 58–59, 144–45, 148–49
leadership and ethics, 153–82; ambiguities, 163–65; civic virtue, 175–77; common good, 173–77; content, 153–55, 162–72; personal responsibility, 173–74; process, 153–55, 155–62; self-interest, 174
leadership and headship, 43–44, 50

leadership as influence, 30, 52, 62, 79–82
leadership and larger transformation of society, 99–101
leadership and management, 43, 129–52, 177–79
leadership and morality, 124–27, 165–67
leadership and postindustrial society, 99–101, 126–28, 179–87
leadership relationship, 105–7; multidirectional, 105; noncoercive, 105–7; number of people in, 109–12; unequal, 113
leadership and shared goals, 51–52, 58
leadership and social psychologists, 24–26
leadership studies, 1–2; importance of periphery and content, 2–6; multidisciplinary, 1, 15, 25, 182; research, 183–84; training and development experts and, 184–86; unidisciplinary, 15–16, 25; universities and, 182–83
leadership theories/movements, 17–23, 24, 26, 28; alternative, 29–31; attribution, 30, 62–63, 88–89; behavioral, 18, 22, 53–55, 58–59; contingency/situational, 18, 22; critical, 35–36, 83–84; excellence, 18–19, 22, 28, 83–84, 116; exchange/transactional, 30, 60–62, 121–23; great man/womn, 18, 22, 26, 70–75; group, 16, 48–50, 50–51, 55–56, 58–59, 75–77; political, 25, 52, 54–55, 64–65; traits, 18, 22, 43, 82, 56, 141; transformational, 30–31, 82–88, 121–23, 164–65
Levinson, Harry, 82
Lewin, Kurt, 51
Likert, Rensis, 33
Lippitt, Ronald, 51, 56
Lombardo, Michael, 135–36
Long, N. E., 54
Lord, Robert, 61
Lowry, R. P., 53

Maccoby, Michael, 28, 82
MacIntyre, Alasdair, 176

management, 77–79, 141–49; benefits of, 141–43; definition, 145–48; denigrating, 140–45; distinguishing from leadership, 129–52; effectiveness, 148–49
McCall, Morgan, Jr., 135–36
McElroy, James, 7, 28
McFarland, Andrew, 55, 72
McGregor, Douglas, 33
Mantz, Charles, 36, 74, 82
Marinoble, Rita, 184
Mason, C. W., 48
Massarch, Fred, 56
Mazzarella, Jo Ann, 76
Merton, Robert, 55
Miner, John, 26
Mintzberg, Henry, 20–21, 35, 91, 138
Misumi, Jyuzi, 71
Moloney, Margaret, 58
Montgomery, B. L., 53
Moore, B. V., 47
Morgan, Gareth, 88–89
Morley, Ian, 6, 19, 25, 83, 91, 139–40
Morris, Frederic, 80
Mouton, Jane, 33
Moyers, William, 7–8

Nannus, Bert, 5, 28, 75, 82, 87, 133, 141, 165
Naylor, James, 80–81
Neustadt, Richard, 73, 159–60
New Dictionary of the English Language, 39
New English Dictionary Based on Historical Principles, 40
Nicoll, David, 71

Osborn, Richard, 59, 78, 80
Owen, Harrison, 85
Oxford English Dictionary, 38, 41, 42

Paige, Glenn, 57, 64
paradigm shift, 186–87
Pastin, Mark, 160–61, 168, 170, 171–72

Pendleton, Bertha, 183
Pennington, L. A., 49
periphery and content of leadership studies, 2–6
persuasion, 105, 159–60
Peters, Thomas, 35, 82, 83, 85, 87
Peterson, Mark, 5, 28, 33, 79
Pfeffer, Jeffrey, 57, 62
Piele, Phillip, 76
Pigors, Paul, 47
Plachy, Robert, 59
Pondy, Louis, 20, 35
Popper, Samuel, 81
Posner, Barry, 28, 33, 81, 82, 141
power, 106, 131
Prince, Howard, 72
Pritchard, Robert, 80–81
purposes, mutual, 118–23; common purposes, 120–23; distinguished from goals, 118–19; reflecting, 119–20

Rachels, James, 169, 170
Randabaugh, J. N., 53
Random House Dictionary, 42
Rauch, Charles, 76
Reagan, Ronald, 166
Redl, F., 48–49
Rejai, Mostafa, 76
relativistic ethics, 171–72, 173
republican tradition, 121–22
Reuter, Edward, 48
Ridge, Warren, 72, 82
Ritscher, James, 85
Roberts, Weiss, 72, 82
Rosenthal, Stuart, 82
Royal Standard Dictionary, 39
rule ethics, 169–70, 173

Sarkesian, S. C., 72
Saville, A., 58
Sayre, Shay, 183
Schatz, Kenneth, 73
Schatz, Linda, 73
Schenk, Carroll, 47
Schlesinger, Joseph, 54
Schmidt, Richard, 48
Schmidt, Robert, 55–56
Schon, Donald, 135, 185

Schriesheim, Chester, 76, 137–39
Seeman, Morris, 53
Segal, D. R., 76
Sekaran, U., 78
Selznick, Philip, 29–30, 130, 134
Sergiovanni, Thomas, 36, 72, 76, 82
Shartle, C. L., 51
Sims, Henry, 36, 74, 82
Sinder, Riley, 75, 76, 83
Smircich, Linda, 21, 88–89
Smith, Peter, 5, 28, 33, 79
Smith, Stuart, 76
Smyth, John, 28, 35, 84
social contract ethics, 161, 170–71
Spencer, Sabina, 86
Steffy, Joan, 83
Stogdill, Ralph, 4, 24, 32, 37–38, 42, 45, 52, 58, 118
Sullivan, William, 176

Tannenbaum, Robert, 55–56
Tarcher, M., 54
Tead, Ordway, 48
Tichy, Noel, 87
Titus, Charles, 52
Tollivar, James, 76
Tosi, H. J., Jr., 73
transformation: and leadership, 123–26; moral requirement for, 124–26; of society, 99–101
Tucker, Robert, 28, 80, 85, 133

United Technologies advertisment, 141
Universal Dictionary, 40
utilitarian ethics, 168–69, 172
utilitarian individualism, 120–21

Vroom, Victor, 33

Waterman, Robert, Jr., 35, 82, 83, 85, 87
Watkins, Peter, 21, 89
Wayson, William, 59
Webster's Dictionary, 39–40, 41, 42
Weiss, Joseph, 71
Weschler, I. R., 56
White, Ralph, 51

Whitehead, Evelyn, 86–87
Whithead, James, 86–87
Whyte, William, 48
Willner, Ann, 80, 85
Wilpert, Bernhard, 135
Winter, B. J., 51

Yetton, Philip, 33
Yoder, Janice, 76
Yukl, Gary, 33, 79

Zaleznik, Abraham, 25, 73, 85, 131, 141
Zander, Alvin, 51

ABOUT THE AUTHOR

JOSEPH C. ROST received his Ph.D. degree in 1973 from the University of Wisconsin-Madison. He did his dissertation research on the passage of the law to merge Wisconsin's two university systems. He then served as superintendent of schools of the Hartford, Wisconsin, Union High School District, northwest of Milwaukee.

In 1976, Rost accepted a position at the University of San Diego as a professor of leadership and administration in the School of Education to begin a master's and credential program in school administration. In 1978, he helped inaugurate a doctoral program in leadership, and in 1981 a leadership minor for undergraduate students was started. Rost has written a number of papers on leadership, politics, and policy making, and consults with organizations on leadership.